Narrative Research on Learning:
comparative and international perspectives

To Barry, Peter and Jessica

Narrative Research on Learning:
comparative and international perspectives

Edited by
SHEILA TRAHAR

Bristol Papers in Education:
comparative and international studies
Series Editors: Michael Crossley & Roger Garrett

SYMPOSIUM
BOOKS

Symposium Books
PO Box 204, Didcot, Oxford OX11 9ZQ, United Kingdom
the book publishing division of wwwords Ltd
www.symposium-books.co.uk

Published in the United Kingdom, 2006

ISBN 1 873927 60 6

Series: *Bristol Papers in Education* Number 2

© Symposium Books, 2006

Typeset by wwwords Ltd
Printed and bound in the United Kingdom by Cambridge University Press

Contents

Acknowledgements

This book emerged from a meeting of the Research Centre for International and Comparative Studies (ICS) at the Graduate School of Education, University of Bristol, UK. My thanks go to Professor Michael Crossley who convened the initial meeting and who had the idea for the book. He has been an invaluable help to me in its development and editing. I should also like to thank all of the contributors, those who are valued colleagues and those who have been so warm and supportive through our 'virtual' relationships. Particular thanks go to my colleagues Jane, Kim, Nell and Tim in the Centre for Narratives and Transformative Learning (CeNTRAL) for their creative energy and their encouragement. Finally, thanks to all at Symposium Books.

Foreword

RUTH HAYHOE
*Ontario Institute for Studies in Education,
University of Toronto, Canada*

Comparative education has often tended to function as a kind of macro-sociology of education, focusing on such topics as differences in educational structures, curricular patterns and modes of educational finance in different national contexts. Issues such as equity and participation at different levels of schooling systems, student achievement in different subject areas and approaches to teacher education are often examined. Yet it is rare that the voices of teachers are heard in the literature, or that distinctive cultural contexts at the local level are given detailed attention. It is thus refreshing to see narrative inquiry being brought into the field of comparative education, as this volume enables readers to become acquainted with individual teachers and learners in contexts as varied as Denmark, England, Jamaica, Kenya, Kuwait, New Zealand, Scotland and Tanzania. Many of the chapters provide the opportunity to hear these voices comparatively. In this way people in different contexts share their thoughts and experiences about educational changes brought about through globalisation, and contribute to the reconceptualisation of comparative research and notions of internationalisation in ways that reflect their distinctive geopolitical locations.

Nor are these narratives mere collections of teacher reflections or commentaries. Thoughtful and theoretically rich explanations are given in almost every chapter, justifying the narrative approach to research, and recounting the kinds of sustained encounter with teachers or students over a significant time period that made possible the presentation and interpretation of their views. The accounts of the process of narrative research provided in this book give vivid insight into the demands made upon both researchers and participants, as they engage in deep reflexivity on many dimensions of experience and learn to tune their inner selves to listen, observe and interpret with empathy. There are also some interesting suggestions for innovative forms of teaching that would enable students to gain narrative understanding through a series of reflective exercises carried out during the reading of published autobiographies.

This challenging and stimulating volume provides a valuable contribution to the field of comparative and international education. It exemplifies forms of research that open up to readers the inner stories of teachers' and learners' lives and the practical knowledge and wisdom embedded there. This is a book that deserves to be widely read. I am sure that it will stimulate further efforts to enrich comparative studies through narrative understanding.

Series Editors' Preface

MICHAEL CROSSLEY & ROGER GARRETT
Research Centre for International and Comparative Studies, Graduate School of Education, University of Bristol, United Kingdom

This is the second volume of the *Bristol Papers in Education: comparative and international studies* to be published by Symposium Books in Oxford. The series was founded in 1992, at the University of Bristol, United Kingdom, with the first seven volumes being published by the Centre for International and Comparative Studies in Education located within the Graduate School of Education. All books in the series focus upon research and scholarship that engages with comparative and international issues and perspectives. The emergence and advancement of the series reflects the contemporary and worldwide growth of interest in such work. This, in itself, has been stimulated by rapidly changing geopolitical relations, the impact of intensified globalisation, advances in information and communications technologies, and paradigmatic challenges and developments that have done much to transform the social sciences, and related professional fields, in recent years.

This volume explores the potential of narrative approaches to research for the field of comparative and international education. In doing so, it focuses upon culture and learning, and draws upon a wealth of experience and innovative practice that is currently attracting international attention within the professional arenas of counselling, ethics and associated research studies. The contributions of linguists, ethnographers and comparativists engaged in detailed fieldwork help to demonstrate how narrative approaches can build upon traditions in case study and qualitative research that have already contributed much to contemporary advances in this multidisciplinary field. While such approaches have helped to highlight the importance of context sensitivity, reflexivity, identity and difference in comparative and international research, the articles in this book bring the personal and intellectual characteristics of the narrative enquirer more directly under the reflexive gaze. This is an original and challenging contribution. Researchers interested in the methodological, paradigmatic and political implications of differing discourses and world-views will, therefore, find much of direct interest in this work – as will a wide variety of other readers who value the diversity, creativity and critical insight that narrative approaches to research are increasingly contributing to advances across the social sciences.

CHAPTER ONE

Introduction. The Contribution of Narrative Research to Comparative and International Education: an editor's story

SHEILA TRAHAR
University of Bristol, United Kingdom

Writing the introduction to a book that explores the contributions that narrative research can make to comparative and international education calls for the telling of a story. It is often only retrospectively that the significance and contribution of particular happenings, actions, and events that link together to form a narrative, in this case the narrative of a book, are known (Polkinghorne, 1995). Martin Cortazzi & Lixian Jin tell us in the opening chapter that stories are often co-constructed by several speakers and that collaboration between the teller and audience is intrinsic to narrative research. Participants and researchers ascribe meanings to events but the stories are also told to other audiences, the readers, who will bring their own meanings. Each of the contributors to this book is re-presenting a range of stories. Some tell stories that were told to them; others tell stories of their own; some do both. This introduction combines elements of those narratives with my own personal story of editing this book. It is thus another story.

The idea for the book emerged from a meeting of the Centre for International and Comparative Studies (ICS), one of the research centres at the University of Bristol's Graduate School of Education's (GSoE), which focuses on the integrative theme of Culture, Learning and Identity in Organisations (CLIO). Professor Michael Crossley, the centre's coordinator, believed that comparative researchers could learn much from contemporary developments in narrative research inspired by trans-disciplinary work being carried out in a diversity of academic and professional fields. In a special number of the journal *Comparative*

Education (2000, Vol. 36, No. 3), entitled 'Comparative Education for the Twenty-first Century', Crossley and colleagues had already recognised a need for more practitioner research and for educational researchers to establish different ways of working in new relationships with others. Here they signalled renewed attention to interpretative traditions and methodologies to address unease with global generalisations and uncritical international transfer, seeing the benefits to be gained from 'a bridging of professional cultures and traditions' and 'increased cross-fertilisation of personnel and research perspectives' (Crossley, 2000, p. 324).

Articulating the themes and interests that connected the planning group in order to bridge our own cultures and traditions was at first problematic. Alexander (2000) suggests that the comparison of education across cultures and academic disciplines 'commands attention to borders and it is a short step from marking borders to defending them' (Alexander, 2000, p. 507). I sensed that potential contributors, unsure about how their work might fit into the proposed framework of the book, were in danger of marking and defending borders. I felt, therefore, that it would be helpful to devise a proposal that would be inclusive of and relevant to an interdisciplinary group of possible contributors. This group comprised counselling practitioners, educators and researchers and those with a strong research profile in comparative and international education. If I could identify shared values and themes, this might be a starting point. Using the word 'learning' rather than 'education' was the first step. Learning is a broad, inclusive term and could encourage people who were not comparative education researchers, but who aligned counselling with the facilitation of learning and change, to feel that their expertise as practitioners and as narrative researchers was essential to the venture.

The natural next step was to reinforce the value of practitioner research and its potential for illuminating comparative and international studies of learning. Polkinghorne (1988), in urging researchers to learn from counselling practitioners, recognised their skills in developing trusting and purposeful relationships within which people could work together to seek solutions to problems or enable richer descriptions of phenomena. Colleagues from the Bristol research Centre for Narrative and Transformative Learning (CeNTRAL) were vociferous advocates of practitioner research and influenced by narrative principles, both as therapeutic practice and as ways of conducting research. Another overarching theme that emerged related to the globalised context of the book. Contributors shared the concern expressed by those such as Rizvi (2004) about globalisation being seen as a Westernised homogenisation of culture caused by uni-directional cultural flows, from the 'West' to the 'Rest'. They also subscribed to the view that as human beings we construct our cultures and identities in the same way that we make our own history (Said, 1993), and that these changing processes of shifting and multiple identities are 'characterised by complex negotiations between past lives and present realities' (Rassool, 2004, p. 206). Finally, it seemed that bringing researchers in comparative and international education together with narrative researchers might have rich potential for explaining how the activities and experiences of teachers and learners in classrooms reflect the values of wider society and enhance understanding of the interplay of education and culture.

Narrative research focuses not only on the experiences of research participants but also on the meaning given to the experiences by those participants. Both narrative and comparative research focus on gathering stories across cultures and contexts and communicating those stories to other audiences. Martin Cortazzi & Lixian Jin in their opening chapter describe how stories are shared in many ways and have different functions in different cultures and communities. In some cultures, the teller expects the listener to supply the story's ending and this dialogical blurring of teller's and listener's roles means that researchers need to examine their own cultural expectations when listening to stories. Cortazzi & Jin, as people from different cultural backgrounds, reveal how their research work together has led to the changing of their own selves and their identification with what they call a 'second complementary culture'. Such shifting of identities is testimony to their assertion that in comparative education, researchers employing narrative methodologies may be led to reflect on their own learning and educational identities and to develop the research activity itself into a story, a fundamental tenet of narrative inquiry (Clandinin & Connelly, 2000). Their moving accounts of white researchers going into communities and distorting the local stories that are told by imposing their own cultural frame of reference, using the language of the colonial narrator to sustain hegemony, contrasts with other narratives that exemplify ways in which more 'international voices' can be heard to avoid the inappropriate dominance of majority voices. Such accounts show how narrative research, with its concern for representation and voice, allows these 'different' voices to be heard.

The 'bridging of cultures and traditions' is taken a step further by Christine Fox. In her chapter she contends that the boundaries between cultures are artificial and can be dissolved. She goes on to argue that narrative needs to be embraced as a way of dissolving these boundaries by listening to voices across borders. Reminding us that one emergent trend in comparative and international research has emphasised the centrality of post-colonial perspectives that challenge binaries such as north/south, black/white and self/other, Fox argues that narrative research is a methodology that needs to drive comparative and international research to assist educators in using dialogue to explore hegemony and create opportunities for change. Sarbin's (2004) concept of imagination as 'it is as if I heard the voice' rather than 'I heard the voice', and the perspective of social cartography, the mapping of imagination to deepen our knowledge of the world around us, are proffered as ways of enabling improved intercultural empathy. Using examples from her own work in Papua New Guinea and the Pacific, Fox demonstrates how her typology of narrative lenses can support researchers to engage in the multidimensionality of narrative research and to make explicit the cultural filtering processes of the analysis of narrative data.

Sue Watson's chapter on the teaching of narrative research is set in her local context of New Zealand. Here indigenous peoples are actively reclaiming their right to conduct their own research, regarding the dominance of white researchers as another form of colonisation. Sensitive to this position as a white European New Zealander, a Pakeha, Watson nonetheless believes that researching across cultures is possible and that narrative research, with its fundamental philosophy of supporting 'other' voices to be heard, is especially respectful of people with oral traditions. She takes the view that it is disingenuous to be respectful in the collection of stories if those stories are then analysed or interpreted within theoretical models that are not cognisant of the culture being studied. In common with other contributors, Watson draws attention to the complex ethical issues inherent in collecting narratives, especially when there are many sources of data. Several other contributors are involved in 'teaching' narrative research, but this chapter is an evocative description of the development of a narrative research course for postgraduate students in New Zealand, grounded in a defined need to show how examples of 'talk' can be systematically and reliably analysed.

Reflexivity and narrative are often bracketed together. Kim Etherington, in her chapter, reinforces the multiple ways of understanding and conducting narrative research, highlighting how the use of reflexivity has emerged from greater recognition of the relationship between storyteller and listener, between the knower and what is known. Defining reflexivity as the capacity of the researcher to acknowledge how their own fluid and changing experiences and contexts inform both the process and outcomes of the inquiry, Etherington draws comparisons between the co-construction of multifaceted and many-layered stories and the messiness and complexity of human life. Using her experience as counsellor and researcher, she describes how the stories that people tell – often painful stories – are constructed and located in the context from which they arise. They are not one story but a family's story, a community's story. Issues of translation and interpretation of narratives are discussed. Both processes can be better understood and validated if readers are informed, through reflexivity, about where researchers stand in relation to the study.

Reflexivity can create a bridge between researcher, practitioner and new knowledge, thus enhancing trustworthiness, an important factor in any research. There are important lessons to be learned here for comparativists, especially when one considers Cortazzi & Jin's plea to take account of culture, ideology and identity of both researched and researcher.

In narrative inquiry the story of the research process and the researcher's own engagement with that process becomes intrinsic to the study. Nell Bridges' personal story about conducting narrative research is testimony to this position. In trying to find her place within this genre with many perspectives, she reveals her desire to carry out research that would do her justice 'in more personal ways' and not betray the principles embedded in her identities as a counsellor and counsellor educator. Bridges grapples with reflexivity, using her own explicitly stated position to challenge reflexivity's dissenting voices. Extracts from her personal journal illuminate an understanding of the processes in which she is involved. Being interviewed by her adviser allows recognition of the completeness and incompleteness of her own stories, leading her to recognise that she too will be selecting what to tell the reader from the stories collected from her participants. Her own awareness of the power that gave her was unexpected. Bridges' acknowledgement of her 'unsettling thoughts' at the myth of mutuality, together with her recognition that, in spite of the desire for research to be beneficial to participants, we as researchers instigate and direct it, raise important ethical issues that are elaborated upon in later chapters. For comparativists this is a chapter that can be helpful in understanding many of the principles that underpin narrative inquiry. For those pursuing doctoral research the critical reflections on the PhD process are both insightful and helpful to those conducting cross-cultural studies.

Angeline Barrett adds her voice to the many that recognise that research in low-income countries with limited funding available is often driven by policy-makers who shy away from in-depth stories of individual teachers or learners. Positioning herself as a comparative researcher, Barrett's doctoral research recognises much continuity between the principles of narrative inquiry and the qualitative methodologies used within international and comparative research in education. She identifies the potential value of using narrative research to understand the motivations of those teachers in low-income countries who are effective in spite of working under difficult circumstances. The stories of Mwl. Makonde and Mwl. Bagohe are vivid explications of the interactions between their professional and personal identities. Mwl. Bagohe bears out Barrett's challenge to the oft-perceived notion that people live storied lives and *tell* stories of those lives. He conveys his life to the researcher by showing her his hens and his garden, and the resources he uses in his teaching. Barrett demonstrates here how the narrative researcher needs to exercise some sensitive judgement in, as she puts it, 'pasting together a series of fairly restricted responses to my questions and describing what he showed me'. Mwl. Bagohe prefers visual modes of expression and therefore Barrett's authorial 'interference' is greater, yet his voice is heard as that of a 'thinking, feeling and doing human being', as a man making decisions about his career rather than a man at the mercy of policy and his environment.

George Bailey's curiosity about the extent to which globalisation has affected the curriculum in schools in Kenya, Kuwait and the United Kingdom (UK) leads him to provide 'curriculum narratives', accounts of conversations with three teachers from those countries, told to determine the extent to which they embed global dimensions into their teaching. Bailey's presence as a white Western researcher and educator is felt. He does not shrink from this position but rather uses it to express his discomfort and frustrations provoked by the stories that are told to him. His wariness that globalisation is a cover for Westernisation reflects Rizvi's (2004) concern about the homogenisation of culture, and through his collection and presentation of teacher narratives Bailey shows how the teachers themselves interpret and deliver this 'global dimension' in their work. These narratives are operating on at least three levels – the individual, the school and the nation – and through this analysis we can recognise how the stories told to the researcher connect with other stories. Bailey is aware of the need for both students and teachers to be conversant with their histories and cultures, but argues that it is through broader understanding of the complexities of the contemporary world that the dominance of the West can be disrupted.

The theme of multilayered narratives and the interaction between personal and professional identities is embedded in Elizabeth McNess's chapter, where she explores how education policy has affected the professional lives of four teachers. McNess is provoked by her curiosity about the differences in the lived experiences of teachers in England and Denmark. Through their stories is heard their commitment, their frustrations and their motivations. The cultures of England and Denmark are remarkably different and both local cultural and policy contexts influence the ways in which the four teachers construct their identities, both personal and professional. In England the focus on and belief in the differences in individual ability is reflected in the feelings of isolation expressed by Jane and Sarah. In contrast, the presence of the *klasselærer* in Denmark results in a much more collective and collaborative environment. Danish teachers studied clearly felt that their professionalism could influence policy, whereas the English teachers felt victims of policy. I was reminded of Alexander's (2000) reference to *obrazovanie*, the Russian word for education. *Obrazovanie* combines personal development, private and public morality with civic commitment, which Alexander (2000) suggests tend to be considered as separate and even conflicting domains in England. Jane and Sarah's narratives suggest they may not be, and that these domains intersect in similar ways to those in Denmark.

Both Beth Cross's and Richard Kiely's chapters focus on the role of language in narrative. Beth Cross's chapter is located within the increasingly global agendas of access and inclusion and uses discourse analysis to uncover the powerful cultural communication embedded in teachers' interactions with their pupils in upper primary classrooms in Scotland and Jamaica. Through the classroom narratives of teachers and pupils, she explicates the ways in which language is used to affirm or negate local community narratives; if the language is constrained by the teacher so too are the broader narratives that enable people to sustain their identities. Her re-presentation of the conversations between teachers and pupils provides us with examples of ways in which narrative navigates spheres of communication building bridges that can both enable and prohibit translation and participation. Cross makes explicit use of Dubose-Brunner's (1994) definition of narrative as fluctuating and shuffling back and forth recursively, thus reflecting narrative's boundless possibilities, including the blurring of boundaries between discourse and narrative analysis. Her ingenious use of fractals as a method of mapping how the classroom narratives are juxtaposed against each other challenges conventional models of discourse analysis by demonstrating how this method may offer a more detailed insight into the dynamics and issues under scrutiny.

Some of the complexities of a multicultural higher education classroom are revealed in Richard Kiely's chapter. Through the exploration of the narrative of Laure, a French student at a British university, Kiely demonstrates how she uses her own narrative to understand her own learning, and how that learning is shaped by her navigation of the English for Academic Purposes (EAP) programme. This is the type of programme taken by 'international' students who speak English as an additional language; thus we have another exemplar of how narrative can enable 'other' voices to be heard in the internationalisation of higher education. As an ethnographer Kiely shows how he draws on aspects of narrative to deepen his understanding both of Laure's experience and of his own experience as a reflexive researcher. Laure's way of using her own conversations with him (essentially *his* research interviews) to provide her with other opportunities for learning that extended beyond the programme exemplify how in any narrative, the teller will have a purpose in telling a story. Through Laure's and Kiely's voices the complexities of the learning process and the importance of attention to its social and cultural dimensions are heard. Kiely's exposition of his own perspectives as researcher and teacher also communicates a strong sense gained of his own judgements and assumptions and of how revisiting his data enables him to construct the

19

episode in a number of ways, thus eliciting and illuminating different meanings from the data (Clandinin & Connelly, 2000).

The value of using narrative inquiry to carry out research into my own practice as a lecturer in higher education is at the heart of my own chapter, which also seeks to embed within itself the central themes of the book outlined above. I am striving to show how narrative inquiry can contribute to practitioner research, to address some of the complexities of conducting research across cultures, and to give voice to some of the perspectives that are often ignored in UK higher education. As a practitioner researcher I draw on some of the stories that have been told to me, as well as my own reflections on how I experience the international community to connect past, present and future, selves and others. Positioning myself as a white British researcher, I reveal how my own identities are shifting and being challenged by my encounters with people whose worldviews are different from my own. Such dynamic intercultural communication is leading me to make changes to my teaching and learning practices and, more importantly, to problematise and explore what whiteness – that 'set of cultural practices that are usually unmarked and unnamed' – means to me.

The first of the next two chapters, exploring ethical issues in narrative research, is an account of the ethical dilemmas that Sue Webb envisages that she will encounter in exploring how female counsellors and clients' constructions of their 'selves' may change through their relationship. Prompted by the need to consider the range of issues inherent in such sensitive researching of her own practice, Webb uses many examples of previous ethical dilemmas that she has faced as researcher and as research participant to demonstrate how such dilemmas are faced by all narrative researchers, especially those working across cultures. She defines the obstacles that can be encountered in seeking permission to conduct research when one has to negotiate with groups for whom narrative research may still be unfamiliar, explores ways of representing with integrity the voices of others, and highlights confidentiality issues. Narrative research seeks to give voice to those who are often marginalised. Participants are often proud to be named, but that naming may lead to others being recognised who may not have given their permission to be included in accounts. Webb, a Pakeha, draws on the Maori concept of *utu*, the returning of what is due, fundamental to the reciprocity of social relations, to provide a useful lens on researchers' responsibilities to participants. This is a theme that is taken up and developed in the subsequent chapter.

Email is the main medium used for the dialogue between Tim Bond and Dione Mifsud to address their ethical concerns about the suitability and wisdom of transferring professional knowledge across cultures. The professional knowledge under scrutiny is Bond's expertise in pastoral care and counselling for young people, gained from his British culture,

20

which he is taking to Mifsud' s Maltese context. They grapple with Crossley's (2000) notion of 'bridging cultures' and move beyond Kazamias' (2001) 'historicity' to challenge their inherited positions of coloniser and colonised. Through their historicising of their respective cultures, represented by Bond's powerful experience in the Hypogeum, sacred to Mifsud, they locate themselves within their current relationship and professional context. They are desirous of understanding their different cultures, wanting to transcend the coloniser and colonised position that they have inherited to gain mutual understanding. Their dialogue highlights the ethical issues that arise in narrative research, which others in this book are struggling with. Who decides what may be disclosed to whom? How can one be respectful to the storyteller and at the same time be mindful of the audience for the story? Together they conclude that the very nature of narrative research means that many of these issues cannot be anticipated; they need to be dealt with continuously as they arise throughout the research process.

In the final chapter I invite the reader to join Jane Speedy and myself as we eavesdrop on the conversations at supper on the eve of the 2nd Oxford Conference of the Association of International and Comparative Narrative Research. Overhearing the post-2009 claret-fuelled conversations of John, Amy, Lampert, Grace, Paula, Naoka and Yi Ling, I am transported back in time to this book's beginnings, its journey, and now as it reaches an end, to my own wrestling with the perspectives that each author has offered. Not being a lover of claret I prefer to sip my chilled sauvignon blanc, an apt metaphor when eavesdropping on such rich, red, erudite conversations. Their chatter reflects some of my own musings. My own dis-ease with one reading of reflexivity, alluded to in my own chapter, is shared by Amy's contestation of the term 'reflexive researcher'. I smile when I recall that, post-2009, Bourdieu, the 'father' of reflexivity, is now a member of the second or third world of European and North American 'cultures'. Grace's attention to the kind of research that is funded in low-income countries reminded me of Angeline Barrett's work with Tanzanian teachers. Yi-Ling alerts me to my own love of Hong Kong and my own struggles with the inherited positions of coloniser and colonised, a dichotomous ambivalence explored through the correspondence between Tim Bond and Dione Mifsud.

I end this introduction by drawing your attention to Parsifnos, one of the gargoyles of Magdalen College, Oxford, who asks, 'Are humans permitted to story their futures?' The 2nd Oxford Conference of International and Comparative Narrative Research is considered a turning point, at which 'it seemed as though all the papers they had intended to give had been given ... as if the original thinking had been thrown up in the air and had landed somewhat differently ... and rearranged the shape of the spaces that these conversations inhabited'. In editing this book I have become aware of the original thinking that has been thrown up in the air and has perhaps landed differently and dissolved some borders. But I also agree with John, who echoes the respect for diversity maintained in Crossley's (2000) 'bridging of cultures' perspective when he asks: 'Why compare *balan* and woman at all? Why not consider several readings and rather than attempt to cross cultures or to integrate methodological positions, celebrate and describe diversity?' There are many, many stories in this book, told by people to people from different parts of the world, who are now telling them to you in yet other parts. We have shown the possibilities of dissolving boundaries of methodological positions in order to reach a kaleidoscope of viewpoints that celebrate and describe diversity. Rather than comparing one story with another, I invite you to engage with the diverse narratives presented, to remain curious about the possibilities for integrating perspectives and perhaps, in doing so, to begin to story your own futures, writing new agendas and creating new knowledges.

References

Alexander, R. (2000) *Culture and Pedagogy: international comparisons in primary education.* Oxford: Blackwell.

Clandinin, D.J. & Connelly, F.M. (2000) *Narrative Inquiry: experience and story in qualitative research.* San Francisco: Jossey-Bass.

Crossley, M. (2000) Bridging Cultures and Traditions in the Reconceptualisation of Comparative and International Education, *Comparative Education,* 36, pp. 319-332.

Crossley, M. with Jarvis, P. (Eds) (2000) Special Issue no. 23 of *Comparative Education* on Comparative Education for the Twenty-first Century, 36(3).

Dubose-Brunner, D. (1994) *Inquiry and Reflection: framing narrative practice in education,* Albany: State University of New York Press.

Kazamias, A.M. (2001) Re-inventing the Historical in Comparative Education: reflections on a *protean episteme* by a contemporary player, *Comparative Education,* 37, pp. 439-449. http://dx.doi.org/10.1080/03050060120091247

Polkinghorne, D. (1988) *Narrative Knowing and the Human Sciences.* Albany: State University of New York Press.

Polkinghorne, D. (1995) Narrative Configuration in Qualitative Analysis, in J.A. Hatch & R. Wisniewski (Eds) *Life History and Narrative,* pp. 5-23. Brighton: Falmer Press.

Rassool, N. (2004) Sustaining Linguistic Diversity within the Global Cultural Economy: issues of language rights and linguistic possibilities, *Comparative Education,* 40, pp. 199-214. http://dx.doi.org/10.1080/0305006042000231356

Rizvi, F. (2004) Debating Globalization and Education after September 11, *Comparative Education,* 40, pp. 157-171. http://dx.doi.org/10.1080/0305006042000231338

Said, E. (1993) *Culture and Imperialism.* London: Vintage.

Sarbin, T.R. (2004) The Role of Imagination in Narrative Construction, in
    C. Daiute & C. Lightfoot (Eds) *Narrative Analysis: studying the development
    of individuals in society.* Thousand Oaks: Sage.

NARRATIVE AS METHODOLOGY

CHAPTER TWO

Asking Questions, Sharing Stories and Identity Construction: sociocultural issues in narrative research

MARTIN CORTAZZI
University of Warwick, United Kingdom
LIXIAN JIN
De Montfort University, United Kingdom

This chapter discusses a number of aspects of narrative research in international and comparative education. In particular, we take up some sociocultural issues in getting narrative data and interpreting stories across cultures and contexts, by focusing on examples of narrative research through interactive questioning and of sharing stories of learning and learner or teacher identity. The title reflects aspects of a common narrative research process in education: researchers ask questions, participants tell stories of learning or teaching, and often these lead to a sense of identity. In comparative and intercultural contexts, narrative researchers may be led to reflect on their own learning and educational identities. The chapter proposes a framework of questions which researchers may ask themselves in planning narrative research projects or in engaging reflexively with narrative data. This framework could therefore be used in reading later chapters of this book.

Sociocultural Issues within a Rationale for Narrative Research

From an ethnographic perspective, narrative research on learning seems important for at least four reasons (Cortazzi, 2001, pp. 385-387), all of which may have problematic aspects in international or comparative contexts. We formulate these issues as four core questions, which will be elaborated later into a framework of ten more specific questions.

First, narrative research – unlike factual data analysis – focuses qualitatively on participants' *experience* and the *meanings* given by them to that experience. As researchers collect and examine accounts of educational events and how teachers or learners interpret those events, they are concerned with the *interpretations* of participants and how these relate to knowing, explaining, or evaluating what goes on in classrooms or institutions. Since narratives are generally memories of one sort or another, narrative research can also explore individual or institutional histories and personal or collective perceptions of the past, and hence how professional and institutional identities are constructed. The problem here is how to obtain and understand these narrative interpretations across cultures and compare them across international contexts. Notice that this is not just a question of physical access but rather one of tellability: a question of what sorts of experiences are narrated to whom. This gives us Question One: *how does a researcher from a different cultural background and from a different country get access to participants' narrative accounts of learning experiences?*

Secondly, narrative research is often concerned with *representation* and *voice*. This means that the focus is on the stories or experiences of particular groups of teachers or learners, often minorities, 'others' who are seen as different, or of those whose voices might otherwise go unheard or unnoticed. The research thus allows for the analysis and comparison of changing interests and different kinds of involvement in education, and may give information about, or publicity to, the ways of learning of minority groups that decision-makers and the public need to know about in more equitable educational contexts. In contexts of increasing globalisation and population movements in education (seen, for instance, in a dramatic rise in numbers of international students and migrants in many countries), there is a pressing need for greater diversity among international voices portrayed in research, not only to avoid inappropriate dominance of majority voices but also to recognise local development and foster awareness of local contexts of learning. Narrative representation of a much wider international range of voices is essential in comparative education, if we are to be aware of the global repertoires of conceptions and practices of learning, knowledge of which is essential for both national and international visions of developing education, and to take account of individual and group differences in multicultural contexts. The problem here is that representation and voice change with audience: something is being represented *to somebody* for a particular purpose, and a different audience – say somebody from another culture – may change both the motivation for telling and the way things are told. Thus, Question Two: *how do researchers get, translate and represent voices authentically in narrative research?*

Thirdly, a collection of narratives of personal experiences of learning in education often has a characteristic that many educational researchers fail to emphasise when they conduct quantitative or qualitative studies. This characteristic is the emphasis given to *personal qualities* of learners or *professional qualities* of teachers. These qualities often emerge as a dramatic point in performed stories and narrative accounts of learning. These humane qualities include dedication and devotion, patience and persistence, enthusiasm, struggle and sacrifice, hard work and humour (Cortazzi, 1991). Narrative research may thus quite naturally find itself tackling the all-important but often neglected humanity of teaching and learning. The problem here is that different qualities may be differently valued across cultures and humaneness can be differently realised in time and place, giving us Question Three: *how do researchers access the human story of teaching and learning in narratives?*

Fourthly, a narrative perspective on learning allows the exploration of *research activity itself as a story.* That is, much qualitative research (not only narrative research) is reported and presented as a story, with a kind of constructed plot, in a rhetorical design aimed at persuading readers of the interest, if not the truth, of the research. Ethnographic studies, for example, are often written up as quests of discovery and interpretation, as a research journey from outsider to insider understanding. The researcher makes a story of the research, and constructs a meta-narrative while relaying and interpreting the accounts of informants (van Maanen, 1988; Atkinson, 1990; Golden-Biddle & Locke, 1997; Wolcott, 2001). The problem here is that the researcher's story may be an imposed version, that of an outsider told to outsiders, and may miss the inside perspectives which are precisely the strong point of narrative research. Even if the researcher is an insider within the participant community, the research story may be an adaptation for outsiders, who are reading the research in another culture. Comparative qualitative research involves more than comparison; it is also implicitly 'translation' from one audience to another, sometimes literally across languages but always between cultures and education systems. As the Italian adage has it, *traduttore traditore* ('translation betrays'), and translators across cultures need to consider whether to remain true to the original (which may distance or exoticise the 'other'), whether to adapt to the target language context or audience (which may distort or falsify the original), and how to compromise between these positions (perhaps using a range of voices). Thus, Question Four: *how do researchers construct narrative accounts of research?*

Narratives are often answers to implicit questions and in research they are typically answers to explicit interview questions. However, it should be clear from this chapter that narrative questioning across cultures needs to be *learned* if it is to be meaningful to all participants.

Anthropological accounts (Briggs, 1986) reveal how specialists in cultural research need to learn how to ask; others specialising in narrative research on learning need knowledge and skills in intercultural questioning for effective international comparisons.

In this chapter we cannot go into detail about the research practices implied by these four questions; rather, we will look at some foundational features of how narratives relate to the cultural contexts in which they are given. We single out three aspects which, we argue, are central for researchers to be aware of when they approach the above questions. These aspects are related to the identity of the researcher as a likely audience in the context of participants telling stories of learning, the cultural variability of stories in narrative performance, and the identity of the teller.

The Identity of the Researcher and the Context of Narrating: who is the story for?

The identity of the narrative researcher can be an important issue (assuming a face-to-face gathering of data), partly in relation to storytellers' perceptions of who usually tells what kind of story to whom (and when, where and why) and partly in relation to community speech styles or the 'ways of speaking' which affect the oral communication of narratives (Hymes, 1974). This is complemented by the teller's identity (which we consider later). How the narrative audience is regarded, in the context of other features of the sociocultural context of interaction, may determine whether a story is told; what kind is told and how; and hence how it is received. Some examples illustrate the complexity of how perceived identity may affect research.

Smith (1999a), in studying the history of nineteenth-century women's education in New Zealand, used biographical accounts alongside other documentary evidence. She found that to understand the historical documentary evidence she needed interpretations through the oral narrative accounts of Maori participants. However, the apparently insider Maori testimonies, in the form of biographies 'as told to' someone else, distorted the participants' perceptions and experiences because the written versions – recorded by white outsiders acting as scribes – were edited into chronological sequences that were quite different from the original order of telling. As a Maori herself, Smith recognised that this obscured the cultural expression of background and details as well as the tellers' own ways of speaking. It ignored any cultural reasons for the original order of presentation. The identity and culture of the researcher and the cultural notions of how research should be carried out are deeply implicated in narrative research.

Like Smith, Brumble (1990) found that white researchers and editors imposed their own values on Native Americans telling their own life stories to make them conform to researchers' own ideas of what an autobiography should be and how it should be told. Many early biographies were stories given 'as told to' (often through interpreters) to white American questioners who wrote the story down and, crucially, edited it in a way that sought turning points and key moments in the unique development of the self, asking about childhood events and arranging everything in a strict chronological order. The narrators, however, were conscious of their lives as the sum total of their deeds as adults and had a collective sense of self oriented to the tribe (childhood episodes were usually irrelevant; chronology was not a great concern); they were what they had accomplished, the sum of their reputations, and therefore their narratives were stories of discrete episodes rather than the Western story of a life. The resultant biography can often be seen as a distortion, which was not corrected until after several generations of misunderstanding. Brumble (1990, p. 80) cites an editor who concluded that:

> Indian narrative style involves a repetition and a dwelling on unimportant details which confuse the white reader and make it hard to follow the story. Motives are never explained – emotional states are summed up in such colourless phrases as 'I liked it'. For one not immersed in the culture, the real significance escapes.

Clearly, this is collecting narrative data without taking into account the participants' cultural views of the telling. These respondents had their own views, however, of the researchers' motives and ethics (Brumble, 1990, p. 90):

> They [the researchers] come here and they say they want to be my friend, then they go away and put down what I say in books and make a lot of money.

The tellers' perceptions of the researchers' motives can align the resulting narrative accounts away from insider perspectives towards fiction. Sarries (1993, p. 254) recalls a Kashaya childhood in California:

> As a child I watched the old timers working with 'the scientists' from the universities. I saw how they edited information. I heard familiar stories told in new ways. I heard stories that I had never heard, and then waited for the elder's trickster wink as the scientist wrote madly, seriously. Two things seemed clear: university people weren't Indians and what was Indian wasn't in books.

Cultural resistance to outsiders, and lack of trust because of perceived motives, can still today lead to defensive distortions, as we ourselves saw in Costa Rica when a Bribri confided to us after a researcher had left his village with a bagful of recounted incidents of indigenous learning:

> That's not what really happened. That's only what we tell the anthropologists so they'll go away and leave us in peace.

This issue can also be interpreted in the light of the Mead-Freeman controversy, in which research conducted by Margaret Mead (Mead, 1943) in the 1920s into adolescence in Samoa was reinterpreted by Freeman (1983, 1996) in the light of later narrative evidence. Mead's fieldwork included living in a Samoan household as 'one of the girls', and she suggested that young Samoan girls did not seem to experience the tensions that American and European adolescents suffer. She concluded that this was because of the kind of social arrangements in Samoa, which made an easy transition from adolescence to adulthood, a crucial point for North American education at the time. Fifty-five years later, Derek Freeman (1996) claimed that one of Mead's main informants (who 61 years earlier had given Mead narrative accounts of local sexual practices) told him that at the time, like other girls she had been teasing Mead, just joking with reports about sex because they were embarrassed by Mead's questions. Freeman concluded that Mead had been misinformed and misled, and that her results were systematically distorted.

Whether the informant's first narrative (to Mead) or the second narrative (to Freeman) was basically 'correct', either may have been influenced by her perception of what the researcher wanted to know or what was appropriate to say, and either may have been shaped by political and religious views in Samoa on the research topic (Freeman took the informant's account as valid because she was willing to swear on the Bible that it was true), such views being part of the changing context of telling. This changing historical context involved the memory of the informant over sixty years, but such remembered accounts may be shaped by distortions of time, by rationalisations from present perspectives, and by changes in the teller's sense of identity (in this case in the postcolonial transition). The context further involves the relationships between the research protagonists of the controversy: a respected world authority, widely recognised as one of America's outstanding academic women, and an Australian challenger who waited until Mead's death before publicising his evidence.

Smith (1999b) argues that indigenous people often have their own research agendas (cultural ways of knowing), and to avoid cultural imperialism and preserve their identities they must research their environments themselves, employing their own culturally appropriate research methods. In much international and comparative narrative research, this larger framework of culture, ideology, and identity – of both the researched and the researchers (and of readerships) – needs to be taken into account. This, however, requires a double vision: that of the insider, with the participants' perceptions of educational meanings, and that of the outsider, with the academic community's conventions and the ability to interpret the research to audiences of readers in other cultural communities. Thus Hejaiej (1996), identifying herself as a Tunisian woman and as a person from a locally known family, was uniquely able to get behind closed doors to unveil women's stories, which in performance empowered women to transcend social conventions but which would not be told to someone apparently unbound by those conventions.

In other cases the inside narratives may need to be gathered by assistants who are seen as members of the community, or at least closer to it than the researcher. Thus Gorkin, in his efforts to collect women's stories, found that as a man in Palestine and El Salvador he was at a disadvantage in interviewing women. His solution was to conduct interviews jointly with local female assistants. When he noticed that the stories were fuller and richer in detail when he was not present, he restricted himself to analysing his and their interpretations and to writing. Ethical problems of authorship and responsibility were solved by recognising the collaboration in joint authorship (Gorkin & Othman, 1996; Gorkin et al, 2000). A joint collaborative solution, which we adopted (Cortazzi & Jin, 1996; Jin & Cortazzi, 1998) in investigating narrative and visual ethnography to study language classrooms in China, is for two researchers from different backgrounds (in this case British and Chinese) to work together and explicitly draw on the strength of their identities and cultures of research for a research synergy. As we have noted, though (Cortazzi & Jin, 2002), this can result in changing the self of the researchers in fieldwork practices, leading to identification with a second complementary culture, and this too is part of the research story.

Narrative Variability: how is the story shared?

The structures and functions of stories can vary enormously across cultures (Cortazzi, 1993, pp. 102-108), and such variations are a significant part of the global repertoire of narrative meanings. For example, evaluative aspects of narratives (structurally, how the teller signals the meaning and perspective of a story) can be seen to work so that the evaluation is *in* the narrative (in a wide range of linguistic devices which are part of the story), or elsewhere in non-story talk so that evaluation is *of* the narrative, or so that the telling itself is implicitly the evaluation of non-story topics *through* the narrative (Cortazzi & Jin, 2000). The balance between these ways, and the ways they actually work with stories, can vary widely across cultures. For example, in many Maori stories the evaluation by the teller is relatively inexplicit, compared with stories told by white New Zealanders: among Maoris the

33

story context is enough for a listener to draw conclusions, but may leave a white listener understanding the words but not realising what the story was actually about (Holmes, 1998).

Here we single out three other aspects of this variation: collaboration, occasioning and performance. One aspect of telling stories of everyday experience among family members or groups of colleagues is that stories are often co-constructed by several speakers simultaneously (rather than having a single teller) when the experience is shared (Ochs & Capps, 2001). This joint recall often gives the telling a celebratory function. However, there are other kinds of collaboration: tellers in some cultures, like Athabascan in North America, wait for the audience to anticipate the conclusion and supply it – the listener gives the ending and the meaning – and if a white audience does not or cannot supply this ending, the teller progressively expands the background, while waiting for an audience completion which may never come (Scollon & Scollon, 1981). Similar teller-audience collaborations among the Kalapalo in central Brasil give listeners the responsibility to put the pieces of the story together and to make evaluations explicit (Basso, 1992). As Heath (1983) has demonstrated in contrasting American communities, these narrative differences can have consequences for literacy practices inside and outside classrooms.

A further telling example is found in chains of learning transmission among health professionals in training (Cortazzi et al, 2001). In these chains, a student shares first-hand experience of a learning event in a clinical placement with a fellow student, who in turn narrates the story to another student, who tells another, and so on, so that vicarious learning is progressively shared through stories by a chain of participants:

> We phone each other up ... when I had my waterbirth [assisting as a student midwife], the next day I had to phone up most of the group and tell them, because I was all excited. I was the only one in the group who had had one. (A student midwife)

> Some stories have gone the rounds when different things have happened, like one of the girls saw a waterbirth so we all talked about that and that all got shared around, and if something bad happens, something really serious, that all gets shared around. (A student midwife)

> I've picked up most of the things from other nursing students further on in the course. More senior students seem able to teach me more. I think it's because they realise what I haven't done ... and then we've got the first-years ... and I've found

myself relaying it back to her [a first-year student] as well. (A student nurse)

A researcher who hears only one story and is unaware of the learning network would miss the narrative chain and thus ignore the informal learning collaboration. A conclusion from these cultural expectations and practices is that in many cultures there is a dialogical blurring of teller and listener roles. They indicate that narrative researchers need to think about their own cultural expectations, to examine interview transcripts to see precisely how the interviewer is implicated in the genesis and construction of oral narratives, and to know how stories function collaboratively in some communities.

The occasion for storytelling and the reason for it is another aspect of narrative variability which can cause confusion. A context in which a British researcher expects a narrative may not yield one, for sociocultural reasons. Another context in which the same researcher does not expect a narrative (or expects a differently aligned one) may elicit one, which since it is unanticipated may be ignored. The following extracts from longer narratives illustrate occasioning (places, names and dates have been changed):

It is a great pleasure to have an opportunity to introduce myself to you ... I was born on January 26th, 1974, in Pusan, the second largest city in Korea. *I am the second daughter having two sisters and two brothers. My father, 59, is a businessman and mother, 54, is there running the Education Advice Centre. They always encouraged me to live in honesty and sincerity, to do my best in anything, and to pursue my self-actualisation.* (A student writing from Korea)

'Set a goal, work hard towards it and achieve it.' My mother, who is primary school teacher, often said this to me when I was a child. Encouraged by this spirit, I progressed myself through achieving one goal after another. Passing the most competitive National College Entrance Examination in China, admitted by *the most prestigious* Hunan Normal University in the province of 64,000,000 people, *I realised my first dream.* After four years' excellent academic performance at University, being one of top 10 in 210 graduates, I won the privilege of serving as an English teacher at Foreign Languages College at Hunan Agricultural University. Growing up in a small remote town, I know more about the importance of education. *My sense of responsibility drives me to devote to teaching. I read a wide variety of books and journals to seek for creative approaches to my class. Sharing laughter with students in group work give me great pleasure; inviting*

35

students with best classroom performance to eat at McDonald's (which is a luxury for village students in China) brings me enormous happiness. I have been awarded the Best Teacher in the past four years. (A student writing from China)

As the only child of my family, I grew *up happily under the ten dance [sic] of my parents* in Xintai, a medium city of Shandong Province, China. Most of my times in primary school and secondary school were well-off. I had been elected as the Learning Commissary and Monitor for many years, which brought up my ability of communication and leadership since I was young ... *Hardworking and devoted, I easily outshone other students* with my academic record, which landed me among the top ten students in the whole grade at University. On the strength of my outstanding academic record, I got the honour to be an assistant to help the professors from my department with data collection and sometimes with their lesson preparation. The chance was rarely available to a third-year undergraduate like me then. In the autumn of 2002, I launched a photo exhibition of educational achievements, aiming to show different educational systems from culture to culture. *Though Chinese traditional systems have its own advantages, the heavy satchels over Chinese students' shoulders as well as piles and piles of papers in their hands, at the disadvantage, made a sharp contrast to the leisurely smiles on Western students' faces. With my efforts* I became a temporary English teacher in the affiliated school of Xintai Normal University. In my teaching, I found my students did the same as I had done when I was a high school student – reading books blindly. Thus I took the trouble to try new learning approaches on my students who learned how to study. *With all the efforts I had made,* both students' extrinsic and their intrinsic interests in language learning have been greatly motivated *and I finally won the respect and trust from the students.* (A student writing from China)

I have been an excellent student all these years. I was born in Dongfang, Hebei Province in China on April 22nd, 1975. *My odyssey in the world of knowledge began* in 1981 when I went to Dongfang No. 1 Primary School. From then on my academic record was always in the upper 5% among the students of my grade and I won various prizes and honours during my school years. *Since being a teacher was one of my dearest dreams,* I became a college student in the Foreign Languages Department of Dongfang Normal University after I finished my secondary education. Because of my outstanding academic performance, I was honoured the First Prize Academic Scholarship and Excellent Student by the college in two consecutive years. In the summer of 1994, *my dream came true*: I became a teacher of English at Dongfang No. 6 Middle School, an ivy league middle school in Hebei Province. *I began to experience the happiness in helping others achieve progress. Those years hard work bore abundant fruit*; nearly 90% of my students passed the entrance examination to senior high school successfully and some of them are now studying at prestigious universities of the country. Years later, most of them still have a strong interest in language learning. *When I receive their letters of thanks, I come to realise that what I have taught to them might have helped them to change their lives. It is such a great pleasure that I have never experienced in my life. I am a person insatiable for knowledge and graduate study helped me to foster diverse interests in learning.* After six months preparation, in 1996, I successfully defeated some 90 candidates around the country and became one of the only three postgraduate students with scholarships at Chongqing Foreign Studies University, majoring in English and American Literature. *It was not easy, especially for an associate graduate, but I made it!* (A student writing from China)

These written narratives are all from postgraduate application letters for British Master's degree courses, in which the writer needs to establish a relevant academic and professional identity and, preferably, a distinctive voice as a worthy applicant. The italicised portions are, in our experience, unlikely to occur in similar self-presentations by British students. This is because British graduates are more likely to be tuned in to the postgraduate admission tutor's expectation that such self-descriptions will establish worthiness through a narrative rooted in factual evidence of achievement, with a rationale of how the course will benefit the applicant in his or her professional context (for this, demonstrated professional or academic qualities are relevant but not claimed personal ones). We see here, however, how these East Asian applicants follow a cultural trend of using their narratives to establish their identities as moral persons ('honesty', 'sincerity', 'my sense of responsibility', 'won the respect and trust'), of sound family background (frequent mention of parents, sometimes even grandparents), with humane qualities ('happiness', 'gives me great pleasure'), who will work hard ('hardworking', 'years hard work', 'devoted', 'with all my efforts') with the dedication to realise their dreams ('my first dream', 'my dearest dreams') in their education ('my odyssey in the world of knowledge'). To them, such narratives are connected to real life; they are the evidence of past performance which is shareable with strangers, evidence which will arouse a reader's emotions to enhance the chance of acceptance. The East Asian bridging assumptions are that this is a narrative occasion where family standing and moral or personal stance are significant, but such assumptions may lead to inappropriate narrative alignment for a British academic. The British reader might read this very positive personalisation as over-claiming through exaggerated boasting or poetic irrelevance; conversely, a Chinese reader of a typical British application letter might wonder why the expected exposition of the moral identity of the person is absent. Either intercultural reading could lead to an inappropriate evaluation of the application. With cultural conceptions of different narrative purposes, interpretations can slide past each other; they may be missed or misconstrued when the occasioning varies.

A third aspect of variability which narrative researchers often underestimate is performance. Primary teachers often give memorable performances of narratives which feature children: voices are vividly performed through pitch changes and wide intonation contours, gestures and facial expressions are exaggerated, as dramatisation combines with entertainment and the professional presentation of the self as a competent teller of stories to adults as well as children (Cortazzi, 1991). This can be institutionally ritualised in schools in events such as celebrations and staff retirements, when more experienced raconteurs talk of each other or of school history. Yet performances vary cross-culturally even among children, as Minami (2002) has shown among 5-9-year-olds: Japanese children's stories of personal experiences were highly succinct accounts of multiple events, whereas American children gave longer stories elaborating single events with more emotion and evaluation. This reflects cultural patterns of the children's interaction with their parents: Japanese parents were less directive and more subtle or ambiguous, whereas American parents encouraged and directed verbal elaboration through many evaluative comments. The stories of the Japanese children resembled the three-line, seventeen-syllable *haiku* verse form, while those of the Americans could be said to be more like longer ballads.

An important oral performance variable for researchers is the discourse organisation of narratives into lines and stanzas (Hymes, 1981, 1996; Scollon & Scollon, 1981; Gee, 1989). This is a matter of transcription and analysis by hearing the unseen ordering of meaning through intonation and clauses into lines, and sets of lines into verses or stanzas cohering round a single topic and structured rhythmically and syntactically by such means as parallelism, repetition and change of viewpoint. This is an implicit cultural pattering through speech: while many North American cultures employ verses of three or five lines (with a central line), others have four-line verses (made of two pairs). As

Hymes (1996) demonstrates, different analyses can give quite different interpretations of the verbal patterning of meaning.

Identities in Narrative: who is the teller?

As a comparer across cultures, perhaps, a narrative researcher can work in one culture but draw conclusions about others personally experienced or known vicariously through research literature. Researchers travelling among cultures can make direct cross-cultural comparisons. Sometimes participants, as tellers, make intercultural comparisons from their own first-hand experience; this brings researchers the advantage of other's interpretations. Here is an example from a Malaysian parent where the narrating implicates the teller's identity and that of her child, whose identity is challenged.

> Malaysian students do not ask questions in class. It's probably because they respect the teacher, the teacher as a guru, but they do ask after the class, you know, by going up to the teacher after the lesson. My son [aged eight at the time] was in Scotland for nine months and during that time he learned to speak up in class, ask questions and all that, but when we came home to Malaysia there was a real problem for about six months. He wanted to talk a lot in class, ask lots of questions. He would volunteer to go up to the front and write on the board but all the other children, you know, called him 'matsalleh' [an insulting reference to a white person] and he was disturbed and unhappy. It's better now. He has quietened down and doesn't ask questions any more, just sits there like everyone else. (A Malaysian teacher who had studied in Scotland)

This narrative was shared in Malaysia. It portrays the homecoming as a reverse culture shock in which British verbal interaction patterns for classroom learning, into which the child had been successfully acculturated, became a source of racial insults to the Malay child in the Malaysian classroom. The parent elaborated later that the problem of the disturbance to the child was severe enough to warrant calling in a clinical psychologist. The teller's understanding of the British ways of learning – as a teacher herself she visited British primary schools – sharpens the contrast in reported patterns of questioning. Her final comment was given with irony but not sadness, implying a cultural adaptability to and for between educational philosophies of interaction, which emerged later in interview as part of her own professional identity.

  In another example, a Singaporean Chinese writer recounts how as a student she answered exam questions. She focuses on the remembered experience of visualising 'the other' (the British examiners, of whom she had no direct experience) and the voices they most frequently read, and deliberately constructing an individual – and different – voice, in distinction to others of her own cultural group (fellow Singaporean candidates). The narrator saw this vocalisation as a key to her successful educational identity. She makes the intercultural comparison herself:

> Unlike my classmates, I never thought of exams as mere regurgitation of information. I imagined a long table of examiners, neither men nor women, but all English, reading these hundreds of thousands of essays pouring in from the British Empire ... These readers formed a formidable audience, for, reading as fast and tediously as they had to, only a different voice could reach them through those fortress walls of exam booklets.
>
> I thought of that voice as the voice of the mind, but a distinct mind, one at ease with information but not burdened by it, a mind that worked with rules and patterns but that manipulated them playfully or deviously or adroitly rather than repeating them. It was a mind that collected and arranged. Sometimes the collection was impressive enough; sometimes the arrangement was surprising or fresh. Because the mind was full and confident, it could suggest that what it said was inadequate, that something else eluded it. The memorisation was never mere data collection, as many of my classmates believed. The selection of 'facts' to memorise was itself a painstaking, necessary, and formative preparation for the final task of analysis and presentation. (Lim, 1996, pp. 132-133)

There are sometimes particular occasions when the act of narrating itself constitutes a context for enhancing awareness of learner identity and realisation of its problematicity (rather than the narrative simply reflecting pre-existing identity). This point emerged in Khalaf's (2001) study of Lebanese students who had returned to Lebanon, having spent long periods of often disrupted education in several countries during the civil war (roughly 1975-1992). A group of such students found a 'third space' shuttling between the two cultures (Lebanese and other), to which they felt they did not belong. This space was a creative writing class, which was midwife to the following narrative extracts from several students (Khalaf, 2001, pp. 96-149 and *passim*):

> I wrote to express my feelings of not belonging anywhere. No matter where I went, I felt alienated, and it seemed like I could only express my feelings on paper ...

Because I have never lived in one place for very long I feel like
an exile everywhere ... people ignore what I say and pretend
that I'm not around because they don't consider me a real part
of their society. Maybe this is why I turned to writing ...

I encompass a spectrum of personalities because my life has
been interrupted so many times that I have not experienced
continuity. My existence is choppy and disconnected ...

Sometimes I think I have multiple personalities, and at other
times I console myself that it is natural to have all these
differences in one personality. However, I believe that I have
probably worn so many masks that I forget who I am in
reality ...
I have been forced to adapt to so many different places,
people, and situations so my personality has not developed in
a linear fashion. I have a special mask for every occasion.
Rarely do I take it off and relax my face ...

It was only when I joined this creative writing class that I
began to feel comfortable ...

In my writing I can express the way I feel. It is refreshing and
encouraging to know that the people in this class feel the way I
do. Together we create our own little niche.

Significantly, the narratives were engendered with a teacher-researcher
who had experienced a similar culturally discontinuous background;
they were written with others who shared a fragmented sense of self.
Over time, however, such narratives help to formulate a reconfigured self
through reflexivity. Narrative reflexivity – the awareness of how our self
relates to social context and how we know it; how that self shapes it yet
is shaped by it – is not only for researchers; participants sometimes
engage with it too, and this can be seen in snapshot form in some
narratives.

A Framework for Reflexive Questioning: what shall we ask?

We conclude with ten socioculturally oriented questions that ask about
narratives in research.

1. What Kinds of Narrative Are There in This Community? Any
particular narrative may need to be seen as having characteristics of a
particular narrative genre within a repertoire of cultural resources of
ways of communicating. We should not expect all cultural groups to

have similar repertoires of narrative types, and the meanings of some types are likely to vary.

2. Why Is the Teller Sharing a Narrative? The motivation and intention of the teller needs to be ascertained in relation to the cultural resources of narration; different kinds of narrative may have different purposes but such purposes may not be transparent to audiences across cultural communities.

3. How Do We Compare Narratives? The obvious approach to comparing narratives is to obtain narrative data on the same topic and analyse them using the same model; however, this needs to be done with awareness of the cultural ways of speaking, as realised or performed in internal structures of narratives and in their functions in social contexts.

4. How Much Context Is Needed to Interpret a Narrative? More than most other genres, narratives contain their own contexts: sufficient contextual and background information is included for the audience to understand the main meanings. Cross-culturally, this often depends on the teller's awareness of what the audience already knows and understands about contexts and about ways of telling; there may be a false presumption of common ground.

5. What Are the Relations between the Teller, the Story, the Audience and the Researcher? The telling of any narrative is likely to vary in content, structure, style, and performance according to the teller's perception of the identity, role and interest of the researcher compared with the teller's self-perception of role and identity, yet the telling itself is part of a developing context. Early stories in an interview may be different, therefore, from later ones.

6. How Do We Account for Performance Features in Narratives? In oral narratives, the teller's notions of drama, performance and self-presentation are crucial, but these may be overlooked in transcription and analysis (see Question 9, below).

7. What Model of Narrative Analysis Is Appropriate? The main criterion should probably be fitness for purpose, since different models are designed to include different features, with different presuppositions and ways of working within different disciplines. Researchers generally consider several models before choosing or adapting the most suitable one.

8. How Does the Researcher Know When Interpretations of Narratives and Their Evaluations Are Appropriate to What the Teller Means? A standard way to check procedure is to check interpretations with the teller or a significant member of the teller's cultural community. However, this is logistically difficult when the tellers are in another country, and member validation is not without pitfalls. Since interpretations are fashioned for different audiences, the researcher may need to translate an academically oriented interpretation into a more publicly accessible format. Since narrating is often occasioned by time and circumstance, a teller re-examining the telling under other circumstances often feels the impulse to change or add to the original text (recall Mead's and Freeman's informant). The researcher probably assumes this editing is an improved final version rather than a change of mind or heart. Both the researcher and the participant need to be aware that the editing of a written text (the transcription) of an oral narrative also needs to take account of the ways in which oral and written communication normally differ.

9. How Does the Analysis Represent Meaning, Voice and Human Qualities? There are standard ways in linguistics to represent prosodic and phonetic characteristics or to analyse gestures and movement from video recordings. For some research, a multimedia approach to analysis, writing up and reporting will be the only solution to the problem of treating narrative text as frozen or fossilised. However, most researchers recognise that the process of standardisation of data to make it manageable across cases risks the loss of characteristics which may later turn out to be interesting and important. One solution, which has particular advantages for cross-cultural research, is to take some representative narratives and treat them as performance texts (Denzin, 1997, pp. 93-123). Here the researcher, as ethnographer, re-enacts the original narratives to recover, yet interrogate, the meanings of the lived experience in an embodied dramatic performance. Such performance suggests that the research is an interpretive event (as were the original narratives) in which the audience is also part of the interpretation (as in the original narrating), reconfiguring relationships between the teller, story, narrative audience, researcher and research audience.

10. What Are the Standards or Criteria to Judge Narrative Analyses? Answers to this final question include coherence, trustworthiness, plausibility, persuasiveness, generalisabilty, verisimilitude, reflexiveness, harmonisation with results from other data sources, and member validation. Since the narrative researcher needs to gain participants' trust and confidence to get narrative data and access to valid knowledge of meanings, the researcher is not impartial, and this needs to be allowed for in interpretation.

This framework would, in most cases, lead to further, more case-specific, questions which need to be asked in research about narratives. Narrative sharing is a natural process in our lives and often the most telling stories are those that prompt the most reflection and the most questions, including questions about identity. For novice researchers, as well as the more experienced, asking the right sorts of questions helps us to feel our identity as researchers. Taking account of this identity is particularly important, as indicated earlier in this chapter, in comparative and international research in education.

References

Atkinson, P. (1990) *The Ethnographic Imagination: textual constructions of reality*. London: Routledge.

Basso, E. (1992) Contextualization in Kalapalo Narratives, in A. Duranti & C. Goodwin (Eds) *Rethinking Context: language as an interactive phenomenon*, pp. 253-269. Cambridge: Cambridge University Press.

Briggs, C.L. (1986) *Learning How to Ask: a sociolinguistic appraisal of the role of the interview in social science research*. Cambridge: Cambridge University Press.

Brumble, H.D. (1990) *American Indian Autobiography*. Berkeley: University of California Press.

Cortazzi, M. (1991) *Primary Teaching, How It Is: a narrative account*. London: David Fulton.

Cortazzi, M. (1993) *Narrative Analysis*. London: Falmer.

Cortazzi, M. (2001) Narrative Analysis in Ethnography, in P. Atkinson, A. Coffey, S. Delamont, J. Lofland & L. Lofland (Eds) *Handbook of Ethnography*, pp. 384-394. London: Sage.

Cortazzi, M. & Jin, L. (1996) Cultures of Learning: language classrooms in China, in H. Coleman (Ed.) *Society and the Language Classroom*, pp. 169-206. Cambridge: Cambridge University Press.

Cortazzi, M. & Jin, L. (2000) Evaluating Evaluation in Narrative, in S. Hunston & G. Thompson (Eds) *Evaluation in Text*, pp. 102-120. Oxford: Oxford University Press.

Cortazzi, M. & Jin, L. (2002) Cultures of Learning: the social construction of educational identities, in D.C.S. Li (Ed.) *Discourses in Search of Members: in honor of Ron Scollon*, pp. 49-78. Lanham: University Press of America.

Cortazzi, M., Jin, L., Wall, D. & Cavendish, S. (2001) Sharing Learning through Narrative Communication, *International Journal of Language and Communication Disorders*, 36, pp. 252-257.

Denzin, N. (1997) *Interpretive Ethnography: ethnographic practices for the 21st century*. Thousand Oaks: Sage.

Freeman, D. (1983) *Margaret Mead and Samoa: the making and unmaking of an anthropological myth*. Cambridge, MA: Harvard University Press.

Freeman, D. (1996) *Margaret Mead and the Heretic*. Harmondsworth: Penguin.

Gee, J.P. (1989) Two Styles of Narrative Construction and Their Linguistic and Educational Implications, *Discourse Processes*, 12(3), pp. 287-307.

Golden-Biddle, K. & Locke, K.D. (1997) *Composing Qualitative Research*. Thousand Oaks: Sage.

Gorkin, M. & Othman, R. (1996) *Three Mothers, Three Daughters: Palestinian women's stories*. Berkeley: University of California Press.

Gorkin, M., Pineda, M. & Leal, G. (2000) *From Grandmother to Granddaughter: Salvadorean women's stories*. Berkeley: University of California Press.

Heath, S.B. (1983) *Ways with Words: language, life and work in communities and classrooms*. Cambridge: Cambridge University Press.

Hejaiej, M. (1996) *Behind Closed Doors: women's oral narratives in Tunis*. London: Quartet Books.

Holmes, J. (1998) Narrative Structure: some contrasts between Maori and Pakeha story-telling, *Multilingua*, 17(1), pp. 25-57.

Hymes, D. (1974) Ways of Speaking, in R. Baumann & J. Sherzer (Eds) *Explorations in the Ethnography of Speaking*, pp. 433-452. Cambridge: Cambridge University Press.

Hymes, D. (1981) *'In Vain I Tried to Tell You': studies in Native American poetics*. Philadelphia: University of Pennsylvania Press.

Hymes, D. (1996) *Ethnography, Linguistics, Narrative Inequality: towards an understanding of voice*. London: Taylor & Francis.

Jin, L. & Cortazzi, M. (1998) Dimensions of Dialogue: large classes in China, *International Journal of Educational Research*, 29, pp. 739-761. http://dx.doi.org/10.1016/S0883-0355(98)00061-5

Khalaf, R.S. (2001) Creative Writing, Identity and Change: a case study of American University of Beirut students in post-war Lebanon. Unpublished EdD thesis, University of Leicester.

Lim, S.G-L. (1996) *Among the White Moonfaces: memoirs of a Nyonya feminist*. Singapore: Times Books International.

Mead, M. (1943) *Coming of Age in Samoa*. Harmondsworth: Penguin.

Minami, M. (2002) *Culture-specific Language Styles: the development of oral narrative and literacy*. Clevedon: Multilingual Matters.

Ochs, E. & Capps, L. (2001) *Living Narrative: creating lives in everyday storytelling*. Cambridge, MA: Harvard University Press.

Sarries, G. (1993) Keeping Slug Woman Alive: the challenge of reading in a reservation classroom, in J. Boyarin (Ed.) *The Ethnography of Reading*, pp. 238-269. Berkeley: University of California Press.

Scollon, R. & Scollon, S. (1981) *Narrative, Literacy and Face in Interethnic Communication*. Norwood: Ablex.

Smith, L.T. (1999a) Connecting Pieces: finding the indigenous presence in the history of women's education, in K. Weiler & S. Middleton (Eds) *Telling Women's Lives: narrative enquiries in the history of women's education*, pp. 60-72. Buckingham: Open University Press.

Smith, L.T. (1999b) *Decolonizing Methodologies: research and indigenous people.* London: Zed Books.

Van Maanen, J. (1988) *Tales of the Field: on writing ethnography.* Chicago: University of Chicago Press.

Wolcott, H. (2001) *Writing Up Qualitative Research.* Thousand Oaks: Sage.

CHAPTER THREE

Stories within Stories: dissolving the boundaries in narrative research and analysis

CHRISTINE FOX
University of Wollongong, Australia

Introduction

The lens through which we see our world and the world of others is made of the stories we hear. Our earliest received and exchanged texts are from the cradle: the first words, the nursery rhymes, the sounds and senses of the immediate world. Our identities form and develop through narrative. Paul Ricoeur (1991) talks about narrative identity: 'the sort of identity to which a human being has access thanks to the mediation of the narrative function', the narrative being a fusion of both historical and fictional (Ricoeur, 1991, p. 73). Narrative research is therefore that of individual and social histories and identities, through space and time. Colette Daiute & Cynthia Lightfoot (2004), in discussing narrative research, state that 'narrative discourse and metaphor are excellent contexts for examining social histories that influence identity and development' (Daiute & Lightfoot, 2004, p. xii).

In comparative and international education, researchers have traditionally been concerned with comparisons, especially across national systems and cultural boundaries. Today, comparisons of either/or, black /white, East/West, self/other – dichotomies of one sort or another – are challenged, deconstructed and re-analysed in the light of the researchers' greater critical awareness of the complex nature of the different discourses of power and ideology (Thompson, 1990; Masemann & Welch 1997; Crossley & Watson, 2003; McCarthy et al, 2003). Comparativists have critiqued the power of the colonial narrator compared with the silenced voice of the subaltern, which distorts or confines the boundaries of understanding and interpretation (see Tikly,

2001; Fox, 2003; Hickling-Hudson et al, 2004). Human life is narratively structured and constructed; narrative research captures the lived experience of human interaction. In an essay on narrative criticism, Mark Freeman claims that narratives 'serve as means of access to social reality, signifying the worlds through which people have moved' (Freeman, 2004, p. 69).

In this chapter, I argue that the need for narrative research as a driving methodology in comparative and international research is essential. The twenty-first century is a postcolonial era of globalisation, fused borders and diasporas, and a challenge to human development at a critical stage of contemporary society (Crossley & Tikly, 2004). Every education system has now become affected, not only by a globalised information technology and a globalised market, but also by a global spread of natural disasters, terrorism, mass dislocation through migration, environmental pollution and degradation. In these diverse sociocultural and economic contexts of education, a qualitative approach to research is required, going beyond statistical, decontextualised data or national systems analysis. I argue that there is a need to embrace narrative as a method of listening to and heeding the voices of experience across borders; a method of dissolving the artificial boundaries that divide one culture from another. The following section looks at the need for narrative research from the perspectives of comparative and international education. The next section discusses narrative method and narrative analysis from an intercultural perspective, and the last section calls for the dissolution of boundaries and the establishment of finely-tuned sensitivities in narrative inquiry.

Significance of Narrative Research in Comparative and International Education

From the late twentieth to the early twenty-first century, a discernible shift in research approaches to comparative and international education has occurred, from the scientific rationalist tradition towards a post-colonial critique. Initially led by such world-renowned theorists as Edward Said (1978, 1994, 2001), Gayatri Spivak (1990) and Homi Bhabha (1994), to name but three, recent research in comparative and international education has emphasised the centrality of a post-colonial context, one that challenges the colonial agenda and disrupts the narrative of the powerful/powerless dichotomy (Arnove & Torres, 2003; Hickling-Hudson et al, 2004; Crossley & Tikly, 2004). Welch (2003) provides a detailed historical perspective of the shift in comparative education research from the positivist agenda of the enlightenment and the notion of scientific reason towards a more critical, qualitative agenda. He states that Vandra Masemann signalled a turning point in comparative research in the 1980s in her challenge to researchers to take on board the notion of critical ethnography and to include indigenous knowledge. On the other hand, by the 1990s, researchers were confronting postmodernity with some alarm at the seeming fragmentation and diversity of approaches that not only sidestepped issues of comparative education systems, but also seemed to ignore the critical theoretical agendas of social justice, gender equity and other forms of social 'reality' (Masemann & Welch, 1997, p. 398; Levinson et al, 1996; Fox, 2004).

It is a challenge for educators to take up an agenda that does not accept the dichotomies implicit in the terms colonisers and colonised, us and Other, developed and developing, but rather explores the relations of power through dialogue, creating spaces for transformation. Some of the chapters in this volume refer to the issue of teaching narrative research, bringing to light the various ways in which dialogue can be used as a tool for understanding the speakers' points of view. When reading these chapters, the reader needs to focus first on the describing, but then move on to 'scribing' (writing new agendas); on deconstructing, but then on constructing (creating new knowledge). The space can be created through narrative research.

An example of scribing and constructing rather than describing and deconstructing is taken from an attempt to construct a new history through an analysis of writings of several hundred years ago. Maria Cristina González has provided an account of her ethnographic studies into her family's history in Mexico (González , 2003). She describes how she has traced the relationships between her ancestors to 'relationships of ethnographic origin' (p. 78). Her indigenous cultural ancestors in Mexico, who met the first Spanish explorers to arrive in Mexico, were the focus of the records kept by the scribes accompanying Hernán Cortés. These records:

> [provided the] prototype for colonial writing of culture, or
> ethnography ... Although meticulously and rigorously written,
> with rich description and cultural insights, what must be
> acknowledged in order for these early colonialist
> ethnographies to be fully appreciated, is that they were written
> in order to justify, legitimise, and perpetuate the colonization
> of those about whom the texts were written. (p. 78; see also
> Clair, 2003)

She goes on to observe that as researchers we tend to assume that historical literature is scientifically constructed, rather than a combination of viewpoint and fiction. Ricoeur's (1984-1988) monumental work *Time and Narrative* discusses the union of history and fiction, a reminder that history is phenomenology, a researcher's comparative methodology of remembering (Kellner, 1990, p. 229). As Foucault has stated:

> Criticism is no longer going to be practised in the search for
> formal structures with universal value, but rather as a
> historical investigation into events that have led us to
> constitute ourselves and to recognize ourselves as subjects of
> what we are doing, thinking, saying .... Criticism will not seek
> to identify the universal structures of all knowledge or of all
> possible moral action, but will seek to treat the instances of
> discourse that articulate what we think, say and do as so many
> historical events ... (Foucault, 1984, p. 46)

An interesting way of discussing narrative research from a comparative perspective is to examine the notion of 'imagination'. Theodore Sarbin (2004) claims that imagination is related to action and is not the same as imagery or 'seeing'. The origin of the word 'imagine' is *imago,* to imitate or copy, following the idea that behaviours are copied rather than the more popular idea of creating pictures in the mind. He therefore contrasts imagery with imaginings, which he defines as 'storied sequences of actions in which self and others are involved. Imaginings are emplotted narratives carrying implications of causality and duration' (Sarbin, 2004, p. 11). He notes that self-report means 'I heard the voice'. Imagining means 'it is as if I heard the voice', which liberates human beings from the constraints of the immediate environment (Sarbin, 2004, p. 11).

Social cartography is another perspective on narrative inquiry, and is best suited to the comparativists' work (Paulston, 1996). Although Paulston uses the imagination as a way of 'seeing', his basic message is similar to that of Sarbin; his metaphor of mapping the imagination is a contribution to constructing knowledge spaces and sites through narrative and metaphor. His claim is that without the thick description of the world around us, there is no basis for comparative study or analysis (Paulston, 1996, p. 8). In Paulston (1996), I have argued that narrative inquiry is the necessary tool of a comparativist researcher or consultant in the consultancy 'field' of education in less industrialised countries, since research, consultancy and practitioner action require a building of relationships between inquirer and subject. The practical role of the comparativist in imagining action is through dialogue and the reporting of interactions:

> Lasting change usually occurs as a result of a change in
> interrelationships. It may be the result of changing
> fundamental structures, changing values or changing ways of
> doing things. People's relationships with each other also
> change in order to bring about that modification or
> transformation ... The role of a consultant is [therefore]
> expected to be that of a change agent rather than a program
> deliverer, since to consult is to ask advice from, to consider, to

refer to something or someone for information. (Fox, 1996, p. 292)

Sara deTurk (2001) developed a similar argument for intercultural empathy, and went on to discuss the interpretation of narrative inquiry from the perspective of the 'subject' of Western inquiry. She warns of the dangers of assuming straightforward scientific translation:

> Subordinates learn that direct, honest reactions are dangerous, and that open communication is possible only with each other. Dominant groups are left ignorant both of their own impact on others and of subordinate group members' true identities and experiences. (p. 379)

It is through the voice of the 'other', spoken in the context of their own situation, that 'the perspective of the "other" permits various cultural irrationalities or inconsistencies to emerge into clearer view' (Swigonski, 1994, cited in deTurk, 2001, p. 380).

Narrative Method

The following typology of contextual lenses illustrates one method of engaging in the multidimensionality of narrative research: how the researcher needs to go beyond the text to the context. These categories are useful in making cultural filtering processes explicit. They should be seen as macro categories, corresponding to whole systems of making meaning. By deliberately recognising these filtering (and sometimes translating) processes, it should be possible to understand how narrative data can be analysed. The categories identified are shown in Table I.

Cognitive Lens

The construction of meaning through language is one of the systems of meaning that constitute culture. As Jerome Bruner has elaborated throughout his career in interpreting cognitive meaning, cognitive classifications are the structures and landscapes of action and of consciousness (Bruner, 1983). Metacognition and cognitive recategorisation thus function as a filtering process in communication, whether it includes a value orientation, a moral attitude, a perception of persons, or a classification of physical stimuli. These filtering processes, according to Bruner, are 'categories by which a person sorts out and responds to the world about him [and it] reflects deeply the culture into which he is born' (Bruner, 1983, p. 10). To take a simple example in a complex area, one person may categorise a similar belief as *religion* for their own culture and *magic* for another. Teachers, to take another example, may describe children's behaviours as inattentive or uninterested, or unintelligent, whereas the children themselves may

51

have withdrawn because they find the teacher's behaviour culturally offensive or inappropriate.

Lens	Definition
Cognitive	The classification of objects, ideas and knowledge in metacognition
Semiotic	The use of metaphor and innuendo in creating new meaning
Experiential	The researcher's mindfulness of self in relation to narrator/text; of affective behaviours, aesthetic and sensory experience; of relationships between verbal and non-verbal communication – the embodiment of experience in body and spirit
Ethical	The degree of ethical validity in context, including understanding of the continuum from personal morality to political and legal ethical contexts
Hermeneutic	The critical interpretation of the context of culture, situation and the narrative event, especially from the cultural dimensions of time and space, both in the bounded situation and in historical text

Table I. Typology of narrative lenses (adapted from Fox, 1992, 1996).

The following example of narrative is taken from a recorded situation that occurred in a Pacific nation between an inexperienced consultant and two indigenous educators while discussing the contents of a career counselling textbook for students. The consultant had classified certain jobs as 'indoor' jobs or 'outdoor' jobs, including secretarial, farming, scientific and so on. The conversation moved to farming, which the consultant construed as an outdoor job. The indigenous educators had further classifications in mind, namely 'subsistence' and 'commercial'. They were discussing the inclusion of a picture showing a commercial tractor, and whether the farmer should be pictured in the garden or next to the tractor. The Pacific island participants wanted to take the tractor out of the picture.

> *Consultant (C)*: But we are only interested in finding out about their interest in outdoor activities [compared to indoor activities].
> *First Pacific Island teacher educator (P)*: We want the picture to look like subsistence farming, not commercial farming.
> *C*: All we want to know [is] if they are interested in working in a garden. It doesn't matter if it's commercial or subsistence.
> *First P*: But if we put in a tractor we are encouraging them to go into commercial farming. Villagers do not use tractors.

Second P: Those are outdoor jobs – two different types of operations going on there. The student can choose which one he [*sic*] likes best.
C: What we're looking at is the skills involved in an outdoor job. Planting etc. It doesn't matter if it's commercial or village. Just the skills.
First P: We need a good variety .... We've also got nursery work.
Second P: Could we change that commercial farming to ploughing a farm?
C: We have to fit in only a few extra pictures. We have to cut down.

The consultant was looking at skills, at general classifications of 'indoors' and 'outdoors'. But these were not relevant to the Pacific educators, given the far more significant cultural and economic differences denoted by jobs in commercial or subsistence farming. Yet the consultant failed to come to grips with this classification. Had the consultant reflected on the situation, she would have had an opportunity to discover the ethical, metaphorical dimensions of the interaction, and possibly found other ways to resolve the dilemma.

Detweiler's (1978, 1980) early work on the process of categorisation and its effect on intercultural interaction has shown there is a strong connection between ways in which individuals organise information into categories and ways in which they adapt to new situations in unfamiliar contexts. Detweiler argues that categorisation is a way of giving meaning to stimulation from the world and that individuals who are socialised in the same culture will categorise and interpret situations and behaviours similarly, and therefore have similar expectancies (Detweiler, 1980, p. 279). It appears from his research that the broader the categories into which an individual organises narrative information, the more likely it is that new contexts can be tolerated, since different meanings can be accommodated more easily within broad categories. Narrow categorisers were more likely to make stereotypical assertions.

Semiotic Lens

Metaphor is a powerful mechanism for inducing insight into meaning. Metaphor has the power to bring two separate domains into cognitive and emotional relation by using language directly appropriate to the one as a lens for seeing the other. Metaphor acts as a bridge to allow common meanings to emerge. Ricoeur's notion of metaphor as a mediating device emphasises that there is no self-understanding that is not mediated by signs, symbols and texts. Metaphor creates meaning through the use of pictures projected into the minds of the interlocutors who are seeking to describe the relationships between ideas and objects. Given different cultural backgrounds, it is not surprising that these relationships are very revealing of how people perceive their reality. With practice at listening carefully, the hearer can anticipate different interpretations and possibly evidence of bias through cultural filtering. For example, an educator may use a number of military metaphors in relation to her or his task, indicating the strategic nature of the vision of the 'captive audience', 'going in' or 'setting targets'. Alternatively, the teacher may use metaphors connoting care or collegiality, using more reflective words.

In narrative inquiry, the use of metaphor for everyday occurrences can alert those from other cultures to differences that might exist about the interpretation of a seemingly common idea. One metaphor, related to the interpretation of history, illustrates my point well, and is taken from Muecke's (1992) fascinating account of Australian Aboriginality, and colonial versus post-colonial interpretations of Aboriginal history. Imagine that history is a reservoir of water. An Aboriginal person who wishes to understand history might swim in that reservoir and become immersed in it. A European historian might instead take a small container, dip it into the reservoir, remove a small sample and examine the water. The sample, once analysed, is casually tossed back in, or cast aside. By alluding to such a metaphor, it is possible to understand how any intercultural discourse on history will have to take these approaches into account. Where a common cultural background is taken for granted, the metaphor acts as an easy filtering process to create meanings in shorthand. In intercultural narrative discourse, the metaphor alerts participants to differences in conceptualisation.

Experiential Lens

Much of the early literature on situational discourse in comparative education treated the act of communicating as a behavioural one, isolating 'culturally different behaviours' such as those relating to eating habits, shopping, use of alcohol, cleanliness, sexism, touching, writing conventions and so on. Of course, most behaviours are of profound complexity, and no matter how often or how elaborately we describe normative differences, the question still remains: what happens when two people with very different discourse norms try to communicate with each other? Meanings cannot be explained only in normative terms, because all the other filters are operating at the same time. The impact of one set of norms on another depends on the interrelationships between people, their positioning as self, and their positioning in relation to the other.

An example from the author's experience in Papua New Guinea illustrates the need to interpret the narrative differently depending on the experiential lenses of the observers (Fox, 2003). In 1995, a team of consultants (including the author) undertook an exploratory study of the levels of participation of females in Papua New Guinea in education and training. In the course of this visit, the consultants interviewed a number of women to discuss their perceptions of the ways in which girls and women were able to participate in schools and in further education and university. The structural inequalities were obvious: girls' participation was far lower than boys', their job opportunities were fewer, and their status in society on the whole was far lower than for boys and men. It appeared that the greatest negative influence on female participation was an overwhelming and systemic subordination of women in much of Papua New Guinea society.

Some of the men interviewed during the same visit claimed that the subordination of women was a time-honoured cultural factor in Papua New Guinea society. These interviewees claimed that any transformation of the role and status of women in society was a Western imposition of their concept of equity and equality, which went against traditional culture. When pressed, those in high-status positions who were responsible for implementing gender equity in the education system maintained that cultural traditions were stronger than school-based ideas and that gender equity policy was not likely to be implemented easily. While the narrative of the educational leaders pointed to change, the experience showed that such statements were at best an illusion. The reality for these educators was different.

Ethical Lens

One of the most complex filters employed in communication is that concerning the ways in which people identify questions of justice and rightness. Within this category lies the narrators' sense of morally justifiable action. It is a question of a personal sense of morality, of personal worth and value. It is also a filtering process with political implications, since it is within this category that questions of power and authority lie. Theodore Sarbin states that all narrative has a beginning, middle and an ending, but more importantly, has the presence of a moral issue as an essential criterion for telling a story (Sarbin, 2004, p. 6). Are there universal ethical rules or norms that explain peoples' actions, duties, obligations and rights? There may be general principles, but not without a cultural filtering process that a narrative researcher needs to take into account in comparative educational research. In a monocultural situation, it could be assumed that people have a general view of what is right, and of what general principles may be acceptable. In an intercultural situation, any expectations of universality or of absolute rightness would need to be spelt out in ways that match the experience of each participant's cultural background.

There is no space here to elaborate on the philosophical and moral arguments regarding universality or relativity; however, some of these ethical dilemmas are explored in later chapters that focus on the ethics of narrative research.

Hermeneutic Lens

Different cultures interpret their history differently, as pointed out earlier. The hermeneutic lens concerns the interpretation of time and space, the near and far, the present and the past. As James Wertsch's work shows, narrative is a cultural tool for representing the past (Wertsch, 1998, p. 73). It is hermeneutic understanding, the ability to reflect critically and interpret the text and the context of that text (Gadamer, 1989), which may be differently applied from different cultural and linguistic perspectives.

Wertsch takes his cue from Bakhtin's account of social languages and speech genres, where 'the notion of a form of speaking *belonging* to someone or to some situation is central' (Wertsch, 1998, p. 78; and see Austin, 1962, who discussed the differences between what the interlocutor says, what they intended and what the listener experiences and interprets). Bakhtin's well-known work *The Dialogic Imagination* (1981) is fundamental reading for narrative researchers. He believes there is no narrative without a context and a particular situation in which to locate the intention of the narrator. When researching past narratives, as compared with current ethnographic research, understanding and interpreting this context of situation is crucial for any analysis.

It is possible to look at this taxonomy of lenses, or filters, as a method of analysis for narrative research, and each of the chapters that follow concentrates on one or more of these lenses.

Conclusion: dissolving boundaries

Almost a decade ago, I discussed the issue of bridging boundaries between cultures through intercultural communication strategies (Fox, 1997, p. 86):

> The question [is], what happens when discourse norms are different, but there is an intention to reach an understanding? Why should it be assumed that groups of people who identify themselves as of a different race, ethnic or cultural group, and whose discourse norms are different, cannot successfully communicate? To put the question in another way, are there really such separate discourse norms for social interaction that cultural boundaries cannot be bridged?

In the twenty-first century, it is important not so much to leap across boundaries as to dissolve boundaries, to break down barriers and to reinterpret two-dimensional dichotomies as fictions of the imagination.

The present volume should enable researchers to recognise and dissolve the dichotomies of us and them, East and West, black and white, North and South, since in the world of experience they are meaningless. In gender studies, for example, the male-female dichotomy was argued relentlessly in the social sciences. Today, the complexity of images of masculinity and femininity takes into account numerous interpretations of subjectivities, social and economic contexts and cultural experience. The boundaries dissolve; instead, there is a kaleidoscope of viewpoints, all within reach of our own interpretation through the recording of narrative.

Incompatibility is a term related more to politics and power than to cultural difference. This does not rule out cultural misunderstanding, even when there is a genuine attempt to look at the dynamics of intercultural communication. Although certain values and truths are incompatible, discourse narratives can be developed that signify important and authentic communication (Fox, 1997, p. 88).

> An important feature of colonial discourse is its dependence
> on the concept of 'fixity' in the ideological construction of
> otherness. Fixity, as the sign of cultural/historical/racial
> difference in the discourse of colonialism, is a paradoxical
> mode of representation: it connotes rigidity and an unchanging
> order as well as disorder, degeneracy and daemonic repetition
> ... The stereotype ... is its major discursive strategy. (Bhabha,
> 1994, p. 66)

How easily the visual can represent stereotypes in relationships of unequal power! Take, for example, typical paintings of early 'culture contact' in the Pacific: the arriving ship with its tall sails rests in a distant harbour, the sun's rays lighting up the centre of the picture where the stately ship lies, its upright and lordly British or other uniformed conquerors on board gazing down at the darkened shores, while 'hordes' of 'natives', usually depicted in a bowed position or in disarray, sometimes brandishing futile weapons, always out of the sunlight, appear lower in the picture or in a corner, and are always relationally minuscule and indistinguishable compared with the large figures, features clearly painted, who are supposedly in command of the situation. Similarly, in maps drawn with Europe or the United States at the centre without the advantage of a Peters' projection, the countries of the 'South' appear as either smaller, or marginal, in relation to the central power.

Mapping denotes boundaries that are in the real world no more than a fiction. Today, even a mountainous border or a wide river is a physical boundary, not a mental boundary, as new technologies dissolve the geographic barrier. However, it should be stressed that to dissolve

Christine Fox

boundaries is not to welcome homogeneity, but to find new ways to understand the specific contexts of narrative.

As long as narrative research focuses on the individual speech, the unique historical book or the particular conversation, the danger of moving into a globalised, homogenised, impoverished system of meaning is averted. Historically, the ideal of a global culture is not new, as the utopian globalism of the 19th century demonstrated (Tomlinson, 1999, p. 75). To take the most obvious example, Marx presented a:

> particularly bold picture of a global culture in which the division of nations disappeared ... a world with a universal language, a world literature and cosmopolitan cultural tastes. (Tomlinson, 1999)

Today these views would be seen as ethnocentric and tasting of cultural domination or cultural imperialism. It is for comparativists to locate themselves within these dialogues, and to be aware of all the ways in which we filter the information received through narrative.

References

Arnove, R. & Torres, C. (2003) *Comparative Education: the dialectic of the global and the* local, 2nd revised edn. Boston: Rowman & Littlefield.

Austin, J.L. (1962) *How to Do Things with Words* (William James Lectures delivered at Harvard University in 1955). Oxford: Clarendon Press.

Bakhtin, M. (1981) *The Dialogic Imagination.* Austin: University of Texas Press.

Bamberg, M. (2004) Positioning with Davie Hogan: stories, tellings and identities, in C. Daiute & C. Lightfoot (Eds) *Narrative Analysis: studying the development of individuals in society.* Thousand Oaks: Sage.

Bhabha, H. (1994) *The Location of Culture.* London: Routledge.

Bruner, J.S. (1983) *In Search of Mind.* New York: Harper & Row.

Chandler, M.J., Lalonde, C.E. & Teucher, U. (2004) Culture, Continuity and the Limits of Narrativity: a comparison of the self-narratives of native and non-native youth, in C. Daiute & C. Lightfoot (Eds) *Narrative Analysis: studying the development of individuals in society.* Thousand Oaks: Sage.

Clair, R.P. (Ed.) (2003) *Expressions of Ethnography: novel approaches to qualitative methods.* Albany: State University of New York Press.

Crossley, M. & Tikly, L. (2004) Postcolonial Perspectives and Comparative and International Research in Education: a critical introduction, *Comparative Education,* 40, pp. 147-156. http://dx.doi.org/10.1080/0305006042000231329

Crossley, M. & Watson, K. (2003) *Comparative and International Research in Education: globalisation, context and difference.* London: RoutledgeFalmer.

Daiute, C. & Lightfoot, C. (Eds) (2004) *Narrative Analysis: studying the development of individuals in society.* Thousand Oaks: Sage.

deTurk, S. (2001) Intercultural Empathy: myth, competency, or possibility for alliance building? *Communication Education,* 50, pp. 374-384.

Detweiler, R. (1978) Culture, Category Width and Attribution: a model building approach to the reasons for cultural effects, *Journal of Cross-Cultural Psychology*, 9, pp. 259-284.

Detweiler, R. (1980) Intercultural Interaction and the Categorization Process: a conceptual analysis and behavioral outcome, *International Journal of Intercultural Relations*, 4, pp. 275-293.

Foucault, M. (1984) *The Foucault* Reader, ed. Paul Rabinow. New York: Pantheon.

Fox, C. (1992) A Critical Analysis of Intercultural Communication: towards a new theory. Unpublished PhD thesis, Sydney University.

Fox, C. (1996) Listening to the Other: mapping intercultural communication in postcolonial educational consultancies, in R. Paulston (Ed.) *Social Cartography: mapping ways of seeing social and educational change*. New York: Garland.

Fox, C. (1997) Metaphors of Development: an analysis of information flow between cultures, in T. Scrase (Ed.) *Social Justice and Third World Education*. New York: Garland.

Fox, C. (2003) The Question of Identity from a Comparative Education Perspective, in R. Arnove & C. Torres (Eds) *Comparative Education: the dialectic of the global and the* local, 2nd revised edn. Boston: Rowman & Littlefield.

Fox, C. (2004) Tensions in the Decolonisation Process, in A. Hickling-Hudson, J. Matthews & A. Woods (Eds) *Disrupting Preconceptions: postcolonialism and education*. Brisbane: Post Pressed.

Freeman, M. (2004) Data Are Everywhere: narrative criticism in the literature of experience, in C. Daiute & C. Lightfoot (Eds) *Narrative Analysis: studying the development of individuals in society*. Thousand Oaks: Sage.

Gadamer, H.-G. (1989) *Truth and Method* (2nd revised edn, translation revised by J. Weinsheimer & D. Marshall). New York: Crossroad.

González, M.C. (2003) An Ethics for Postcolonial Ethnography, in R.P. Clair (Ed.) *Expressions of Ethnography: novel approaches to qualitative methods*. Albany: State University of New York Press.

Habermas, J. (1981) *The Theory of Communicative Action*, vol. 1, trans. T. McCarthy. Boston: Beacon Press.

Hickling-Hudson, A., Matthews, J. & Woods, A. (Eds) (2004) *Disrupting Preconceptions: postcolonialism and education*. Brisbane: Post Pressed.

Kellner, H. (1990) 'As Real as It Gets...': Ricoeur and narrativity, *Philosophy Today*, 34, pp. 229-242.

Levinson, B., Foley, D. & Holland, D.C. (1996) *The Cultural Production of the Educated Person: critical ethnographies of schooling and local practices*. Albany: State University of New York Press.

Masemann, V. & Welch, A. (Eds) (1997) *Tradition, Modernity and Post-Modernity in Comparative Education*. Hamburg: UNESCO Institute for Education.

McCarthy, C., Giardina, M., Harewood, S. & Park, J.-K. (2003) Contesting Culture: identity and curriculum dilemmas in the age of globalization, postcolonialism, and multiplicity, *Harvard Educational Review*, 73, p. 449.

Muecke, S. (1992) *Textual Spaces: Aboriginality and cultural studies.* Kensington, NSW: New South Wales University Press.

Paulston, R. (Ed.) (1996) *Social Cartography: mapping ways of seeing social and educational change.* New York: Garland.

Ricoeur, P. (1979) *Rule of Metaphor: multi-disciplinary students of the creation of meaning in language.* Toronto: Toronto University Press.

Ricoeur, P. (1991) Narrative Identity, *Philosophy Today,* 35(1), pp. 73-81.

Ricoeur, P. (1984-1988) *Time and Narrative*, trans. K. McLaughlin & D. Pellauer. Chicago: University of Chicago Press.

Said, E. (1978) *Orientalism.* Harmondsworth: Penguin.

Said, E. (1994) *Culture and Imperialism.* London: Vantage.

Said, E. (2001) The Public Role of Writers and Intellectuals, *The Nation*, 17-24 September, 273, pp. 27-34.

Sarbin, T.R. (2004) The Role of Imagination in Narrative Construction, in C. Daiute & C. Lightfoot (Eds) *Narrative Analysis: studying the development of individuals in society.* Thousand Oaks: Sage.

Spivak, G.C. (1990) *The Post-Colonial Critic: interviews, strategies, dialogues,* ed. S. Harasym. New York: Routledge.

Thompson, J.B. (1990) *Ideology and Modern Culture,* p. 107. Cambridge: Polity Press.

Tikly, L. (2001) Globalisation and Education in a Postcolonial World: a conceptual framework, *Comparative Education,* 37, pp. 151-171. http://dx.doi.org/10.1080/03050060124481

Tomlinson, J. (1999) *Globalization and Culture.* Chicago: University of Chicago Press.

Welch, A. (2003) Technocracy, Uncertainty and Ethics: comparative education in an era of postmodernity and globalization, in R. Arnove & C. Torres (Eds) *Comparative Education: the dialectic of the global and the local,* 2nd revised edn. Boston: Rowman & Littlefield.

Wertsch, J. (1998) *Mind as Action.* New York: Oxford University Press.

CHAPTER FOUR

The Stories People Tell: teaching narrative research methodology in New Zealand

SUE WATSON
Massey University, New Zealand

It is through the hearing of stories ... that children learn what the cast of characters may be in the drama into which they have been born and what the ways of the world are. (MacIntyre, 1981)

The stories people tell about themselves are interesting not only for the events and the characters they describe but also for something in the construction of the stories themselves ... It is this formative – and sometimes deformative – power of life stories that makes them important. (Rosenwald & Ochberg, 1992, p. 1)

Narrative research allows us to see lives as simultaneously individual and social creations, and to see individuals simultaneously as the changers and the changed. (Personal Narratives Group, 1989, p. 6)

Introduction

Narrative research has been described as 'both pervasive and elusive' and 'in all of its various manifestations, deeply implicated in contemporary conflicts over theory, methodology, and politics in scholarly investigation' (Casey, 1995, p. 211). This chapter is a description of a course constructed for postgraduate students in education and other social sciences within a university faculty of education in New Zealand.

The task was to find a way to introduce students to a particular form of qualitative research methodology, one which would lead them towards appreciating that narrative research was not simply capturing examples of talk and reconstructing new versions of them, but would show that examples of talk could be as systematically and reliably analyzed as much traditional quantitative research data. Narrative research must be grounded in a particular theoretical commitment so that there is a focus to the enterprise of relating individual instances to larger explanations, and the particular to the general (Chase, 1995).

In teacher education and professional development, as well as counselling and psychology, narrative research based on collecting and examining autobiographical stories is becoming increasingly popular. Goodson & Walker (1991) promote narrative methodology in research to get beyond the 'surface realities' to the 'deep structures' of schooling (p. xiii). Understanding what might be called 'biographical method' provides a better understanding and facilitates process in reflection on practice (Mezirow, 1990). There have been many recent calls for teachers' voices and teachers' knowledge to be valued in educational research (Casey, 1995), but the voices of all sorts of people engaged in their work and their lives are relevant to praxis research.

An understanding of social constructionism alerts potential researchers to the group effects of social conditions, and an awareness of individual agency in the course of a life and the performance nature of the telling of the life story allows researchers to demonstrate that social conditions can be responded to in different ways. The value of narrative research is that it can elicit evidence of the variety of constructions and responses made by human agents that can indeed change conditions, or enable people to resist changes imposed on them. With this methodology, the constructivist aspect of narrative is honoured. Narrative researchers must be aware of multiple realities and the political aspects of explanations; for example, which version of the truth is privileged. It is also important for potential researchers to become aware of the many sources of data for narrative research, and the range of methods appropriate for analyzing these materials.

Although narrative research may seem attractive to students of research methods, they need to be alerted to the difficulties inherent in the method. In the doing of the research, many issues and details arise that require a close examination of the literature in search of guidance. Questions that require data about people's lives, feelings and attitudes produce ethical problems, which can prevent proposed research from being carried out or published (Josselson, 1996).

In New Zealand there is strong support for qualitative research in sociology, anthropology, women's studies and education (Davidson & Tolich, 2003). Narrative methodology is seen to be particularly appropriate for studying people with an oral tradition. In the first instance, this is because narrative research is perceived to be the collecting of traditional stories so they are not lost, and the opportunity to collect the voices of 'other' individuals to allow diverse voices to be heard. There are many projects, official and unofficial, collecting oral history and autobiographical stories, justified as countering the past silences of groups within the population. Potential researchers, however, must be cautioned about venturing into projects which will be rejected as unethical. They need to see how they may be patronising the people they wish to interview and how what they may be doing is another form of colonisation or paternalistic activity, even if their interest is genuine and caring. Ethics committees have clear guidelines for working with groups of people who are of a different language or ethnic group to the researchers.

Collecting autobiographical stories is really only data collection: something needs to be done with the data to clarify and find meaning in multiple instances. In narrative research with different cultural groups, this next level needs to be conceptualised carefully. Just as sociologists tend to be uncomfortable with psychological analyses of autobiographical stories and vice versa, different cultural groups are uncomfortable when their stories are analyzed or interpreted using theoretical models that they see as foreign, unrelated to real life, and ignorant of the meanings held in the culture being studied. For these reasons, Maori are now encouraged to do research on Maori issues, Pacific islanders to do research on their own people, and both to develop their own models to underpin the research being conducted (see Tolich, 2002). The task for the teaching of narrative is to show how current theories are applicable in any cultural context if the underlying principles are understood.

The Context

The decision to offer a course on narrative arose out of the orientation of the Human Development department. This can be described as life-span, ecological-contextual, organicist and constructivist. Over recent years, the discipline of Human Development has found itself straddling several social science, humanities and science fields, for example psychology, sociology, anthropology, history, linguistics, biology, genetics and literary criticism. In many of these fields, changing views of the nature of knowledge, methodology and the purposes of studying humans by humans has produced increasing emphasis on qualitative research. To write a course specifically around narrative research promised to be a valuable, forward-thinking approach to the teaching of the discipline and research methodology. Most of the Human Development postgraduate courses are taught extramurally through printed study materials sent out to students, with online or telephone support and a two-day on-campus course contact session at Easter or during the mid-year break. This delivery system imposes certain limitations on the content of the course and the tasks that can be supervised at a distance.

Planning Issues

A course on narrative research was seen as a way to offer two vital intellectual activities for students: to challenge them to develop more complex ways of thinking, and to persuade them that theory can be a desirable object of study. It was (and remains) apparent that many students saw no need to address theory and had difficulty accepting that 'theories' were anything other than conflicting viewpoints, viewpoints which had no more status than personal opinion. Such students do not want to know about different theories, only which one is the most correct. They fit the descriptions by Belenky et al (1986) of 'received' and 'subjective' knowers.

To teach narrative research, it is necessary to find an autobiographical text to examine. In other courses students had been given assignments based on interviewing family and friends. This type of assignment has been abandoned with extramural students because of ethical problems: with distance students it is difficult to manage the relationship of students with their sources of data. Initial applications of theory to interview data often produce clumsy judgments that may be hurtful to the people who have contributed their personal stories.

It was therefore decided to make use of published autobiographies. This pragmatic decision had excellent outcomes. Rather than a set book or list of suitable autobiographies, students were advised to find the autobiography of a person who interested them. It needed to be book-length (not part of a collection) and be written by someone about his or her life up to at least the age of 40, covering family origin and some adult life, and it needed to contain personal information, not just an account of career successes or the history of the person's workplace. Although it was assumed that autobiographies by New Zealanders might be most often selected, autobiographies could be from anywhere, and did not have to be in English.

This decision had several unexpected and desirable effects. It has allowed overseas students to make use of material from their own countries; through the application of the course's ideas to people from other cultural backgrounds, all involved had their understanding expanded. Students can discuss with others the way their chosen autobiography provides examples of ideas in the readings, but they have little opportunity to get themselves into trouble by plagiarising. They engage in personal dialogues with the story and the subject of the autobiography. It is also obvious to students that they do not need to produce the 'correct' interpretation, but justify the interpretation that they are making. It is clear that original thinking is required for this course.

Comments by students suggest that they enter the course because they have enjoyed other Human Development courses and are attracted to studying an autobiography. As Bruner (1990) has pointed out, there is nothing more attractive and more meaningful to people than stories, especially about people's lives. All students gain information about many lives, data for appraising how well these lives seemed to fit different theories of human development.

One of the chief concerns was how to increase the complexity of thought of those students who were still concrete thinkers and literal readers, those who did not recognise metaphor and had difficulty finding a theme or underlying principle. If students do not recognise a metaphor, they do not understand a great deal that lecturers are saying, or even understand that they are reading about theory. Much of the literature discussing narrative as a research methodology requires understanding of meta-theory. Learners entering the social sciences are exposed to terms such as 'postmodernism', 'cultural relativism', 'dialectical thinking', 'paradigmatic revolutions', 'narrative truth', 'feminist epistemologies' and 'irony in the rhetoric of policy documents'. All these are higher-order abstractions; before they can be understood, students require some understanding of lower-order abstractions such as the principles on which traditional psychological and sociological theories are based. Unfortunately, what students often think is that learning of theory is the rote learning of descriptions of a theory, with little understanding of the key concepts. To achieve a higher level of learning, a number of pedagogical principles are invoked: saliency of the content, the construction of knowledge, transfer and intrinsic motivation.

Saliency

New learning must be able to be linked by students to their own knowledge base and interests. The perception that the new learning will be useful will sustain continued engagement through difficult aspects. The study of published autobiographies as life-story data for analysis and interpretation has the advantage of linking leisure reading interests, a natural interest in people's lives and motivations, and a desire to understand people better. Students begin to read for this course with enthusiasm.

Constructing Knowledge rather than Receiving Knowledge

The course material, which is summarised later in this chapter, provides students with readings accompanied by guidelines and further explanation to draw attention to specific concepts or theoretical issues.

Students must do their own mental work to derive an understanding of the concepts presented to them, which they are expected to apply to the life story they have selected. This means the teacher must order the tasks so that simpler ideas can be acquired as the basis for more complex ideas. As assignments come in, the shifts in thinking of some students are clear. Students report flashes of insight and how exciting they are. A number of very competent students who have been struggling with conflicting information about knowledge, society and theory are thrilled to find ways of making sense of unassimilated data. The relevance of theory for the organisation of information becomes more obvious for students.

Transfer

With practice, these concepts and their application are organised into higher-level operations, which can be used to examine other bodies of knowledge, other language and cultural media, as well as the students' own interpersonal relationships and lives. Applying ideas derived from this course to their own lives is inevitable.

Intrinsic Motivation for Further Intellectual Engagement

The introduction to the possibilities inherent in narrative analysis or qualitative research in general can lead students to want to study more in specialised areas which previously seemed esoteric, for example, the study of linguistics for discourse analysis, the study of sociological and feminist theory for the analysis of dominant and suppressed discourses, the usefulness of telling life stories in psychotherapy, and the relevance of these ideas in writing history, biography and literary analysis.

Content of the Course

Having chosen an autobiography, students are invited to write their initial responses, assisted by several questions. This work is not marked, but is simply a way to record their beginning understandings so that when they complete the course they can read what they were thinking and assess how much they have learned. This activity is based on the recognition that many students appraise their learning by the grade they are given for the course. To sustain learning, it is more effective for individuals to realise how much has been learned by their own efforts, and that learning is not what is supplied by the teacher or measured by grades

The study guides contain readings and commentaries on them. The introductory section begins with a reading from Mary Gergen (1994). Her article is an excellent introduction to the notion of social construction of personal histories. Her account of research into the gender differences in autobiographies by socially successful and prominent women and men has wide appeal to students. This is followed by Dan McAdams's (1988a) introduction to a special issue of the *Journal of Personality,* which was devoted to the new uses of life narratives in psychobiography and social research.

The second and third topics are concerned with the concepts of context, culture and cohort, to expand students' understanding of the social construction of human lives. Students have to make parallel time-lines of what was happening in history at the same time as the events of the autobiography were taking place. This is modelled on the work of Elder et al in *Children in Time and Place: developmental and historical insights* (1993). Students are then required to write a sociocultural description of the family of origin, and a two- or three-page description of one historical event that has had a significant effect on the life opportunities of the autobiographer, making mention of Bronfenbrenner's (1979) systems. This assignment encourages students to explore areas of social history and cultural beliefs that are relevant to the autobiography they are studying, underlining the differences in attitudes and opportunities that operate in people's lives. In brief, the first part of the course looks at the external influences on an individual.

To move students' thinking from the macrosystem perspective to the microsystem, the Vygotskian research of Helen Haste (1987) leads students through thinking about how we learn our original and most basic meanings about the world in the microsystems of the family and in our mother tongue. Hence differences and similarities in families can be appreciated as seedbeds, the growing media for the developing child's learning about everything. Our learning is embedded in our culture. Our understanding of who we are, whether we are worthwhile and whether the world is a safe and interesting place, or chaotic and dangerous, is constructed by us in the environment of our families and the social worlds they inhabit. From this, students acquire a rich base for understanding recent research interest in such areas as situated learning (Rogoff & Lave, 1984), an understanding that is not simply social learning theory recast and attributed to Vygotsky. This approach also allows a deeper understanding of what sociologists call 'cultural capital', and of why differences in cultural capital set individuals on life trajectories that can be predicted by group statistics from quantitative research methods. Life stories also allow the examination of variations in the expected stories, such as information about severely deprived or abused children who become happy and competent adults (Higgins, 1994).

The next topic, Myths and Storylines, is designed to allow students to come to understand the social constructionist notion that within a culture there are conventional story forms, and when people are telling stories about their own lives they unconsciously use a conventional storyline. (If a story is told with a form that is not familiar to the listener, it will not be heard as a coherent story.) Using readings from Schank (1990), Hankiss (1981) and others, some of the features of narrative structure and their purposes are discussed. These are followed by readings where narrative devices and story construction are used so obviously that literal readers should be able to gain insights into such things as the efficacy of using metaphor for the transmission of ideas, while other students can be amused by the play between substance and form. The final reading of this section consists of extracts from Pearson (1989), which use the concept of archetypal hero to demonstrate that the way people construct their understanding of themselves in relation to the world can be meaningfully organised as appropriations of cultural stories. Interested students can then branch off to investigate the original masters of cultural stories and archetypes, Carl Jung and Joseph Campbell, if they so desire.

Following this section of the course, students submit a brief essay on what is meant by 'personal myth' in autobiographical writing, and what myth is apparent in the autobiography they have selected. Some students struggle to find the myth, but once they have found it they have cleared a major epistemological hurdle. The importance of this breakthrough is considerable. Once they understand that emergent themes and concepts can be recognised by many readers and listeners, they realise that what are called 'subjective' meanings can be shared and 'observed' as if they were objective phenomena.

Topic Five deals with the controversial topic of 'self', what is meant by 'identity', and what narratives reveal about aspects of self. Readings come from social psychology (Potter & Wetherell, 1987) and personality psychology (McAdams, 1991). Topic Six moves into constructivist ideas, including some examples and discussion of thematic analysis of autobiographies, especially aspects of personality and identity and the purposes of people that are revealed in narratives. Topic Seven is concerned with research into autobiographical memory in children and the elderly, and the notion that nuclear memories (McAdams, 1988b) and self-defining memories (Singer & Salovey, 1993) are more useful in psychotherapy than probing the unconscious. Topic Eight is focused on different perspectives on the changes that occur in meaning-making over the life span, with discussion of stage theories such as Kegan (1982, 1994) and epistemological development (Perry, 1970; Belenky et al, 1986). Topic Nine is a brief introduction to the place of language in narrative analysis. Topic Ten provides a number of research articles as examples of narrative research, which together review some of the issues and concepts addressed in the earlier sections of the course.

At the end of the first semester there is an assignment, a report on the identity revealed in the autobiography, based on McAdams's Life-Story Model of Identity (1988b). This model, which is conceptually very challenging for students, has been described in the readings, and other readings have been chosen to elaborate aspects of the model or to show convergences with other theory and research. The model has four components: Ideological Setting (the culture in which the ideology has been formed), Imagoes (the valued and avoided aspects of significant characters in the stories), Nuclear Episodes (the highlighted and significant incidents reported) and Generativity Script (what a person is doing in life that makes them feel their life has value). Two basic dimensions run through each component: Thematic Lines (especially Intimacy and Power motives) and Narrative Complexity (which reflects ego stage or epistemological development).

Outcomes from the First Semester Work

Students' responses to these tasks demonstrate their efficacy as learning opportunities. Younger students write in a way that reveals that they have experienced and are highly responsive to the insight that social structures put people into social classes that distribute opportunities inequitably. This is a very powerful intellectual development, which we may fail to appreciate years after such a concept becomes commonplace to us. Once people have understood that there are indeed invisible patterns and that they do indeed have palpable and predictable results, they are responsive to further exploration of theory. Students today are coming fresh to the insights that excited young intellectuals last century when Marxist theory provided a new way of viewing the social world. As teachers we should know that such insights are rarely achieved by being told; we have to grow into the knowledge through our life experience.

It is not possible, however, to allow these ideas to mellow if we want students to gain understanding of more recent theoretical ideas; we must push them onward. Not all students are ready to make the shift required by the course to understanding that as well as these social influences there are other interacting strands of influence in people's lives. After students have reflected on how history and society have influenced the life course of the person in the selected autobiography, they are asked to immerse themselves in how the world looks to the person writing the life story. Students need to know how individual and idiosyncratic acts of perception, conception and intention also shape people's lives. This is an exercise in empathy or connected knowing (Belenky et al, 1986).

It is instructive to note how some students make useful comments about what they have learned from examining the autobiography in this way, without having yet mastered the ability to think about abstractions. McAdams's terms can be understood on several levels. Some students talk about their person's generativity script as if it is a real thing, which exists as an entity that the person is deliberately following. The ideological setting can be thought of as the material world imposing its values on the person. Imagoes can be people who have been role models. Narrative complexity is a mystery to a few students because their own facility with abstractions needs further development.

On the other hand, the majority of students produce assignments and letters that are a pleasure to read. They are writing about what they have discovered about the person they have selected, and seem to fall naturally into giving definitions of complex terms and providing examples and quotations as evidence from their book and their reading. They are fascinated that McAdams's elements are intertwined, providing them with examples of multidimensional causality and dialectic action. They are intrigued to see the continuities in their person's life and speculate whether this is an artefact of the public presentation of the story, an unconscious process of selecting incidents and linking them to make better sense of the present, or a modification over time of some memories. They report how valuable the course has been in giving them insights into their own lives; some have been motivated to seek oral histories from their families, so that they can understand better the hidden influences on themselves and family members. They comment that they ask their children and their friends different sorts of questions since they have done the course. They comment about their irritation with television once they are aware of how it constructs our reality and shapes shared meanings.

Doing Narrative Research

Having introduced students to an appreciation of the information that can be found in autobiographical stories, the next step is to focus their attention on applying that knowledge to a research question that is best approached with a narrative methodology. Novice researchers often have little understanding of the logistics of the task they are proposing. They do not realise how long it takes to transcribe an interview, the difficulties of establishing a satisfactory coding scheme for their analysis, or the difficulties of managing the fragments of data they are finding and seeking to group in some way. Narrative researchers can be overwhelmed by the quantity of words on paper. Computer programs designed to get around these problems are better suited to some sorts of analyses than others, and even if the program is suitable for the task, it is still necessary to learn how to use it.

Finding the Research Question

In the middle of the year, extramural students gather at an on-campus contact course. On the first day, students share what they have learned from their examination of autobiographies. The issues that arise from these brief reports can stimulate discussion that can go beyond one full day. Students also come to the contact course with an idea of a research question that is best examined using narrative methodology. In the second semester, the task is to try out a narrative methodology that could be preparation for a Master's research project or thesis. On the second day, individual students put forward their questions and any ideas they have about how to go about investigating them. The ethical implications are discussed by the group, as well as other methodological issues, often changing the focus of the original question. Some questions are abandoned and new ones generated. After sorting out the best way to approach a question for one student, other students see new questions and new possibilities for ideas they have had vaguely formulated previously.

As a creative group experience, this is very exciting. The life experience of the entire group can be drawn into finding solutions to real problems. At the end of the contact course, students should have a clear idea of their question and procedure and go home to write up a draft proposal in two weeks, including a brief account of any ethical issues and how they might be dealt with. This includes the construction of an Information Sheet for any interviewees who might be involved. The use of children as participants is usually excluded because ethics committee approval is required, and this can be too time-consuming for a trial project. These abbreviated proposals are good practice for later research proposals. Usually some correction or modification is necessary for the submitted proposal, but in most cases it does not take long before the students can be given approval to go ahead with their planned procedures.

The Purpose

The object of the exercise is not to produce findings, except in a limited form to show that the procedure proposed produces the kind of data that can address the question. The intention is to give the students the opportunity to learn from doing and to appraise what happened. The final assignment requires them to evaluate the use of narrative methodology for the research question, the process that they went through engaging in the research, and the key issues that arose for them.

Some important lessons are learned in these trials of methodology. More than one student has learned the hard lesson of finding that an interview has not been recorded; one found a blank tape after a two-hour interview with a busy politician. Others learn quickly how much time and paper are consumed by a one-hour interview, and modify their approach. Many see that what they expect to find in their data is not there, or is ambiguous and very difficult to code.

Those who choose to interview people become aware of many ethical issues. Ethics committees and advice from textbooks on research methodology have led to the widespread acceptance of several issues that do not appear problematic until encountered in real situations. First is the issue of informed consent. Students often believe that if an interviewee has been informed of the research and there is no deception, then consent is freely given and consequently all is well. They can be taken aback when it is pointed out that the researcher still has a responsibility of care for the interviewee and needs to be confident that he or she understands what has been agreed, and is not motivated simply by friendship or a desire not to offend.

Another common expectation is that a promise to allow a research participant to read the transcript and the final report for approval covers issues of data ownership and power relationships between researcher and researched. This can be seen belatedly to be a real problem. One student became very worried about her final report because she feared her two participants would be offended by some of the interpretations. She dealt with this by ringing them and discussing the problem of confidentiality that would arise if she allowed each to read about the other. Experiences such as this mean such issues can be addressed by the student in subsequent research, and can be used as a warning to be considered by students in later groups planning their trial research.

Examples of Trial Research

Many trials of narrative methodology have now taken place. One student chose to examine the stories of women in Jane Tolerton's (1994) book *Convent Girls*. She experienced difficulty in finding what she thought she was looking for in the text, but in the process became aware of other themes emerging that reflected deeper issues, which she felt were important to pursue. This led her to further reading about feminist epistemology and suppressed discourses, and stimulated a continued desire to continue this study. She went on to produce an MEd research project entitled '"Once You're a Catholic ... ": how their Catholic education and upbringing is expressed in the personal identity of eight New Zealand women in their mid-thirties'.

Another student who was a guidance counsellor in a secondary school was concerned about the problems adolescents had in forming an identity in New Zealand in the late 1990s, when there was a great deal of despondency in expectations for employment of young people. The method of data collection used was for 15- to 17-year-olds in his school to write, as a normal lesson activity but acknowledging the extra research purpose, essays on the topic: 'The best form of education for people at my age would be ...' The researcher's expectation was that this topic would produce several pages of writing that would reveal statements of values and some self/other descriptions. As a method to collect data about adolescent identity, it was disappointing. However, the researcher's reading of the essays allowed him to see how certain attitudes, values and identity factors could be derived from other textual features and use of language. He found differences in number of words, language use, spelling, grammar and essay planning between girls and boys. He found differences in the use of 'I' between Maori and Pakeha (non-Maori New Zealanders) students. He found a link between the use of 'boredom' and 'jobs', but no reference to boredom by students who used the word 'career'. He demonstrated to himself that the use of a collection of writing can be a substantial although indirect method of data collection.

A third student proposed to examine the autobiography of Donna Williams (1992), who wrote about what it was like to be autistic. The student was already an experienced psychotherapist and she felt this exercise would add to her professional understanding of autism. While reading professional accounts of autism and sensitising herself to story lines and the politics of different discourses, she became aware that accepted explanations about autism had changed very little since the condition was first named, and that Donna Williams was not using the conventional explanations in her account of herself. This student's research exercise then became one of grouping the types of explanations of autism, and at the same time exploring further clues in the autobiography that suggested aspects of autism absent from the professional accounts. The whole topic became even more salient when newspapers suggested that the Donna Williams story was the second Australian literary fraud emerging at that time.

Conclusion

Everyone is interested in people's lives, so using a life story as an object of study engages students' attention. Beginning with social constructionist concepts that make sense whether they are understood in concrete or abstract ways invites students to think from different theoretical perspectives. Applying these concepts to the life story in a book that the teacher may or may not have read produces original thinking. Interpreting aspects of people's lives highlights the importance of justifying the position taken. Because the central ideas are presented in a form that can be used by most students, the more mature thinkers quickly gain access to important ideas and move on to think about the many layers, or many perspectives, that can be examined through narrative methodology about human lives. The study of autobiography works as an introduction to narrative research. Students say it has been stimulating, but feel no sense of closure because the course has the effect of sending them off on a journey: there are many more questions they want to investigate.

Has this course achieved its aims? Many writers suggest that a good university education requires courses that encourage reflection, critical thinking and deep learning techniques so that students become independent and life-long learners (Mezirow, 1990). Teaching narrative provides an excellent framework for students to do just that. The narrative research course contains practices that are recommended for adult learners: self-direction by the student, negotiation between student and teacher, ownership of one's own learning, self-evaluation (Broadbent, 1995) and group problem-finding and problem-solving (Arlin, 1989), and thus offers real potential for comparative and international research in education. Having been engaged with the issues raised by studying narrative, students emerge enthusiastic and wanting more. Narrative research may be controversial and complex, but the students who engage with this course emerge knowing the value and the limitations of this methodology, and with a great deal more besides: a deeper understanding of people through the stories they tell.

References

Arlin, P.K. (1989) Problem-solving and Problem-finding in Young Artists and Scientists, in M.L. Commons, J.D. Sinnott., F.A. Richards & C. Armon (Eds) *Adult Development (vol. 1): comparisons and applications of developmental models.* Westport: Praeger.

Belenky, M.F., Clinchy, B.M., Goldberger, N.R. & Tarule, J.M. (1986) *Women's Ways of Knowing: the development of self, voice and mind.* New York: Basic Books.

Broadbent, F. (1995) Innovation and Excellence in Teaching, *Tertiary Education News,* 5, pp. 2-5.

Bronfenbrenner, U. (1979) *The Ecology of Human Development: experiments by nature and design.* Cambridge, MA: Harvard University Press.

Bruner, J. (1990) *Acts of Meaning.* Cambridge, MA: Harvard University Press.

Casey, K. (1995) The New Narrative Research in Education, in M.W. Apple (Ed.) *Review of Research in Education, 21, 1995-1996,* pp. 211-253. Washington, DC: American Educational Research Association.

Chase, S.E. (1995) Taking Narrative Seriously: consequences for method and theory in interview studies, in R. Josselson & A. Lieblich (Eds) *Interpreting Experience: the narrative study of lives,* vol. 3, pp. 1-26. London: Sage.

Davidson, C. & Tolich, M. (Eds) (2003) *Social Science Research in New Zealand: many paths to understanding.* Auckland: Pearson.

Elder, G.H. Jr., Modell, J. & Parke, R.D. (Eds) (1993) *Children in Time and Place: developmental and historical insights.* New York: Cambridge University Press.

Gergen, M. (1994) The Social Construction of Personal Histories: gendered lives in popular autobiographies, in T.R. Sarbin & J.I. Kitsuse (Eds) *Constructing the Social*, pp. 19-44. London: Sage.

Goodson, I.F. & Walker, R. (1991) *Biography, Identity and Schooling: episodes in educational research*. London: Falmer Press.

Hankiss, A. (1981) Ontologies of the Self: on the mythological rearranging of one's life history, in D. Bertaux (Ed.) *Biography and Society: the life history approach in the social sciences*, pp. 203-209. London: Sage.

Haste, H. (1987) Growing into Rules, in J. Bruner & H. Haste (Eds) *Making Sense: the child's construction of the world*, pp. 163-195. London: Methuen.

Higgins, G.O. (1994) *Resilient Adults: overcoming a cruel past*. San Francisco: Jossey-Bass.

Josselson, R. (1996) *Ethics and Process in the Narrative Study of Lives*, vol. 4. London: Sage.

Kegan, R. (1982) *The Evolving Self*. Cambridge, MA: Harvard University Press.

Kegan, R. (1994) *In Over Our Heads: the mental demands of modern life*. Cambridge, MA: Harvard University Press.

MacIntyre, A. (1981) *After Virtue*. Notre Dame,: Notre Dame Press.

McAdams, D.P. (1988a) Biography, Narrative and Lives: an introduction, *Journal of Personality*, 56, pp.1-18.

McAdams, D.P. (1988b) *Power, Intimacy and the Life Story: personological inquiries into identity*. New York: Guildford Press.

McAdams, D.P. (1991) Self and Story, *Perspectives in Personality*, 3(B), pp. 133-159.

Mezirow, J. (1990) How Critical Reflection Triggers Transformative Learning, in J. Mezirow (Ed.) *Fostering Critical Reflection in Adulthood: a guide to transformative and emancipatory learning*, pp. 1-19. San Francisco: Jossey-Bass.

Pearson, C.S. (1989) *The Hero Within: six archetypes we live by*. San Francisco: HarperCollins.

Perry, W.G. (1970) *Forms of Intellectual and Ethical Development in the College Years*. New York: Holt, Rinehart & Winston.

Personal Narratives Group (1989) *Interpreting Women's Lives: feminist theory and personal narratives*. Bloomington: Indiana University Press.

Potter, J. & Wetherell, M. (1987) *Discourse and Social Psychology: beyond attitudes and behaviour*. London: Sage.

Rogoff, B. & Lave, J. (Eds) (1984) *Everyday Cognition: its development in social context*. Cambridge, MA: Harvard University Press.

Rosenwald, G.C. & Ochberg, R.L. (Eds) (1992) *Storied Lives: the cultural politics of self-understanding*. New Haven: Yale University Press.

Schank, R.C. (1990) *Tell Me a Story*. New York: Scribners.

Singer, J.A. & Salovey, P. (1993) *The Remembered Self: emotion and memory in personality*. New York: Free Press.

Sue Watson

Tolerton, J. (1994) *Convent Girls: New Zealand women talk to Jane Tolerton*. Auckland: Penguin.

Tolich, M. (2002) Pakeha 'Paralysis': cultural safety for those researching the general population of Aotearoa, *Social Policy Journal of New Zealand*, December, pp. 164-175.

Williams, D. (1992) *Nobody Nowhere*. London: Corgi.

CHAPTER FIVE

Reflexivity: using our 'selves' in narrative research

KIM ETHERINGTON
University of Bristol, United Kingdom

Introduction

Behind every piece of research, even research described as objective or positivist, there is a human being, or several human beings, who have chosen to design or undertake research for their own purposes, whether personal or professional, and whether they are aware of that choice or not (Devereux, 1967; Ellis & Berger, 2003). Sometimes our choice of topic is pragmatic and/or related to career development or progression; sometimes we have a burning passion to understand something that relates to our own lives or those of significant others; sometimes we begin without knowing why we are interested and find out as the process unfolds, being led through the research into new and unexplored areas of our lives.

Narrative research, as described earlier in this book, has a variety of meanings that depend on the beliefs and worldviews of those involved, usually based upon the notion that narratives are constructed between a teller and an 'other' – even when the 'other' is a different aspect of oneself. Reading or listening to people's narratives creates a response in us, verbal or non-verbal. Those responses might lead us to ask questions that invite new stories to be told; we might respond by silently filling in the gaps in other people's stories with our own ideas and assumptions; or we might influence which stories are extended or negated by smiles that encourage or frowns that disallow. Simply by being there we influence the research that is being created.

As I write this chapter, which is my current story about reflexivity in narrative research, I am influenced by a variety of ideas, feelings and thoughts. My ideas have been generated through connections with many different sources: learning from others who have written on this topic, and my personal experiences of using reflexivity in research (Etherington, 2000, 2003). I gained a great deal through undertaking a narrative study entitled 'Becoming a Reflexive Researcher: using our selves in research' (Etherington, 2004), which gave me the opportunity to converse with a range of people, mainly in the social sciences and humanities, who were at different stages – in their life and in their development as researchers – and who valued reflexivity in research. Later in this chapter, where I refer to 'my participants', it is these people to whom I am referring and whose words I use.

My feelings as I create this narrative are related to my personal and social history and the experiences that have shaped my sense of self and identity, as a woman, a counsellor, a reflexive researcher and a writer.

As I write this I also think about you, the reader, and wonder how you will respond to the stories I am telling. So already (indeed, even before I sat down to write) this story has become a relational activity between you and me, even though I may not know you. Therefore my assumptions about you partly shape this story and influence my choice of language, and the tentativeness with which I put forward my ideas, not wanting to create the impression that my point of view is 'right' or 'wrong', rather that it is one story among others: and that this too is a story of its time.

Societal Background

Research in general has been greatly influenced by the changing traditions and trends in society as a whole, and to understand reflexivity we need to locate it within those changes. Following the powerful influences on society of superstition and dogmatic religion, science provided a belief in a measurable and knowable reality and encouraged people to create a better and more predictable world based on certainty independent of subjectivity; this led to a sense of power and progress. However, these ideas were brought into question by a growing recognition that even the most objective observers or interpreters inevitably brought themselves, and their prior knowledge and personal and cultural histories, into the equation.

During the 1970s and 1980s the Women's Movement led the challenge to the dominant discourses of patriarchy, recognising that *women's* views of women's lives needed to be placed alongside the views of men, and that women's ways of knowing and relating were different from those of men (Alcoff & Potter, 1993). Researchers began to address power issues that were of concern not only to women, but also to other oppressed groups, and provided platforms from which previously marginalised and oppressed voices could be heard: gay men and women, abuse survivors and ethnic minorities. Research was used to effect changes in society by revealing the sources and symptoms of powerlessness as well as promoting the idea that people could work together to change oppressive and disempowering practices within society (Freire, 1972, 1985). In the wider context of comparative and international research, in education and other fields, the silenced and forgotten voices of indigenous people are being heard, drawing attention to the effect of power discourses on the stories that can be told (Masemann & Welch, 1998).

Feminist research approaches (and there are many) espoused greater equality in research relationships, which called for different ways of collecting and representing data. Researchers were required to become transparent about the values and beliefs that lay behind their interpretations and were called upon to emerge from behind the safe barriers of objectivity from where they had been making their 'expert' interpretations, unchallenged because they were hidden and unknown, and therefore a source of mystery that could be oppressive (Foucault, 1980). Researchers were encouraged to take responsibility for their views, and to use the first-person pronoun 'I', thus losing the anonymity of 'the researcher', or 'the passive voice that distances subject from object' (Crotty, 1998, p. 169).

Later, with the postmodern shift in society, we came to the narrative 'turn' in the world, which continued the challenge to orthodox research methods, thus stimulating arguments between those who want to privilege 'scientific truth' and who value 'rigor over imagination, intellect over feelings, theories over stories, lectures over conversations, abstract ideas over concrete events', and those who value meaning, agency, difference, and subjective involvement that includes emotionality (Bochner, 2001, p. 134). The narrative 'turn' is away from reification of grand narratives or dominant discourses and towards the valuing of local stories; away from the idea that there is a single 'right' way to approach social research and towards a pluralist tradition and multiple ways of knowing and learning (including multiple ways of understanding and conducting narrative research and reflexivity).

Thus, postmodern ideas have contributed to a greater recognition of the importance of the relationship between the storyteller and the listener and between the knower and what is known, and what each brings with them into the research relationship to create meaning and understanding of the topics under exploration. This recognition has, in turn, led to the use of reflexivity in research.

Reflexive inclusion and valuing of the process have sometimes been described as 'feminine', a quality of both men and women, although it is often less developed in those socialised into what Bochner (2001, p. 144) describes as the traditional orthodoxy of scientific monolithic research, which he sees as 'unmistakably macho'. Women have typically been seen to pay greater attention to relationships in general, and the relationships between storyteller and listener are no less central to women's knowing and learning simply because orthodox research has not valued them:

> The process that comes from this way of knowing has to be at the centre ... of a woman's scholarship ... the point is to integrate ideas about love and healing, about balance and connection, about beauty and growing, into our everyday ways of being. WE have to believe in the value of our own experiences and in the value of our ways of knowing, our ways of doing things. (Aptheker, 1989, quoted in Clements et al, 1998)

This view was also reflected in a conversation I had with one of my participants, Sue, who saw reflexivity as something that might come more naturally to women and men who are comfortable with women's ways of knowing and relating:

> It [reflexivity] fits with women's culture more easily than objectivity. The notion of the existence of objectivity is something that belongs within patriarchal traditions. The notion of 'the Judge' who is completely removed from the sides of the case and *therefore* can see clearly what is truth and what is not – I think that's a very patriarchal notion. I think it's obviously been important along the way and I'm not denying its right to exist, but I think it's not a particularly female way of approaching the world .... Because if you don't have the model of the world of 'the Judge', establishing Truth with a capital T, then everything that happens is constructed by those involved in it, and therefore *not* to be reflexive, not to self-examine, and not to put that process and the results of that out there, is to withhold some of the information that exists about the context which you're examining. (Etherington, 2004, pp. 44, 48)

Personal Influences

The principles that underlie my own thinking as I set out this chapter are built upon my training as a holistic practitioner in occupational therapy in the United Kingdom in the early 1960s, a profession that introduced creative ideas to the world of medicine that challenged the patriarchal medical model, and my later training as a humanistic counsellor in the 1980s, when feminist ideas also came to my attention. As an experienced counsellor and researcher, I have come to embrace postmodern and social constructionist ideas, valuing local stories and appreciating the impact of culture and language on our stories of identity.

Postmodernist ideas, generally characterised by a sense of fragmentation and uncertainty and a falling away of traditional values, led me to question the psychological idea of a firm sense of self with which I had become familiar in my counsellor training. Social constructionism invited me outwards 'into the fuller realm of shared language' (Gergen & Gergen, 1991, p. 79), away from a purely psychological view of people, which provides 'no exit from personal subjectivity', and towards a balanced view that takes into account the influences of our personal psychology *and* how our history affects our identity. However, these ideas too are social constructions clearly related to shifts in societal thinking that influenced my own.

Reflexivity in Research

My current understanding (and it constantly changes) of what is meant by researcher reflexivity is that it refers to the capacity of researchers to acknowledge how their own experiences and contexts (which are usually fluid and changing) inform the process and outcomes of inquiry. This is sometimes called critical reflexivity or critical subjectivity (Alvesson & Skoldberg, 2000).

Reflexivity is not the same as subjectivity, but rather opens up a space between subjectivity and objectivity that allows for an exploration and representation of the more blurred genres of our experiences. Reflexivity requires self-awareness but is more than self-awareness, in that its use creates a dynamic process of interaction within *and* between ourselves and our participants, *and* the data that informs decisions, actions and interpretations at all stages of research. By this means we co-create multifaceted (Richardson, 2000) and many-layered stories (Lather & Smithies, 1997) that come close to representing the messiness and complexity of human life (Geertz, 1973, 1983) and enable us to create meaning out of experience (Bruner, 1986, 1990).

By positioning our 'selves' within the text, *alongside* the stories others tell about their lives, and viewing those stories within the contexts of dominant discourses (Derrida, 1981), without privileging one story over another, we can create new and reflexive knowledge (Hertz, 1997) that can include the researcher's story, thus making transparent the values and beliefs that have inevitably influenced the research process and its outcomes. Behar (1996, p. 14) reminds us that the use of our 'selves' in research is a means to an end and not an end in itself: reflexivity does not mean anything personal goes, rather it means that:

> The exposure of self who is also a spectator has to take us
> somewhere we couldn't otherwise get to. It has to be essential
> to the argument, not a decorative flourish, not exposure for its
> own sake.

Purposes of Using Reflexivity

Reflexivity is a term that has been debated across the social sciences and used across the qualitative paradigms to a greater or lesser extent. For some traditional qualitative researchers, it might mean little more than a way of checking against possible sources of subjective bias creeping into their research (Stiles, 1993). If we can be aware of how our own thoughts, feelings, culture, environment and social and personal history inform us as we design the research, gather and transcribe the data and write our representations of it, then perhaps we can come close to the rigour that is required of good qualitative research.

From a non-traditional position, using reflexivity might itself be the primary method of inquiry, viewing our own stories and experiences as primary material and placing them within a social and cultural context, as in auto-ethnography, autobiography, heuristic inquiry, narrative inquiry or social poetics (Moustakas, 1990; Ellis & Flaherty, 1992; Ellis, 1995; Ellis & Bochner, 1996; Katz & Shotter, 1996; Riessman, 2002; Sparkes, 2002).

Reflexivity can create a bridge between researcher, practitioner and new knowledge (Reason, 1994; Heron, 1996; Etherington, 2000) when used in practitioner research. By viewing our relationship with participants and clients as one of consultancy and collaboration, we encourage involvement and a sense of personal agency. When we enable other people (and ourselves) to give voice to our experiences, those voices create a sense of power and authority (Hertz, 1997; McLeod, 1997).

Reflexive research encourages us to display in our writing the full interaction between ourselves and our participants and our relationship with the topic of inquiry and the data collected, so that our work can be understood, not only in terms of *what* we have discovered, but *how* we have discovered it. For myself and other like-minded individuals, this is both a moral *and* a methodological issue (Frank, 1995; Josselson, 1996; McLeod, 2001).

One important methodological issue is that our interpretations can be better understood and validated by readers who are informed about the position we adopt in relation to the study and by our explicit questioning of our own involvement. This means 'interpreting one's own interpretations, looking at one's own perspectives, and turning a self-critical eye onto one's own authority as interpreter and author' (Alvesson & Skoldberg, 2000, p. vii). In my view this enhances the trustworthiness of the findings and representations of the research.

For some people, greater transparency about their personal involvement as a researcher, and acknowledgment of prejudices towards or personal connections with the topic of study, may feel too great a challenge. Giddens (1991, p. 20) observed that doubts and uncertainties created by this challenge to familiar practices are 'not only troubling to philosophers but [are] *existentially troubling* for ordinary individuals'.

Reflexivity at Different Phases of the Research Process

Reflexive awareness of our involvement potentially affects *all* phases of research: deciding on our topics, planning our methodologies, doing the research and its final representation. As I said earlier, our motivation for undertaking research usually connects at some level with our 'personhood', whether for pragmatic or more personal reasons. One of my research participants, Dori, described her own recognition of her connection:

> It just seemed that the question was *there* inside of me, my
> question, my topic was there already. (Etherington, 2004,
> p. 214)

Our choice of methodology is based on the personal beliefs and philosophies that inform our worldview (ontology) and our ways of relating to and understanding how knowledge is created (epistemology). Our research methods, whether these involve conducting interviews, having conversations, co-creating stories or creating knowledge in other ways, link with our motivations and philosophies. The ways we choose to analyze or represent knowledge need to be consistent with all that has gone before.

Reflexive interviewing can follow the usual format of researchers asking questions that participants answer. It may be different if the interviewer also notices and/or includes personal experience of the topic and comments on the unfolding communication between both parties. Ellis & Berger (2003, p. 162) see the researcher's disclosures as 'more than tactics to encourage the respondent to open up; rather, the researcher often feels a reciprocal desire to disclose, given the intimacy of the details being shared by the interviewee'. In this way a new story is co-constructed:

> The interviewers might reflect deeply on the personal
> experiences that brought them to the topic, what they learned
> about and from themselves and their emotional responses in
> the course of the interview, and/or how they used knowledge
> of the self or the topic at hand to understand what the
> interviewee was saying. (Ellis & Berger, 2003, p. 162)

Each meeting with participants is like a snapshot of a moment in time, with each of us being uniquely embedded in our current lives. As we converse we are changed by our interactions, each person's story affecting the other's, and new selves are forming through this constant reconstruction:

> Storytelling is for another just as much as it is for oneself. In
> the reciprocity that is storytelling, the storyteller offers herself
> as guide to the other's self-formation. The other's receipt of
> that guidance not only recognises, but values the teller. The
> moral genius of storytelling is that each, teller and listener,
> enters the space of the story for the other. (Frank, 1995, p. 18)

Each story is told for a purpose and how it is told, and how it is heard, will depend on the listener as much as the narrator.

Reflexivity in audiotaping and transcription is rarely acknowledged in research reports (Lapadat & Lindsay, 1999). If we are explicit about our own involvement in such reporting, we are less likely to misrepresent our data. Even as we listen to and transcribe audiotapes of interviews, conversations and stories, we will almost certainly have begun to analyze the data, making choices based upon the theories and attitudes we hold that are informed by our personal and professional context.

Researchers make decisions about whether or not to use audio or video equipment, whether or not to transcribe, what to transcribe, and how to represent the transcription in their representation, but without explicit knowledge of this process the reader will end up with 'an impoverished basis for interpretation' (Kvale, 1996, p. 167) and be denied an opportunity to understand how the data have been used. However, it is important to acknowledge that transcripts are themselves social constructions: re-tellings and re-creations of stories that have already happened and not a faithful copy of a static world (Lapadat & Lindsay, 1999).

Reflexive research that overtly acknowledges the life and presence of the researcher as part of the research, dealing with issues of gender, culture, race and class, has contributed to what has been called a 'crisis of representation' (Denzin & Lincoln, 2000). This crisis came about in response to the falling away of traditional notions of truth, reality, and knowledge that previously provided us with familiar structures for presenting our 'findings'. If there is no objective truth to be found, then there can be no 'findings'; what we are left with is the voice and experiences of our participants and ourselves, and a need to find new ways of representing them.

Although the content and process of the research may become seamlessly interwoven stories that affect each other, the voices of researchers and researched need not be merged and reported as one story, which is actually the researcher's interpretation. By reporting each part and showing how the different roles and voices are separate, differences and problems encountered are discussed rather than ignored. Sparkes (2002) refers to these as 'confessional tales'.

Ruth Behar (1996) reminds us that we need to ask ourselves *where* we locate ourselves as the researcher in the field; how much we reveal of ourselves; and how we reconcile our different roles and positions. She invites us to see the researcher, writer, participant and interview not as separate entities but as intertwined in a deeply problematic way. In doing so we allow our biases and taken-for-granted assumptions to be seen, and provide the reader with the opportunity to make different interpretations of the data we have gathered.

One of my participants, Sue, told me how she saw this leading to the possibility of a more human interaction:

> Yes, they're [the readers] better informed about the process, they're better informed about the particular light that I might have chosen to shine on that particular topic. And I also think that it's more likely that the reader or the listener will access *their* personal response if I've done that. ... If I have said as author, 'This is who I am in relation to this topic', then the reader/listener is freer to decide who *they* are in relation to the topic and to declare that to themselves or others, as the case may be. So it makes for a more human interaction, it makes for a more dynamic energy around the research and its ongoing life.

Reflexivity and Voice

The academic community has traditionally discouraged the inclusion of our 'selves' in our writing, and academic writers can find this habit hard to break. Writing about ourselves can be experienced as both an opportunity and a risk: the opportunity for personal growth and development, or the risk that accompanies self-disclosure – disclosure of our selves to ourselves and to others.

Michael, a research participant in an earlier study who had offered to contribute his story as part of a collective auto-ethnography (Etherington, 2003) had previously written profusely within academia. In response to my request to see examples of his writing during the selection process for the study, he sent me several pieces of writing that all used the passive, objective voice. I wrote to him: 'You write very well in an academic genre. However – can you write [personal] stories? I notice that you leave yourself out of what you write almost entirely and of course what I am planning would be all about you!' However, we persevered and eventually co-constructed his story of childhood trauma, which reconnected him in the process with aspects of his experience hitherto forgotten, thus enriching the stories that he told.

When we use 'I' and write from inside our lives, we are better able to connect with feelings and senses that help us to *show* the experiences we want to share as research stories, rather than writing from the sidelines and 'telling' *about* our lives. This does however require an ability to *engage* with emotions without being overwhelmed, and for some people this is not always possible, especially if their way of managing painful lives has been to separate aspects of their experiences in order to survive them.

One way of developing a personal voice can be to keep a reflexive journal as part of the research process. Keeping a journal can help us to focus on our internal responses as researchers and capture our changing and developing understanding of method and content. We might use the journal to reflect on our roles; on the effect of the research on our personal and professional lives; on our relationships with participants; on our perception of the effect we may have on *their* lives; and our negative and/or positive feelings about what is happening during the research process.

In a reflexive journal we can capture dreams or images that might inform the research even while sleeping or daydreaming; poems that reflect the essence of something barely known to us, which provides new insights; conversations with colleagues about the research; drawings, cartoons or doodles that represent events, people, or telephone conversations; photos of places or people that may have become part of our research journey; indeed, anything that might be useful as data or to inform our process. The journal can provide a means by which we can make the most of the complexities of our presence in the research setting, in a methodical and regular manner (Holliday, 2002) or even an unmethodical and irregular manner.

One of my participants, Ruth, explained how she has different journals for different purposes. She observed that she uses different 'voices' in these journals: a critical voice and a freer creative voice.

> But what I have found that I've really loved doing (and this is
> relatively new), is including bits and pieces, playing around in
> a very scrawly way, creatively with ideas and so on, and I
> don't feel my critic comes into this bit. So I put dreams in it ...
> but also things I need to do to get finished on time, which of
> course I break all the time ... I read that [journal] last night and
> I thought 'Well, I've already broken four of those!' So I have to
> keep using it as a way of disciplining myself. But I use the
> other one much more than this one [she takes a journal from
> her bag]: this one is about thinking multi-dimensionally, and
> I've got a very bad memory, and if I don't jot down a concept
> I'll not remember I've ever read the thing, whereas if I have a
> metaphor I'll be able to remember.

Using the private space of a journal to record and process our thoughts and/or feelings can enable us to 'clear' or free up our communications with participants if they become stuck. Unacknowledged negative thoughts and feelings may block our ability to hear participants clearly or influence how we make sense of what we are hearing. On the other hand, being aware of our thoughts and feelings can help us to notice our biases. Ely et al (1997, p. 350) quote Jane Marsh, who asserts that 'a bias that we are aware of, a passion deeply felt may be an entrée into the experience we are studying'. They go on to describe this as 'an "enabling" not a blinding bias. The difference between the two would seem to lie in self-awareness'. This seems to me a very good argument for writing a journal as a way of reflecting and processing internal and external responses and behaviours.

Reflexive Texts

Reflexive texts are notoriously complex and multilayered and therefore difficult to manage: the line between text and context is blurred. In my recent attempt to capture such complexity I found myself writing:

> Trying to arrange this book has been like trying to dress an over-active baby in a Babygro! No sooner had I pushed one leg in, than the other came out: as soon as I tucked that leg back in, an arm was free, and so on. Postmodern texts are notoriously messy to handle and as a person who likes some degree of order and clarity, this has caused me more than a few problems. (Etherington, 2004, p. 21)

If we are able and willing to know and relate to the data differently, we may open ourselves up to creative and transformative opportunities for personal growth and new learning. One of my participants, Mel, who conducted an auto-ethnographic study for her Masters degree, told me:

> It has been an incredible upward, inward and outward spiral of growth. It has been the catalyst which has propelled me forward on another leg of my journey: physically, emotionally and spiritually. (Etherington 2004, p. 139)

Sometimes researchers are constrained by accusations of solipsism, narcissism and self-indulgence from critics who view subjectivity as a contaminant of research, judgements that stem from their positivist beliefs. Within academia the dominant stories of positivism still hold enormous influence that can be hard to challenge as simply *one* of the ways of doing research. There might be a great deal to lose if we expose ourselves to those who reject our personal involvement as valid and useful (Mykhalovskiy, 1997; Bochner, 2000; Sparkes, 2002).

Even researchers who value reflexivity may not always use themselves in their research because they lack the necessary awareness of their fluid changing process. Yet others are constrained by lack of self-confidence; anxiety about exposure; fear of judgement; shame about confessing their blunders or owning their personal connection with the topic; or a wish to retain their personal privacy. Clandinin & Connelly

(1994, p. 423) comment on how researchers might risk criticism when 'putting their heads above the parapet':

> The researcher is always speaking partially naked and is
> genuinely open to legitimate criticism from participants and
> from audience. Some researchers are silenced by the invitation
> to criticism contained in the expression of voice.

William, one of the participants in my research, summed up his own feeling about using reflexivity by referring to it as a process of 'coming out'. I have reported his words in stanza form, using some of the ideas described by Gee (1991). I have broken the lines where a natural pause or hesitation occurs in the transcription, and separated the stanzas where a new theme is introduced, such as exposure and hiding; being seen; coming into print and taking a risk.

'Coming out'

What's kind of coming up for me
is a sort of ambivalence
about my *own* exposure
          and my *own* hiding,
that, yes I want to be in print
and, no I don't,
          you know?

It's like I want to be seen
and I don't want to be seen
          and, yes,
I want to be on the stage
and I want to be hidden under the chair
at the same time.

My coming into print,
          and coming out as a reflexive researcher
          and coming out heuristically,
has been a gradual process of:
is this going to be OK?
And then pushing it a bit further
and selecting the media,
          the journal
          or the conference,
where I can go that next step.

Yes, it's all a risk
and it's all a kind of a question
of knowing what I can ...

knowing what I can get away with.
(Etherington, 2004, p. 242)

And Finally

I have located reflexivity within the traditions and trends in society as a whole and within the literature and my own research in order to convey my understanding of some of the theories, meanings and related issues; its history; uses and applications in research; the dilemmas it might create; and arguments for and against including ourselves in our writing as researchers. In summary, my story has shown that there are many ways of understanding and using reflexivity; that the judicious use of our 'selves' in research needs to be essential to the argument, not just a 'decorative flourish', for it to be described as reflexivity; that reflexivity requires self-awareness but is more than self-awareness; and that reflexivity recognises a circulating energy between the context of researcher and researched and that both have agency. Reflexivity enables us to provide information on *what* is known as well as *how* it is known.

Reflexivity challenges us to be more fully conscious of our own ideology, culture, and politics and those of our participants and our audience; this adds validity and rigour by providing information about the contexts in which data are located and enables us to recognise and address the moral and ethical issues and power relations involved. Reflexive awareness therefore is particularly relevant for those involved in comparative and international research in education, as indicated by other contributors to this book.

As I finish this chapter I am aware that my understanding is still incomplete and ever-changing, and that by the time this book is published I will probably have reached a different stage of my journey. I invite you to read this chapter as my way of telling a 'story of reflexivity' using my academic, personal and researcher's voices, and as an attempt to balance my own voice(s) with those of my participants and those whose shoulders I stand upon who have gone before me in the exploration of using our 'selves' in research.

References

Alcoff, L. & Potter, E. (1993) Introduction: when feminisms intersect epistemology, in L. Alcoff & E. Potter (Eds) *Feminist Epistemologies*, pp. 1-14. New York: Routledge.

Alvesson, M. & Skoldberg, K. (2000) *Reflexive Methodology*. London: Sage.

Behar, R. (1996) *The Vulnerable Observer: anthropology that breaks your heart*. Boston: Beacon.

Bochner, A.P. (2000) Criteria against Ourselves, *Qualitative Inquiry*, 6, pp. 266-272.

Bochner, A.P. (2001) Narrative Virtues, *Qualitative Inquiry*, 7, pp. 131-157.

Bruner, J. (1986) *Actual Minds, Possible Worlds*. Cambridge, MA: Harvard University Press.

Bruner, J. (1990) *Acts of Meaning*. Cambridge, MA: Harvard University Press.

Clandinin, D.J. & Connelly, F.M. (1994) Personal Experience Methods, in N.K. Denzin & Y.S. Lincoln (Eds) *Handbook of Qualitative Research*. Thousand Oaks, CA: Sage.

Clements, J., Ettling, D., Jenett, D. & Shields, L. (1998) Organic Research: feminine spirituality meets transpersonal research, in W. Braud & R. Anderson (Eds) *Transpersonal Research Methods for the Social Sciences: honoring human experience*. Thousand Oaks, CA: Sage.

Crotty, M. (1998) *The Foundations of Social Research: meaning and perspective in the research process*. London: Sage.

Denzin, N.K. & Lincoln, Y.S. (2000) *Handbook of Qualitative Research*, 2nd edn. London: Sage.

Derrida, J. (1981) *Positions*. Baltimore: Johns Hopkins University Press.

Devereux, G. (1967) From Anxiety to Method in the Behavioural Sciences, in P. Reason & J. Rowan (Eds) *Human Inquiry: a sourcebook of new paradigm research*. Chichester: Wiley.

Ellis, C. (1995) *Final Negotiations: a story of love, loss and chronic illness*. Philadelphia: Temple University Press.

Ellis, C. & Berger, L. (2003) Their Story/My Story/Our Story: including the researcher's experience in interview research, in J.F. Gubrium & J.A. Holstein (Eds) *Postmodern Interviewing*. Thousand Oaks, CA: Sage.

Ellis, C. & Bochner, A.P. (Eds) (1996) *Composing Ethnography: alternative forms of qualitative writing*. Oxford: AltaMira Press.

Ellis, C. & Flaherty, M. (Eds) (1992) *Investigating Subjectivity: research on lived experience*. Thousand Oaks, CA: Sage.

Ely, M., Vinz, R. Downing, M. & Anzul, M. (1997) *On Writing Qualitative Research: living by words*. London: Falmer Press.

Etherington, K. (2000) *Narrative Approaches to Working with Male Survivors of Sexual Abuse: the clients', the counsellor's and the researcher's story*. London: Jessica Kingsley.

Etherington, K. (2003) *Trauma, the Body and Transformation*. London: Jessica Kingsley.

Etherington, K. (2004) *Becoming a Reflexive Researcher: using our selves in research*. London: Jessica Kingsley.

Foucault, M. (1980) *Power/Knowledge: selected interviews and other writings*. Brighton: Harvester.

Frank, A.W. (1995) *The Wounded Storyteller: body, illness and ethics*. Chicago: University of Chicago Press.

Freire, P. (1972) *Pedagogy of the Oppressed*. Harmondsworth: Penguin.

Freire, P. (1985) *The Politics of Education: culture, power and liberation*. London: Macmillan.

Gee, J. (1991) A Linguistic Approach to Narrative, *Journal of Narrative and Life History*, 1, pp. 15-39.

Geertz, K.J. (1973) *The Interpretation of Cultures: selected essays*. New York: Basic Books.

Geertz, K.J. (1983) *Local Knowledge: further essays in interpretive anthropology*. New York: Basic Books.

Gergen, K.J. & Gergen, M.M. (1991) Towards Reflexive Methodologies, in F. Steier (Ed.) *Research and Reflexivity*. Newbury Park: Sage.

Giddens, A. (1991) *Modernity and Self-Identity: self and society in the late modern age*. Cambridge: Polity Press.

Heron, J. (1996) *Co-operative Inquiry: research into the human condition*. London: Sage.

Hertz, R. (Ed.) (1997) *Reflexivity and Voice*. Thousand Oaks, CA: Sage.

Holliday, A. (2002) *Doing and Writing Qualitative Research*. London: Sage.

Josselson, R. (Ed.) (1996) *Ethics and Process in the Narrative Study of Lives*, vol. 4. London: Sage.

Katz, A.M. & Shotter, J. (1996) Hearing the Patient's 'Voice': toward a social poetics in diagnostic interviews, *Social Science and Medicine*, 43, pp. 919-931. http://dx.doi.org/10.1016/0277-9536(95)00442-4

Kvale, S. (1996) *InterViews: an introduction to qualitative research interviewing*. Thousand Oaks, CA: Sage.

Lapadat, J.C. & Lindsay, A.C. (1999) Transcription in Research and Practice: from standardization of technique to interpretive positionings, *Qualitative Inquiry*, 5, pp. 64-86.

Lather, P. & Smithies, C. (1997) *Troubling the Angels*. Oxford: Westview Press.

McLeod, J. (1997) *Narrative and Psychotherapy*. London: Sage.

McLeod, J. (2001) *Qualitative Research in Counselling and Psychotherapy*. London: Sage.

Masemann, V. & Welch, A. (Eds) (1998) *Tradition, Modernity and Postmodernity in Comparative Education*. Hamburg: UNESCO Institute for Education.

Moustakas, C. (1990) *Heuristic Research Design, Methodology and Applications*. London: Sage.

Mykhalovskiy, E. (1997) Reconsidering 'Table Talk': critical thoughts on the relationship between sociology, autobiography, and self-indulgence, in R. Hertz (Ed.) *Reflexivity and Voice*. London: Sage.

Reason, P. (Ed.) (1994) *Participation in Human Inquiry*. London: Sage.

Richardson, L. (2000) Writing: a method of inquiry, in N.K. Denzin & Y.S. Lincoln (Eds) *Handbook of Qualitative Research*, 2nd edn. Thousand Oaks, CA: Sage.

Riessman, C. (2002) Doing Justice: positioning the interpreter in narrative work, in W. Patterson (Ed.) *Strategic Narrative: new perspectives on the power of personal and cultural stories*. Oxford: Lexington Books

Sparkes, A.C. (2002) *Telling Tales in Sport and Physical Activity: a qualitative journey*. Leeds: Human Kinetics.

Kim Etherington

Stiles, W.B. (1993) Quality Control in Qualitative Research, *Clinical Psychology Review*, 13, pp. 593-618. http://dx.doi.org/10.1016/0272-7358(93)90048-Q

CHAPTER SIX

Learning and Change through a Narrative PhD: a personal narrative in progress

NELL BRIDGES
University of Bristol, United Kingdom

Introduction

My aim in writing this chapter is to offer a personal narrative, to show some of my lived experience as a PhD student and novice narrative researcher and to hint at some possibilities that my chosen approach to narrative research brings. This is not so that others may follow my path but that they may be roused to find a path of their own, their own narrative adventure that emerges from their particular context, culture and history.

Narrative research inevitably involves the re-presentation of stories that are in some way collected, usually from others but sometimes from the researcher's own experience. Decisions about the nature of this re-presentation are influenced by the values, preferences, skills and assumptions of the researcher. In my PhD I am attempting to use creative, evocative and transgressive forms of re-presentation (Richardson, 1992, 2000; Clough, 2002) to produce a multiply-storied (Speedy, 2001) rather than a simple, unitary story. I will attempt to do likewise here in the (dis)organisation of this chapter, where I turn my attention from the lived experience of others to my own lived experience. As I am only using my own story it also seems a good opportunity to be a little playful.

At the time of writing, it is Summer 2004 and I am in the middle of my period of study, funded by the Economic and Social Research Council (the United Kingdom's leading research funding agency addressing economic and social concerns), for a PhD using narrative inquiry to investigate counsellors' experiences of maintaining ethical practice despite contrary demands. This is to some extent a point of balance, from where I am able to look back to the beginning and forward in anticipation of the end. I am aware, though, that the true endpoint cannot be clearly seen or predicted from here, and may not even exist at all. I am also increasingly aware, as I look back through my memories and my narrations of these memories, that what I recollect and what I tell is likewise neither there to be recalled clearly by myself nor straightforwardly revealed to others. As I turn my attention to the beginnings and the events that I have lived through so far, I sift, I select, I remember some things and fail to remember others. I also realise that I am struggling to access and disclose a version of my 'self' that no longer exists (Drewery & Winslade, 1997). More than that, I am trying to do this while describing the period of my life that brought about those changes and fundamentally re-constituted that self, and in the telling I will be further constituted (White & Epston, 1990; Anderson, 1997; Wortham, 2000). A tall order! So where shall I start? With a story of course.

In the Beginning

Like most big adventures this one started modestly. A middle-aged woman in a small, pavement café on a sunny, spring day, sipping coffee and opening her newspaper. She was yearning for adventure, something to change her life. There always was something otherworldly about her and so she usually took adventure and transformation in her stride. But she was not prepared for the transformation that would start that very day. She opened her newspaper and there in front of her was an advertisement to study for a narrative PhD at the University of Bristol. And although she only had a vague idea of what narrative meant at that time, she knew that it meant stories, and that stories meant fun.

This is in many ways a true account, but of course there was more to it than that. Soon after embarking on this period of study I had a sense of being almost overwhelmed by the situation that I had put myself into. I was clearly at an exciting point in my professional life; I had gained a place at a prestigious university to study something that really interested me. However, it was also very daunting: I had left secure employment as a professional practitioner and the success of my future career would now depend on what I was able to make of the opportunity that I had been given. Clearly, I was keen that my research would be well-regarded and seen to be of an acceptable standard, but I was also keen that it would do me justice in more personal ways, that it would not betray the ethics, standards and values that I had developed throughout my life, and particularly through my years of experience as a counsellor, counselling supervisor and counselling educator. However, as I have already mentioned, the self that held these values was in a process of transformation. I was trying to remain true and constant to a self that was itself remaining neither true nor constant.

Time Trials

Like most big adventures this one contained unforeseen trials and tasks to be completed. And being a lover of stories, she knew of many heroes. So each time the wise ones said, 'Go forth into the unknown, slay dragons and bring me back evidence of your journey' she knew the kind of heroic thing to say. And though shaky inside, she smiled and heroically replied 'Easy!' (or something similar). And once she had completed the legendary funding trials, the mystical research training trials and the mythic upgrading trials the real adventure began.

When studying for a PhD, the research is only part of the work. There are many other hurdles to clear; these may include securing funding, completing research method courses (some are likely to be compulsory) and (in the United Kingdom) passing through the upgrade from registration as an MPhil student to registration as a PhD student. Each represented a risk to my progress, a potential to fall on my face, to end with nothing, no PhD and no job. But as a mature student with substantial professional experience I thought that I should be able to take these things in my stride, so I tried to hide my insecurities.

Finding My Feet

Along the way, she came to a place where the main track separated into many different paths. She stood bewildered, not knowing which way to turn. She knew that some would lead to confusion, some to betrayal, and some nowhere. She hoped with all her being that at least one might lead to illumination, but the signposts were unclear.

Our need for our research to be credible or convincing leads us to lay our process open for others to examine and to defend that process as legitimate human enquiry to be taken seriously. In order to do this we need to clearly account for our theoretical perspective and its underlying epistemology. Although I had chosen to use a narrative approach, this can encompass a wide range of disparate perspectives and I had to find my own position and coherence within this range. According to Carr (1995), values are vital in influencing choices in research; he is critical of attempts to use research strategies infused by one set of values in order to study practices that are infused by another. I thus attempted to identify my values and relate them to my research choices and practices. However, throughout this period of study the self that I had known, and the values that I had used to navigate my life by, began to mutate and my insecurities grew. So I struggled to keep up, to 'find a position' that I could adhere to, to establish a reliable standpoint. An excerpt from my research journal illustrates this:

> Today I really need to focus – to get somewhere. I have this hope that today will be a turning point. Today I will come to some sort of resolution about my philosophical focus. Is philosophy so emotional for everyone? Do I just turn everything into a big emotional issue? [I have since learnt that I am by no means alone in experiencing this.]

Increasingly researchers are embracing improvisation and the creation of techniques for data collection and analysis, which has come to be known as *bricolage*. Denzin & Lincoln (1994) refer to this as the negotiation of a personal route through the methodological terrain, whereas McLeod claims that: 'The bricoleur is someone who both fully understands and "owns" his or her perspective on research' (McLeod, 2001, p. 27). These positions seemed to offer values and an identity that appealed to me, though I was well aware that some writers (Hammersley, 1999) expressed serious concerns about such mixing of traditions. Others (Crotty, 1998) seemed less absolute, focusing on the need to be explicit about the relationships between our methods, methodology, theoretical perspective and epistemology and the need to elucidate our key theoretical influences.

This made sense: I didn't want a haphazard, 'pick-and-mix' thesis, though I did want it to be rich, multitextual, challenging and enjoyable to read as well as to write. And I wanted it to do justice to the stories of my participants, which were in themselves rich, multitextual, challenging and enjoyable. The task then became one of explicating the relationship between the various themes that underpinned the research, while keeping the richness, multiplicity and complexity. Richardson (1992) provided a working solution; she advocates 'drawing freely' from literary, artistic and scientific genres and including different 'takes' to produce a sort of postmodern triangulation. She claims that the metaphor of a crystal is appropriate to represent this, as we can assume no fixed point to triangulate on but instead need to include multiple dimensionalities, various transmutations, angles of approach and so on; this became my aspiration.

Reflections on Reflections

Looking into the deep pool of wisdom, she saw no clear reflection but a shimmering and magical scattering of incomplete images that continuously metamorphosed as they flowed into each other. She endeavoured to distinguish figure from background but the harder she tried the giddier she became.

I did not come to this PhD naïvely. I have long known that researchers cannot be assumed to be neutral in the research process and I was very aware that at least part of my motivation to undertake research in this area had roots in some of my more difficult professional and personal experiences. Bochner & Ellis (2003, p. 508) see this 'deep and abiding connection between one's own life history and one's research and writing' more positively than I did at that time. My intention had been to make my 'vested interest' clear while maintaining appropriate confidentiality and boundaries about the situations and events that had so motivated me. In short, I intended to practise reflexivity in a bid both to minimise the effects of my own history and also to make its influence explicit. I wanted reflexivity to provoke me, as a researcher, to take greater responsibility for my actions and to reflect on the impact of my research (Warner, 2004). I wanted to 'close the illusory gap between researcher and researched and between the knower and what is known' (Etherington, 2004, p. 32). I was, however, wary of accusations of non-productive 'navel-gazing' or narcissism (see for example, Mykhalovskiy, 1997; Sparkes, 2002) and wanted to engage actively and critically. Lynch (2000) is also sceptical about reflexivity, relating it to academic privilege. I did not and do not experience it as privilege, but as an exposing and demanding but immensely worthwhile process.

A particular difficulty for me was that throughout my adult life I have held a strong personal value of honesty and authenticity. I also valued creativity and freedom of expression, but saw this as distinct from the honesty and sincerity that I so prized. I did not consider how comfortably authenticity and creativity might sit alongside each other. These challenges hit me with full force and I struggled to maintain, or rather to regain some equilibrium. I was of course caught between the two worldviews of realism and poststructuralism, trying to force a realist or essentialist framework to coexist with poststructuralist perspectives. I knew that truth and experience are not simple but multilayered and are constructed in a continually evolving social and cultural context, but there was a nagging discomfort with the excessive relativism that this could lead to. Again I used my journal to try to work these things out:

> I believe that there are some truths and there are also lies. And
> the difference between them is profoundly important. And the
> difference between them is extremely problematic because
> there are not simple truths, or unitary truths.

I was particularly wary of the powerful truth claims of the grand narratives. I think we have to be very careful about accepting theories or concepts as 'truth', particularly with regard to interpreting other people. Such theories can lead to people being interpreted, classified, diminished, dismissed and even incarcerated. Once we think we have found a truth we become dangerous. Holly Near makes this point in her song 'I Ain't Afraid' (2000): 'The ones who say they know it are the ones who will impose it on you'.

One of my most treasured values is that of uncertainty and mystery, particularly with regard to other people. Bauman expresses it thus:

> [Uncertainty] is the very soil in which the moral self takes root and grows. Moral life is a life of continuous uncertainty, and it takes a lot of strength and resilience and an ability to withstand pressures to be a moral person. Moral responsibility is *unconditional* and in principle *infinite* – and thus one can recognise a moral person by their never quenched dissatisfaction with their moral performance; the gnawing suspicion that they were not moral enough. (1994, p. 44-45)

Once we accept not knowing, really not knowing, then we can meet each other and the world with openness and innocence. Then we can create something truly fresh and valuable. This is what I must strive to do in my research.

Dipping My Toe in the Water

In order to gain a rich understanding of the narrative interview process and to inform my own approach to the interviews that I would conduct with my respondents, I was interviewed by my research adviser. This proved to be an immensely valuable first stage for an iterative, heuristic research process (Moustakas, 1990; Etherington, 2000).

As she stepped into the enchanted pool, she felt as if some incredibly penetrating eyes were watching her and she yearned for a cloak of invisibility, but none could be found.

During my experience of being interviewed I felt vulnerable and wondered what my adviser was thinking of me, and whether she had an agenda. In retrospect, of course she did, we all do. I had hoped to be able to fence off some aspects of myself, as recommended by phenomenological researchers, and as I had attempted to do in my practice. Such fencing off seemed increasingly impossible, but I was yet to see this as an advantage.

The transcript shows me telling some stories, starting to tell some stories and not managing to tell others. This is a testimony to the pervasive nature of narrative (Mischler, 1986; McLeod, 1997), and I realised that I would not be able to focus on all of the stories of my participants; there would inevitably be some selection. I became aware that I would be more powerful in this process than I had expected.

Power and the Myth of Mutuality

It was soon time for her to meet other travellers and in doing so she realised that, because of the particular path she had taken, she stood in a powerful position. She carried a power that the others did not have and she felt uncomfortable, as she had learned that power was dangerous. So she tried to give it away and share it, but each time she tried it just kept coming back to her, as the giver of gifts is inevitably powerful. Then she tried to pretend that she did not have this power and that it did not exist, but an evil smell immediately began to emanate from it. Eventually she realised that, although she would receive help, it was a burden that only she could carry on this particular journey and she must do this with all the integrity she could muster.

The potential power of the interviewer became evident when I first read the transcript of my own interview. My journal says:

> I am struck by a sense that it seems to represent what the interviewer heard, rather than what I said. For instance at one point I referred to someone called Jill but this was heard as John and the name John appeared in the transcript, i.e. what the interviewer heard not what I said. This jars as I read it and I have a sense of alienation from it. The question, 'whose transcript is it?' occurs. Other inaccuracies in transcription seem to misrepresent people and, even though this was simply a learning exercise and no further use will be made of it, I am still uncomfortable when I read it.

I then understood more clearly why my adviser's research practice is to return the transcript for checking, as she did with me. Such inaccuracies are thereby amended. Not all researchers do so and this was an important lesson for me. In carrying out my own interviews and transcriptions, I soon came to realise that total accuracy is impossible and that research participants are much more likely to know what they said or meant than the interviewer. They are the ones who have lived through the experience and the context that they are describing. In any case, in my research I attempt to hear previously suppressed or submerged narratives, and so privilege the voice of the participant over my own. I acknowledge, though, that this will be impossible to fully achieve and share Sparkes's (1998) 'unsettling thoughts' about this.

My adviser pointed out that researchers are legitimately more directive than therapists:

> I believe that although there are many similarities between my roles as therapist and researcher, there are also differences.
> The main difference being that as a therapist my purpose is to assist my clients re-search (into themselves and their lives)

and in my role as researcher the positions are reversed – they are there to assist me in discovering something about a topic or concept that I am curious about. As a counsellor people seek *me* out: as a researcher I seek them. (Etherington, 2004, p. 110)

To her, the research is primarily 'for' the researcher, and this is clearly the case for me as well: I am the one who hopes to gain a PhD. Having dispelled the myth that this research is intended simply to benefit the participants, it feels more important than ever that I treat them with respect, honour their stories and give appropriate credit for their contribution. I still hope that they will benefit from their involvement in the research, but I have to admit that the whole project has been brought into existence primarily by me and for me. As Wolcott (1995, p. 140) says, 'It's just a bit awkward having to face up to being our own beneficiaries.'

Out with the Old, In with the New?

She came across a chest of unknown treasure and knew that if she were to take some of this for herself she would have to make space in her knapsack. So she peered in at all of the things that she had brought with her on her journey. She knew that some were precious gifts that she had won on previous adventures, some were empty talismans that had no value on this particular journey and some were just useless clutter. But how to tell which was which?

In starting my PhD I was making a major transition, from counsellor to researcher. However, I was keen that my current role would not bring a stark division from my past, but rather build on it. I was reassured by my adviser's position regarding this:

Sometimes students arrive on research training courses believing they have to leave behind all the knowledge and skills they have acquired through counsellor training ... reflexive research training uses and values all that they bring with them and seeks to develop and add to that. (Etherington, 2004, p. 110)

As an experienced counsellor I had a conception of myself as a skilled listener, yet I didn't know which of my counselling and listening skills would be relevant and useful and which inappropriate to my new role. Clearly some would be unsuitable. My adviser is also a counsellor, and although we have some similar influences on our practice I was also aware of differences. This means that what we bring to our research practice is different, and the decisions that we make about what is or is not appropriate are also likely to differ. Despite this knowledge of the differences in our practice, I was surprised at how active she was when she interviewed me and the number of questions that she asked me. At the time I struggled to know whether this was because of our different approaches to counselling or because my more person-centred approach was inappropriate for a narrative research interview. In my practice I have tried to avoid questions in an attempt to stay in the client's frame of reference, not to intrude, distort or distract. My aim has been to witness deeply, to avoid co-construction. My adviser believes co-construction to be inevitable and embraces it in both her counselling practice and her research.

As my research has progressed, it has inevitably been influenced by both my old values and practices and by my new understandings. I feel that my old skills have enabled me to stay close to, and present with, respondents in the telling of their story; however, my new recognition is that co-construction is inevitable and can also be positive. So my aim is again to witness deeply, though now I do not naïvely separate this from co-construction.

Writing

I initially attempted to use writing as a straightforward aid to my researcher reflexivity. I had written through times of difficulty and dilemma and as part of my personal development for many years, and this seemed a natural way to proceed. I began with journal writing and written reflections on my reading and on key experiences. I also took a more reflexive approach to my traditional academic writing. Increasingly, I sent emails to advisers, participants and peers so that the reflexive process became less individual and more connected. But I still learnt little that I wasn't previously aware of. In fact, I began to bore myself and I became concerned that I would tire of my research topic. Yet something was keeping me connected.

Further on her journey she found a pen, but it was no ordinary pen. It was a charmed pen that would not stop writing. It wrote and it wrote. It wrote of truth and it wrote of fantasy. It wrote of hope and it wrote of despair. It wrote to everyone and it wrote to no-one. And although she knew that she would never write the truth, she began to see that she could write of meaning and of feeling and of understanding.

It is hard to know what happened to enable me to write differently. It clearly wasn't just one isolated occurrence, as ideas entered my consciousness from several directions. One quite hurtful experience was being confronted about my motivations for studying ethical practice in a way that I found unfair. I wrote in my journal:

> That meeting has been in my mind. I have a nagging
> discomfort about how I responded to those challenges. I was

101

defensive. I sold myself short and I sold my research topic short. What was going on for me? That comment – something about monitoring and judging others really got to me. That's just what I'm trying to challenge – that idea that ethics is about rules and negative judgements ... So I did the worst thing. I distanced myself rather than explaining myself ... This says a lot about why I'm really researching this area. It is a very powerful subject for me ... I do have a particular interest in ethics ... All of my life I have been trying to understand it. Trying to work out the bottom line, 'Am I a good enough person?' So what am I really asking in this research?

Another push came from a narrative therapy course where, in a practice session, I recalled powerful experiences and attributions from my childhood that again seemed to link to my motivations regarding this research. An identity that had been imposed in a very negative way in the original context of my evangelical Christian upbringing was given space, acceptance and even honour in this new arena of narrative therapy. This approach shares some of the underlying poststructuralist ideas and values of many narrative researchers (McLeod, 1997; Speedy, 2000).

I began to want to express my connection to my topic more vividly. I needed to find a way to re-present my own stories as well as those of my participants evocatively. Bolton (2001) advises studying our own stories to allow us to work constructively with our experience. In exploring new and more creative ways of writing, one particular piece of advice kept recurring: 'Show, don't tell' (Booth, 1991; Hunt, 2000). Combined, these various prompts enabled me face the page in a new way; to write from the position of 'experiencer' rather than observer; to alternately turn inward to memory and embodied personal experience, then outward to connection with others to be prodded by their curiosity and challenge, and so again turn to self and write within and between these positions. In this way I found that, like Ellis (1995) in her groundbreaking book *Final Negotiations*, I had transformed my understanding and my connection to my field of research. I had moved from seeking participants who felt that they have simply maintained their ethical code and resisted external pressure, to seeking participants who had experienced the complexity of being pulled in different ethical directions. The question that I asked in my journal, 'Am I a good enough person?', began to stop haunting me. The process of creative writing had clearly been healing as well as informative. I found myself allying with an emerging community of others (Richardson, 1992, 2000; Etherington, 2000, 2003, 2004; Bolton, 2001; Clough, 2002; Sparkes, 2002; Bochner & Ellis, 2003). All of these researchers had been discovering and expressing the power of writing for inquiry, creativity, therapy and reflexivity and, in doing so, 'troubling' old boundaries between art, science, therapy and research.

And Finally

In attempting to represent my experience of undertaking a PhD using narrative methods, I have found myself using narrative methods. I have told a story. This has not been a simple linear account with a clear beginning, middle and end, but has taken shape as a sort of patchwork. Different aspects and elements have been presented alongside each other, not always in a neat and tidy way. Some parts overlap, some are masked or hidden, and others are quite clearly revealed. You, the reader, have not had a clear, unobstructed view of what 'doing a narrative PhD' is like, but you may have gained some meaningful insight into my lived experience of my particular narrative PhD. You have not only read of my struggles to make sense of my experiences and of my changing constructions of self, but have also witnessed some of those struggles and changes as I inevitably revealed these processes in and through this narrative. This ever-shifting flux of live experiencing and story is at the heart of narrative inquiry, and I thoroughly recommend it.

Now some say that the grail is a cup, and some that it is a cauldron, but for this particular middle-aged woman it is the freedom to journey and discover creatively, to play with ideas, words and stories and to know that this is worthwhile.

References

Anderson, H. (1997) *Conversation, Language and Possibilities: a postmodern approach to therapy*. New York: Basic Books.

Bauman, Z. (1994) *Alone Again: ethics after certainty*. London: Demos.

Bochner, A. & Ellis, C. (2003) An Introduction to the Arts and Narrative Research: art as inquiry, *Qualitative Inquiry*, 9, pp. 506-514. http://dx.doi.org/10.1177/1077800403254394

Bolton, G. (2001) *Reflective Practice: writing for professional development*. London: Sage.

Booth, W. (1991) *The Rhetoric of Fiction* (2nd edn). Harmondsworth: Penguin.

Carr, W. (1995) *Philosophy, Values and Educational Science: towards critical educational inquiry*. Buckingham: Open University Press.

Clough, P. (2002) *Narratives and Fiction in Educational Research*. Buckingham: Open University Press.

Crotty, M. (1998) *The Foundations of Social Research*. London: Sage.

Denzin, N.K. & Lincoln, Y.S. (1994) Introduction: entering the field of qualitative research, in N.K. Denzin & Y.S. Lincoln (Eds) *Handbook of Qualitative Research*. Thousand Oaks: Sage.

Drewery, W. & Winslade, J. (1997) The Theoretical Story of Narrative, in G. Monk, J. Winslade, K. Crocket & D. Epston (Eds) *Narrative Therapy in Practice: the archaeology of hope*. San Francisco: Jossey-Bass.

Ellis, C. (1995) *Final Negotiations: a story of love, loss and chronic illness.* Philadelphia: Temple University Press.

Etherington, K. (2000) *Narrative Approaches to Working with Adult Male Survivors of Child Sexual Abuse: the clients', the counsellor's and the researcher's story*. London: Jessica Kingsley.

Etherington, K. (2003) *Trauma, the Body and Transformation*. London: Jessica Kingsley.

Etherington, K. (2004) *Becoming a Reflexive Researcher: using our selves in research*. London: Jessica Kingsley.

Hammersley, M. (1999) Not Bricolage but Boatbuilding: exploring two metaphors for thinking about ethnography, *Journal of Contemporary Ethnography*, 28, pp. 574-585. http://dx.doi.org/10.1177/089124199129023569

Hunt, C. (2000) *Therapeutic Dimensions of Autobiography in Creative Writing*. London: Jessica Kingsley

Lynch, M. (2000) Against Reflexivity as an Academic Virtue and Source of Principled Knowledge, *Theory, Culture and Society*, 17, pp. 27-56.

McLeod, J. (1997) *Narrative and Psychotherapy*. London: Sage.

McLeod, J. (2001) *Qualitative Research in Counselling and Psychotherapy*. London: Sage.

Mischler, E. (1986) *Research Interviewing: context and narrative*. Cambridge, MA: Harvard University Press.

Moustakas, C. (1990) *Heuristic Research: design, methodology and applications*. Thousand Oaks: Sage.

Mykhalovskiy, E. (1997) Reconsidering 'Table Talk': critical thoughts on the relationship between sociology, autobiography and self-indulgence, in R. Hertz (Ed.) *Reflexivity and Voice*. London: Sage.

Near, H. (2000) *I Ain't Afraid*, from *Edge*. Ikiah, CA: Calico Tracks Music.

Richardson, L. (1992) The Consequences of Poetic Representation: writing the other, rewriting the self, in C. Ellis & M. Flaherty (Eds) *Investigating Subjectivity: research on lived experience*. New York: Sage.

Richardson, L. (2000) Writing: a method of inquiry, in N. Denzin & Y. Lincoln (Eds) *Handbook of Qualitative Research* (2nd edn). Thousand Oaks: Sage.

Sparkes, A. (1998) Reciprocity in Critical Research? Some Unsettling Thoughts, in G. Shacklock & J. Smyth (Eds) *Being Reflexive in Critical, Educational and Social Research*. London: Falmer Press.

Sparkes, A. (2002) Autoethnography: self-indulgence or something more?, in A. Bochner & C. Ellis (Eds) *Ethnographically Speaking: autoethnography, literature and aesthetics*. New York: AltaMira Press.

Speedy, J. (2000) The Storied Helper: an introduction to narrative ideas and practices and practices in counselling and psychotherapy research, *European Journal of Counselling, Psychotherapy and Health*, 3(3).

Speedy, J. (2001) Singing over the Bones: a narrative inquiry into the construction of research and practice cultures and professional identities by counsellor educators at the University of Bristol and within the UK. Unpublished PhD thesis, University of Bristol.

Warner, S. (2004) Contingent Morality and Psychotherapy Research: developing applicable frameworks for ethical processes of enquiry, *Journal of Critical Psychology, Counselling and Psychotherapy*, 4, pp. 106-114.

White, M. & Epston, D. (1990) *Narrative Means to Therapeutic Ends*. New York: Norton.

Wolcott, H.F. (1995) *The Art of Fieldwork*. Walnut Creek: AltaMira Press.

Wortham, S. (2000) Interactional Positioning and Narrative Self-Construction, *Narrative Inquiry*, 10, pp. 157-184.

STORIES OF LEARNING IN COMPARATIVE AND INTERNATIONAL RESEARCH

CHAPTER SEVEN

African Teacher Narratives in Comparative Research

ANGELINE M. BARRETT
University of Bristol, United Kingdom

Introduction

Narrative approaches are claimed to be applicable across cultures on the grounds that story is a universal way of knowing (Carter, 1993), albeit with differing conventions of structure between (Riessman, 1987) and within cultures (as illustrated, for example, by Rasmussen, 1999). By respecting the texts created by informants, narrative approaches have also been credited with achieving authentic representation of individuals (Riessman, 1993). Given this, narrative should be eminently suited to education research in Africa. While this is borne out by the quality of teacher narratives to be found in African literature, very little use has been made of narrative techniques within formal education research published internationally or within the United Kingdom (UK), although this is slowly beginning to change. One reason for this is that the research context of low-income countries raises particular challenges to the practice of narrative methodologies. This chapter briefly reviews the forms in which the narratives of African teachers appear in literature. It then argues that there is a continuity between the principles of narrative inquiry, as laid out by Clandinin & Connelly (2000), and qualitative methodologies used within the field of international and comparative education. I use two Tanzanian narratives of entry to teaching to illustrate the potential and limitations of narrative, used as a method rather than methodology, for teacher research in Africa. The exemplar narratives emerged from my own PhD research on Tanzanian primary school teachers' identity, which from its inception was conceived as being comparative but not narrative.

Narrative and comparative research both encompass a range of theoretical approaches and defy rigid definition in terms of frameworks or paradigms. Hence, it is worth starting by explaining the understandings of each that I have used in this chapter. Narrative research refers to the methodological use of story and usually is concerned with the stories of individuals, although those of communities or organisations may also be of interest. The stories range from detailed life histories, collected through a series of in-depth interviews over an extended period of time (Shaw, 1996; Munro, 1998), to less detailed life histories collected from a larger group of informants (Casey, 1993) or anecdotes collected through listening in on informal chat or meetings (as discussed by Cortazzi, 1993). One of the most important divisions within narrative approaches is between those who, like Clandinin & Connelly (Connelly & Clandinin, 1990; Carter, 1993), regard narrative as a form of knowing and hence use story as an ontological metaphor, and those who use narrative to refer to the study of texts constructed by informants (Nespor & Barylske, 1991; Maclure, 1993a). This latter group regard narratives as performative texts constructed within a specific set of social relations, and may use techniques of discourse analysis to probe how they have been created (Convery, 1999).

The common-sense understanding of comparative research is research comparing some specific aspect of education in two or more systems, which may be national, subnational or international. However, it is often used as an umbrella term for studies of education that are in some way international, for example carried out by a researcher from another country or with reference to international debate, and theoretically oriented. Comparative research is therefore methodologically eclectic and comparativists have adopted a range of qualitative techniques, including case study, ethnography and open interviews. Whereas narrative research is defined in terms of methodology, comparative research is defined in terms of the research topic, making the two non-exclusive. Nonetheless, there is a correspondence between the principles of narrative inquiry and qualitative research as conducted by comparativists, particularly in low-income counties. This suggests that a growth in the use of narrative methods by comparativists would be continuous with recent developments in the field.

Comparative and Narrative Teacher Research in Africa

Anyone researching education in low-income countries comes up against a hegemonic development discourse (Tikly, 2004). Within this discourse, education in low-income countries is a problem and primary school teachers are an important part of that problem. The problem is how to expand provision concurrent with improving quality in the context of a weak national economy and poor infrastructure. Underpaid, underqualified teachers working in under-resourced schools, and as a consequence ineffective, demoralised and prone to misconduct, are viewed as both causes and casualties of the problem (Lockheed & Verspoor, 1991; World Bank, 1995; UNESCO, 1998). As various development agencies seek strategies to improve the quality of primary education, the question being posed with increasing frequency is, 'What makes teachers tick?' (the title of a research study by Voluntary Service Overseas, 2002).

In other words, those committing funds towards the improvement of education want to know what motivates those teachers who are effective despite their difficult circumstances, and what demoralises others to the point of falling into habits of frequent absenteeism and in the worst cases, corrupt or abusive misconduct. Given their capacity to '[open] up the sealed boxes within which teachers work and survive' (Ball & Goodson, 1985, p. 13), biographic approaches as a subset of narrative research would appear to be eminently suited to answering this question. Yet the research context of the development field is inimical to their use for many of the same reasons that constrain education research generally in low-income countries (comprehensively explained in King, 1991; Mwiria & Wamahiu, 1995; Crossley & Watson, 2003). These include a funding context that means the majority of research is either commissioned, usually by external donor agencies, or carried out by research students based in universities in high-income countries. The funding context also makes it harder for researchers based in low-income countries to work outside positivistic paradigms, which too often exclude local knowledge and local voices (Dzvimbo, 1994; Brock-Utne, 1996). The culture of the development industry imposes time limits and constrains methodologies. For research students, the simple fact of physical distance between research field and place of study restricts access to the field.

It is easier to find examples of insightful teacher narratives from the African continent in literature than it is within formal education research. Wole Soyinka's 'faction' *Ìsarà* imaginatively portrays his father 'Essay', who was a primary school headteacher in colonial Nigeria (Soyinka, 1989). The ease with which Essay moves between the several cultural spheres of school, church and his home village contrasts with the tormented Godfrey Munira, a character in Ngugi wa Thiong'o's *Petals of Blood* (Ngugi, 1977). Possibly Africa's most famous fictional teacher, Munira's fragmented identities in newly independent Kenya ultimately drive him to violence. In *Maru*, Bessie Head beautifully evokes the loneliness of a teacher in a Botswanan village, who belongs to a marginalised ethnic group (Head, 1971). Dangarembga's novel *Nervous Conditions*, set in Zimbabwe, is a study of education from a feminist perspective and includes the character Maiguru, a teacher who despite her Masters degree from England still remains oppressed by patriarchy (Dangarembga, 1988). Isegawa, in his novel *Abyssinian Chronicles,* shows us an unheroic side of teaching in Uganda (Isegawa, 2000). During a brief stint as a secondary school teacher, his main character, Mugezi, distracted by his lucrative illegal brewing business, is unremorseful over missing more lessons than he teaches.

There are a few examples of life history in education research carried out in Africa and published in British or international journals. Beth Cross used a narrative methodology to inquire into the life history and identity of three African postgraduate colleagues at her university in the UK (Cross, 1996). This was life-history research in its purest sense: in-depth, collaborative with ongoing contact between researcher and research subjects over an extended period of time. A more common technique has been a less collaborative approach going into less depth with more informants, as used by Osler to elicit the career biographies of Kenyan teacher advisers (Osler, 1997). Stephens' methodology of cultural inquiry in Ghana included life-history interviews with teachers and pupils, among other methods (Stephens, 1998). He has since argued the case for more use of life-history research in the development field (Stephens, in press).

Although narrative research has, so far, been little used in low-income countries, there is a tradition of qualitative education research that has many points in common with its methods and epistemologies. My own research is located within this tradition and originated out of approaching the question 'What makes teachers tick?' from the other end. When I was a Masters student, recently returned from teaching in secondary schools in Tanzania, the question I asked of educational theory was 'Who does it think we teachers are?' School effectiveness and improvement theories, when applied to developing countries, reduced teachers to input-output functions in cost-efficiency calculations (as observed by Hawes & Stephens, 1990; Pennycuick, 1993). The exception, Harber & Davies' application of the effectiveness approach to school management, arrived at an unoptimistic if realistic theory of school ineffectiveness (Harber & Davies, 1997).

When I went looking for the human stories behind what teachers do, I found a rich resource of literature, but nearly all emerging from and addressed to Anglophone high-income countries (e.g. Nias, 1989; Clandinin & Connelly, 1995; Acker, 1999). To my delight, I also came across a genre of qualitative research carried out in low-income countries and oriented by an attention to context that described educational processes within national contexts of economic scarcity in a way that I could relate to. Guthrie's arguments, that teachers use traditional teaching techniques because these are the most effective within their context (Guthrie, 1990), rang true with my own experience and practice in Tanzanian schools. Serpell (1993), Tabulawa (1997) and Palme (1999) used their intimate knowledge of local culture in Zambia, Botswana and

Mozambique respectively to argue that teachers' practice is influenced by societal values that they share with pupils and parents.

In designing the methodology for my own study into teacher identity in Tanzania, I drew on the advice of Vulliamy, Lewin & Stephens (Vulliamy et al, 1990) and the contributors to Crossley & Vulliamy (1997a). These texts reflected comparative researchers' acute awareness of the importance of context (also demonstrated in two special editions of *Comparative Education*: Crossley & Jarvis, 2000, 2001) and recommended qualitative research methodologies that yield 'thick' description. It is no coincidence that Vulliamy et al's book is essentially a narrative account of the authors' separate experiences of doing research. Qualitative comparative research in low-income countries and narrative research are both rooted in qualitative interpretive traditions and both owe a particular debt to ethnography. For although the funding context in low-income countries may constrain theoretically oriented research, other aspects of context make the insights offered by ethnography indispensable. Weak communications infrastructure and administrative capacity within the education systems of low-income countries can give rise to broad disparities between formal and implemented policy, which may only be apparent through ethnographic observation (Crossley & Vulliamy, 1984). 'Lone ranger' research students may find the logistics of collecting large data sets for quantitative analysis beyond their means, when schools are located up to a hundred kilometres from their mailboxes and roads become impassable during the rainy season. Even governments and international agencies, when faced with these challenges, cannot always guarantee the quantitative data they collect is reliable (Chapman & Boothroyd, 1988). Ethnographic observation, by alerting attentive researchers to actual practices, can assist in interpretation of published statistical data. It can also make the cultural outsider aware of how educational processes are situated in and influenced by their broader social context (Fife, 1997).

Similarities between Narrative and Comparative Research

Narrative research is oriented and structured by story. What distinguishes comparative research from other kinds of qualitative research is that it is structured by place. These different starting points lead narrativists and comparativists to some common principles, albeit expressed in differing terms. These include an awareness of temporal and spatial context, flexibility, alertness to the role and relations of the researcher and criteria of 'relatability' for research texts. In outlining these similarities, I will use Clandinin & Connelly's introductory text to represent the principles of narrative research (Clandinin & Connelly, 2000). They attribute to narrative the property of 'temporality', so that any event is viewed as unfolding over time with a past, present and anticipated future (Clandinin & Connelly, 2000, p. 28). This leads to a view of educational theory and practice as 'historicized' (Clandinin & Connelly, 1998, p. 154).

Comparativists commonly start studies by inquiring into the history of education systems (the value of which has been argued by Fife, 1997; Kazamias, 2001), implicitly viewing their subjects as situated in time. Narrativists view their subjects as situated in place as well as time. It goes without saying that comparativists' work is explicitly located geographically. This leads to an awareness of cultural context as a mediator of educational processes that has been evident in much research conducted in low-income countries (e.g. Stephens, in press). Clandinin & Connelly's argument that narrativists need to be flexible in their research design echoes Bogdan & Biklen's description of qualitative research in general (Bogdan & Biklen, 1998). The particular relevance of this advice to research in low-income countries is demonstrated in Vulliamy et al's tales of research experience (1990).

Both narrative and qualitative comparative researchers have a sense of being immersed in their research field. Clandinin & Connelly talk of narrative inquiry as 'a way of life' (Clandinin & Connelly, 2000, p. 63). Comparativists, at least for the duration of fieldwork, may find themselves living in countries and cultures with which they may be more or less familiar. For ethnographers, of course, immersion is especially intense and prolonged and may extend to learning a new language. Immersion has implications for relations in the field. Clandinin & Connelly describe their position as narrative researchers as 'being in the midst', located not only along the dimensions of time and place but also personal and social dimensions (Clandinin & Connelly, 2000, p. 63). The researchers' personal stories and the story of the research project intermesh with those of subjects. For comparativists, reflection on the relationship between themselves and others is one way of being alert to cultural context. This is often debated in terms of their position and relations as outsiders or insiders (e.g. Choksi & Dyer, 1997; Louisy, 1997). Although comparativists tend to view relations in less personalised terms than narrativists, they have an equal concern with their methodological and political implications. This should include an awareness of how colonial histories and present-day economic inequalities affect and even distort, not only data collection but also the theoretical basis of our research (Tikly, 1999).

Clandinin & Connelly also use the personal and social dimension to express the tension that all researchers 'in the midst' may feel between involvement and withdrawal for reflection. There is a parallel between engagement versus withdrawal and the insider-outsider balance for which comparativists strive. Balance may hinge on an individual researcher's negotiated status and prior experience, or on relations within a cross-cultural research team. Outsiders are credited with being better able to observe phenomena otherwise taken for granted (Judge, 2000, p. 155) or cross-national patterns, and insiders with being better placed to interpret them (Alexander, 2000, p. 269). Osborn (2004) explains how a team of collaborators from each of the countries being studied can engage in in-depth debate to open up educational values that are taken for granted in practice. Team-building has to be worked at, however, and when visitors from high-income countries collaborate with local researchers in low-income countries, funding and power inequalities can threaten the quality of insider-outsider relations (King, 1992).

When it comes to writing, narrativists aim to create texts that allow readers to 'imagine their own uses and applications' (Clandinin & Connelly, 2000, p. 42). This corresponds to the quality of 'relatability', which Bassey (1995) used in case-study research and was taken up by Crossley & Vulliamy in their discussion of teacher research with particular reference to 'developing countries' (Crossley & Vulliamy, 1997b, p. 17). A concern to privilege relatability, in order to render Tanzanian teachers' experiences and perspectives intelligible to readers in other countries, led directly to my own search for and construction of narratives.

One area in which comparativists may learn from narrativists is interpretation. Clandinin & Connelly explain that:

> In narrative thinking, interpretations of events can always be otherwise. There is a sense of tentativeness, usually expressed as a kind of uncertainty, about events' meaning. (Clandinin & Connelly, 2000, p. 31)

Narrative inquiry has emerged at the confluence of several fields: Casey (1995/1996, p. 212) lists literary, historical, anthropological, sociological, psychological and cultural studies. Largely, however, it has been fostered by the therapeutic disciplines, in which research is usually intended to be carried out by practitioners. 'Uncertainty' is rather an unfortunate choice of word for international research aimed at informing policy. Authors expect their reports to be read by time-pressured policy-makers, who are likely to pay little attention to 'uncertain' conclusions. On the other hand, researchers in low-income countries are under pressure from dominant development discourses to produce authoritative solutions to education problems. Narrative approaches may help to counterbalance this influence by standing alongside postmodernist and post-colonial approaches in highlighting the interpretations of marginalised groups within theoretically oriented comparative research (Welch, 1999; Holmes & Crossley, 2004). The two teacher narratives discussed and reproduced below illustrate how narrative method can be used within a comparative study to foreground the voice of teachers in a post-colonial country.

Angeline M. Barrett

Two Teacher Narratives from Tanzania

The methodological correspondence between narrative research and the qualitative tradition in comparative research facilitated the emergence and analytical preservation of teacher narratives in my own work. Primary allegiance to a comparative approach, however, led to dilemmas in eliciting and representing narratives, which are demonstrated by Mwl. Makonde's and Mwl. Bagohe's narratives below. (Mwl. is short for Mwalimu, the respectful Swahili title for a teacher). The overall research aim was to arrive at a description of Tanzanian primary school teachers' collective sense of identity and how it related to their material, systemic and social contexts. The purpose of collecting life histories from Mwl. Makonde and Mwl. Bagohe was to illustrate how professional and personal self-identities interact. As Shaw (1996, p. 329) points out, one of the strengths of life-history research is that it 'ideally, situates the lives of individual teachers within broader historical, social and cultural contexts'.

I had previously carried out over thirty one-to-one semi-structured interviews with individual teachers as well as a week's intensive observation in two schools. Through these activities, I made contact with over fifty teachers. From this group, I invited Mwl. Makonde, Mwl. Bagohe and one other teacher to take part in a series of three unstructured one-to-one interviews, to be conducted alongside classroom observation. In all interviews, life history was one of several topics discussed. The three 'focus' teachers were carefully chosen for their differing ages, educational qualifications, family responsibilities, household incomes and types of posting.

A few informants, all of them long-service teachers, were natural storytellers who spontaneously presented themselves and their knowledge through story. Hadijah Makonde was one such informant. The detail and emotive fluency of her narrative below may give the impression that we knew each other much better than we in fact did. Although we had more time to get to know each other on a casual basis than was possible with Mwl. Bagohe, Mwl. Makonde already had a story that she wished to tell for her own reasons. She explicitly stated these:

> I don't see that because I am a woman it is a reason I should be
> refused an education. Maybe there are others whose parents
> cause them not to study. But a woman is also a human being.
> Many orphans are given a hard time but later they have a
> family, they have a house.

Her unstated reason was that she was adept at using biographic stories to construct her self-identity as a teacher and school leader. Her reputation amongst colleagues and managers suggested that if stories of self are masks, then her mask was intended to be seen through, to borrow from Grumet's analogy:

> Our stories are masks through which we can be seen and with
> every telling we stop the flood and swirl of thought so
> someone can get a glimpse of us, and maybe catch us if they
> can. (Grumet, 1987, p. 322)

Woods recommends only carrying out life-history research with a self-selected collaborator who clearly wishes and is ready for in-depth reflective research (Woods, 1996). Narrativists working intensely with a small number of participants usually select them carefully on the basis of good rapport and their predisposition towards narrative (e.g. Cross, 1996; Munro, 1998), qualities that are more important to narrativists than representativeness. As far as was possible, I invited people with whom I felt I had already established some degree of rapport and trust. Mwl. Makonde taught at a school where I had carried out observation, and hence we had had time to get to know each other before I asked her to be a focus teacher.

I also wished to include a young man posted to a remote school as a focus teacher. The reasons why it was harder to establish rapport with James Bagohe were my very reasons for inviting him to be a focus teacher, and are obstacles familiar to any education researcher who has worked in a low-income country. Mwl. Bagohe worked and lived at a remote school, to which my only available means of transport was a lift on the back of a local education officer's moped. The school was close enough for me to make several visits without imposing too much on the education officer's time. However, travel arrangements meant I could never predict the exact time and date of my next visit and this was detrimental to building a relationship with Mwl. Bagohe. Staff of small remote schools are often socially as well as professionally dependent on their colleagues and hence often present themselves to visitors as a close community. Protocol obliged me to present the request for his participation as a focus teacher to the staff as a whole. Protocol also allowed Mwl. Bagohe, as the youngest member of staff, little space to negotiate individually in the face of his headteacher's and other colleagues' enthusiasm. The earlier round of interviews had shown that young men posted to rural schools tended to be among the most demoralised of teachers and felt the most estranged from the wider education system. Mwl. Bagohe was no exception, and this did not make it any easier for him to trust an outsider. There was, however, a positive reason for my particular interest in Mwl. Bagohe: out of all the young teachers I had previously interviewed, he appeared to be the most reconciled to living in a village environment.

The different qualities of the two informants and my relations with them had implications for how their life histories were constructed in our interviews, and then reconstructed as I translated them and organised them into chronologically ordered narratives. Mwl. Makonde made use of her past experiences to construct a present identity. Mwl.

Bagohe, by contrast, preferred to draw on the physical resources in his environment by preparing visual aids for lessons, showing off his house and garden and preparing a meal out of one his chickens. In this manner, he carefully constructed a self-presentation that was as much visual as oral. In the case of Mwl. Makonde, I have done little more than translate her narrative (itself a deceptively subjective process), cut out repetitions and rearrange sections in chronological order. I constructed Mwl. Bagohe's narrative by pasting together a series of fairly restricted responses to my questions and describing what he showed me. My authorial 'interference' is greater and his own narrative style less distinctively present than that of Mwl. Makonde's. My dilemma is that I do not wish to neglect the less fluent voice. The views of those who do not perceive their world to be storied and do not express themselves through story are equally important to a study of collective teacher identity. The absence or fragmentation of story can tell us as much about a person's identity as an articulate narrative. Mwl. Bagohe lays down a challenge to Connelly & Clandinin's assertion that 'people by nature live storied lives and tell stories of those lives' (1990, p. 2). Although all people's lives may be represented in story, some, like Mwl. Makonde, are inclined to tell stories of their lives, while others, like Mwl. Bagohe, prefer non-narrative modes of expression.

I leave the reader to judge on the basis of these two narratives whether the compromises I have made in reconstructing Mwl. Makonde's and Mwl. Bagohe's life histories are justified. The excerpts concern entry into teaching and, taken together, highlight how social and educational background, as well as early career experiences of posting and educational bureaucracy, contribute towards identification as a teacher. Because I am at heart a comparativist oriented by context, each story is preceded by a brief description of the informant's school.

Mwl. Hadijah Makonde's Story

At the time of the research, Hadijah Makonde was deputy headteacher and class teacher of the first year at a primary school located close to a main road. She had taught at the same school since qualifying nearly twenty years before. In the last two or three years her school had raised its local reputation, following the construction of new classrooms and an improvement in pupils' performance in national examinations.

> The story of how I reached this point is a long one. I have become wise because of my difficulties. I have had many problems in life and maybe God planned it that way because I now thank God for giving me a long life as a healthy adult. When I was young my health was not good, I had so many problems that I did not believe I would live to be the age I am now. I have had an amazing life. When I was with my parents I

was happy, in the way that is normal for people with their children. Later, our situation became bad after the parent on whom we all depended very much departed. My father was ill for a short time and when he died it was a severe blow for my mother. Fortunately, my uncle took me to Dar es Salaam to complete primary school, otherwise my story might have ended there. I was selected to enter [a government girls' school in Dar es Salaam] in 1976 but my mother could not afford the fees. My uncle did not see any reason to continue sponsoring a girl's education. So I had to return to the village to help my mother farm. I lived the life of an old person. A year later, my father's best friend sent me to study accountancy but after I completed the first year the fees for the second year were too expensive for him. Shortly afterwards, I heard that my mother was ill and returned to the village to take care of her.

In 1979, I returned to Dar es Salaam. The sister of my father's friend had just given birth. She asked me to help care for her child for a short while and said she would also try to help me. I started working for her and we got on well with each other. She was a teacher and I helped her with marking. I asked to talk to pupils at her school and was invited to help with teaching. That aunt helped me very much, she placed me close to her. When it was announced that teacher training courses, open to primary school leavers, were to be started, she helped me write a letter requesting admission. Two thousand of us sat the entrance examination for one hundred places. My name was ninety-sixth on the list. Later the examination was declared invalid for various reasons. Aunt was extremely sorry but later two letters arrived, one from Korogwe Teachers' College and one from Kigurunyembe Teachers' College, both offering me a place. Korogwe wanted students who had completed 'O' level and Kigurunyembe wanted those who had completed primary school. I decided to go to Kigurunyembe, although Aunt was anxious because it was an army college and would be physically demanding. I told her I was not afraid of the army, I had already struggled.

...

When I arrived at Kigurunyembe, I was given a medical check-up for the first time in my life. Before, I had not known that there was such a thing as a health check and diagnosis. In the village, the hospital only existed in stories. When I was at home I was afraid to go to hospital because I was worried that should I be found to have serious problems, who would pay for my treatment? I thought that even if I should die it wouldn't matter very much as I didn't have a child at that time. In the health check, it was discovered that I had stomach ulcers, tonsillitis and low blood pressure. Four of us were called by the college principal. One had problems like mine, one had had major surgery recently and another had one leg shorter than the other. These last two were transferred to a civilian teachers' college. As for us, we were told that we had problems but if we exercised we would be able to build up our strength and the college would help us with minor treatment. One officer told us that if we persevered, by the time we finished our course we would be completely fit and asked us if we were ready. I replied that I was ready but my fellow student refused and decided to return home out of fear of army exercises.

It is as if Kigurunyembe caused me to be born anew and built up my strength. Therefore I can live anywhere and with anyone. I can read a person in a short time. Even in my teaching, because I can tell straight away if a student is having difficulties. Even my fellow teachers; I can tell this one is having difficulties so I shouldn't bother him or her. Therefore experience in this work depends very much on your background. Some grow up in a good environment and have never known difficulties. They cannot tell if their colleague is having a difficult time, they just suppose that she or he is sulking when she or he has a serious problem.

When I came to Mandhari, I met a difficult and frightening situation but I remembered that I had already lived a hard life. I believed that I should try my best to help these young people. The school was alarming. When I arrived we were only three teachers for the whole school. If those old students were to come now they would be surprised at the results we have achieved. After I arrived, teachers came and left. They would say, 'I can't live in these conditions'. I saw that the road helped. I could go anywhere if there was a problem, for example, if I needed to go to hospital. Many of the schools were in a similar condition and also needed help. Things were hard for teachers in [this region], in this society and in this district. I saw that I was getting pay rises, even if they came late.

Mwl. James Bagohe's Story

James Bagohe, more commonly known as JB, had been posted to a village school five kilometres from the main road and about fifteen kilometres south of the district headquarters. His school had many of the features of a village school. It was understaffed, with five rather than seven teachers, which meant that all five had an unrealistically packed timetable. It was therefore unsurprising that the timetable was not adhered to strictly, but the extent to which it had slipped was alarming, all the more so because it was not unusual for a village school. I made five visits to the school in total, usually arriving at around eleven in the morning. Each time, most of the classes were unattended by a teacher, and the children seemed to spend much of the afternoon playing outside. There were, however, always at least two teachers marking books in the teachers' office. On one visit, I found the headteacher and JB on top of a dilapidated teacher's house, repairing the roof in preparation for an expected new teacher, who never showed up.

Like most young men interviewed, JB was offered a place at teachers' college on the basis of 'O' level results that had been a disappointment to him:

> When I was studying secondary, I expected I would go to Form 5 [lower sixth form] and that was what I wanted. Because I only achieved division III [reference to 'O' level results, taken after four years of secondary schooling], due to scoring F in mathematics, I failed to find a school for Form 5. I looked for something I could get a place to study quickly with my grades. I saw that if I applied for teaching I would get accepted without any problem.
>
> At the time I finished college recruitment was frozen by the government so there was no employment. For seven months, I was doing clerical work, January to July 1997. After that I worked voluntarily in a primary school in Kibaha, from 1997 to 1999. I went when I felt like it, not every day. In 1999 I got employment at this school.
>
> When I arrived here, I found the environment to be very different from my home or the places I had stayed. Both my parents were employed so we lived in town [Bukoba]. What helped me was that I had been to a college where the environment is similar to here. I was at Nachingwea Teachers' College, Lindi. So I was not a complete stranger when I arrived here. My fellow teachers explained to me the problems of the locality, like the difficulty of getting food, books and water. Water comes from shallow wells. Sometimes it is white like milk and other times it is muddy. There are no rivers or water pipes here. My colleagues advised me that this is normal and I should get used to it. What I did was to buy chemicals to clean the water and leave the buckets standing, so that the mud settles to the bottom. For food, I buy a lot of rice when they start to harvest and store it or sometimes I travel to Mkuranga Town to look for food that is not available here.

I studied in two different primary schools, one for years 1 to 5, and then another for years 5 to 7. At the schools where I studied, the teachers' houses were good and permanent and a teacher was able to live well. They were not mud huts, which fill with dust. Before I started teachers' college, I expected to get a house like those I was used to. I did not know there are schools that are shacks, with houses that are shacks. I thought I would go to a school like those I saw my teachers living in. But the situation I have come across is different from what I expected.

The first few weeks I did not live here, I lived in town. I stayed here Monday to Friday and then left for town because the environment was difficult and alarming. If it starts raining, you haven't a place to sleep. After getting used to the environment I stopped going to town and now stay here the whole time. When I arrived, I didn't receive a salary for a period of five months after starting work, January to May 1999. During that time I depended on myself and my fellow teachers helped me. I received what I was owed at the end of last year [2002].

Despite his early difficulties, JB appeared to be making a go at village life. He lived on the school compound, with two older teachers with families as his neighbours. His house was a low wattle-and-daub construction (fortunately JB was not a tall man), with one room on each side of a short corridor cutting through the middle of the house. The corridor opened at the back into a small courtyard, walled in on all four sides. In the courtyard, there was a shed for wood and for storing his bicycle and two sheds for chickens. JB seemed proud of his hens, regretting that they were all foraging out of sight during my visit. JB had developed a small but intricate garden in front of his house, which must have required regular watering. The walls of the corridor displayed the interests of young men everywhere in the world, decorated with magazine articles on reggae and football posters. Handmade mobiles improvised out of exercise books were hung from the ceiling.

Conclusion

The narratives above illustrate how social background, personal biography and early career experiences contributed to the formation of two teachers' professional identity. Twenty years apart, both teachers were first posted to remote schools where they found living and working conditions to be challenging. Mwl. Makonde was already highly committed to an occupation that she had struggled to enter. Becoming a teacher empowered her in multiple ways, physically, socially and materially. As a primary school graduate, an orphan and a girl, Hadijah's life opportunities had been extremely limited, and hence she appreciated the extrinsic and intrinsic benefits of teaching. Mwl. Bagohe came from a more privileged background and as a secondary school student had started with higher expectations for his career. Hence he was disappointed by his living conditions, late salary payment and heavy workload. Most of all, however, he was frustrated with what he saw as his slow rate of progress, in terms of material welfare, academic qualifications and professional development.

On their own, these narratives offer insight into African teachers' experiences. When they were placed alongside the findings from interview data collected from a larger sample of teachers, some themes emerged as clearly affecting a large number of teachers. For example, Mwl. Makonde was one of several long-service teachers who had entered teaching against the odds and consequently felt committed to teaching and appreciated the life opportunities it offered. Mwl. Bagohe, as mentioned earlier, was one of several short-service male teachers posted to villages who were disappointed with their working and living conditions. These findings suggest that the conclusions of Akyeampong & Stephens (2002) and Hedges (2002) about newly qualified teachers in Ghana are also applicable to Tanzania: namely, it is not easy for young secondary-educated people used to urban environments to adjust to village postings, and hence they should be provided with more support from the education administration once in post.

The reason, however, for reproducing these narratives here is not to discuss the early career experiences of teachers and their implications for policy, but rather to reflect on the potential and limitations of narrative method within international and comparative research. They illustrate how narrative methods can be used alongside other data collection methods, in this case semi-structured interviews, to arrive at conclusions that can inform policy. They also illustrate how narrative can be used as a tool for communicating the perspectives and experiences of African teachers, hence enhancing the authenticity of findings. For although Hadijah Makonde's and James Bagohe's voices are modulated by my interpretation, they also, to an extent, speak for themselves through their stories. Speaking for themselves, they are represented not just as objects manipulated by policy and their environment, but as agents who make decisions within their careers. In this respect, they demonstrate Maclure's observation, made with respect to teachers in England:

> However, the impact of context upon teacher [sic] was by no means one-way. While the context certainly made a difference to the teachers' lives and work, each teacher also partially constructed that context according to her or his *biographical project*: that is, the network of personal concerns, values and aspirations against which events are judged and decisions made. (Maclure, 1993b, p. 314)

Angeline M. Barrett

As teachers, Hadijah Makonde and James Bagohe are located within the improvement projects of policy-makers and educational planners. As people with agency, they locate teaching within their 'biographical project' of achieving independence, material security or academic certificates. Narrative methods can then open up the perspective of African teachers, locate them within the midst of social, collegial and family networks, and hence deepen understandings of the experience and values they bring to their work.

Perhaps the most powerful quality of the narratives is their relatability. The mystery of 'What makes teachers tick?' in contexts of scarcity is resolved into a set of desires to which readers from any country or culture can relate. Mwl. Makonde appreciates independence, material security and a job that is not so physically arduous it threatens her health, and which she believes to be worthwhile and is emotionally and intellectually fulfilling. JB would like to know that one day he will own a house which doesn't let in the rain; he would like his salary to be paid in full and on time; and he would like to develop in his work and have the satisfaction of doing a job well, rather than knowing that in a severely understaffed and under-resourced school, his best is not enough.

Narrative methods, then, appear to have a place in the comparative researcher's methodological toolbox for '[opening] up the sealed boxes within which teachers work and survive' (Ball & Goodson, 1985, p. 13) in low-income as well as high-income countries. Narrative methods may not, on their own, address policy-oriented questions such as 'What can we do to make teachers more effective?' They do, however, help to bring teachers to life as thinking, feeling and doing human beings, and that in itself should be of value to researchers and policy-makers.

References

Acker, S. (1999) *The Realities of Teachers' Work: never a dull moment.* London: Cassell.

Akyeampong, K. & Stephens, D. (2002) Exploring the Backgrounds and Shaping of Beginning Student Teachers in Ghana: towards greater contextualisation of teacher education, *International Journal of Educational Development*, 22, pp. 261-274. http://dx.doi.org/10.1016/S0738-0593(01)00064-5

Alexander, R. (2000) *Culture and Pedagogy: international comparisons in primary education.* Oxford: Blackwell.

Ball, S.J. & Goodson, I.F. (Eds) (1985) *Teachers' Lives and Careers.* Lewes: Falmer.

Bassey, M. (1995) *Creating Education through Research: a global perspective of educational research for the 21st century.* Newark: Kirklington Moor/British Educational Research Association.

Bogdan, R.C. & Biklen, S.K. (1998) *Qualitative Research for Education: an introduction to theory and methods.* Boston: Allyn & Bacon.

Brock-Utne, B. (1996) Reliability and Validity in Qualitative Research within Education in Africa, *International Review of Education*, 42, pp. 605-621. http://dx.doi.org/10.1007/BF00601405

Carter, K. (1993) The Place of Story in the Study of Teaching and Teacher Education, *Educational Reseacher*, 22, pp. 12-18.

Casey, K. (1993) *I Answer with My Life: life histories of women teachers working for social change.* London: Routledge.

Casey, K. (1995/1996) The New Narrative Research in Education, *Review of Research in Education*, 21, pp. 211-253.

Chapman, D.W. & Boothroyd, R.A. (1988) Threats to Data Quality in Developing Country Settings, *Comparative Education Review*, 32, pp. 416-429. http://dx.doi.org/10.1086/446794

Choksi, A. & Dyer, C. (1997) North-South Collaboration in Educational Research: reflections on Indian experience, in M. Crossley & G. Vulliamy (Eds) *Qualitative Education Research in Developing Countries: current perspectives,* pp. 265-293. New York: Garland.

Clandinin, D.J. & Connelly, F.M. (1995) *Teachers' Professional Knowledge Landscapes.* New York: Teachers College Press. http://dx.doi.org/10.1111/0362-6784.00082

Clandinin, D.J. & Connelly, F.M. (1998) Stories to Live By: narrative understandings of school reform, *Curriculum Inquiry*, 28, pp. 149-164.

Clandinin, D.J. & Connelly, F.M. (2000) *Narrative Inquiry: experience and story in qualitative research.* San Francisco: Jossey-Bass.

Connelly, F.M. & Clandinin, D.J. (1990) Stories of Experience and Narrative Inquiry, *Educational Reseacher*, 19, pp. 2-14.

Convery, A. (1999) Listening to Teachers'Stories: are we sitting too comfortably? *Qualitative Studies in Education*, 12, pp. 131-146. http://dx.doi.org/10.1080/095183999236213

Cortazzi, M. (1993) *Narrative Analysis.* London: Falmer Press.

Cross, B. (1996) *Sounding Out the Silences: narratives and absences in African higher education.* Occasional Paper No. 59. Edinburgh University: Centre for African Studies.

Crossley, M. with Jarvis, P. (Ed.) (2001) Special issue No. 24 of *Comparative Education,* on Comparative Education for the Twenty-first Century: an international response, 37(4).

Crossley, M. with Jarvis, P. (Eds) (2000) Special issue No. 23 of *Comparative Education,* on Comparative Education for the Twenty-first Century, 36(3).

Crossley, M. & Vulliamy, G. (1984) Case-Study Research Methods and Comparative Education, *Comparative Education*, 20, pp. 193-207.

Crossley, M. & Vulliamy, G. (1997a) Qualitative Research in Developing Countries: issues and experience, in M. Crossley & G. Vulliamy (Eds) *Qualitative Educational Research in Developing Countries: current perspectives,* pp. 1-30. New York: Garland.

Crossley, M. & Vulliamy, G. (Eds) (1997b) *Qualitative Educational Research in Developing Countries: current perspectives.* New York: Garland.

Crossley, M. & Watson, K. (2003) *Comparative and International Research in Education: globalisation, context and difference.* London: RoutledgeFalmer.

Dangarembga, T. (1988) *Nervous Conditions.* London: Women's Press.

Dzvimbo, K.P. (1994) Qualitative Research in African Education: notes and comments from Southern and Eastern Africa, *Qualitative Studies in Education*, 7, pp. 197-205.

Fife, W. (1997) The Importance of Fieldwork: anthropology and education in Papua New Guinea, in M. Crossley & G. Vulliamy (Eds) *Qualitative Educational Research in Developing Countries: current perspectives*, pp. 87-111. New York: Garland.

Grumet, M.R. (1987) The Politics of Personal Knowledge, *Curriculum Inquiry*, 17, pp. 319-329.

Guthrie, G. (1990) In Defense of Traditional Teaching, in V.D. Rust & P. Dalin (Eds) *Teachers and Teaching in the Developing World*, pp. 219-232. New York: Garland.

Harber, C. & Davies, L. (1997) *School Management and Effectiveness in Developing Countries.* London: Cassell.

Hawes, H. & Stephens, D. (1990) *Questions of Quality: primary education and development.* Harlow: Longman.

Head, B. (1971) *Maru.* Oxford: Heinemann.

Hedges, J. (2002) The Importance of Posting and Interaction with the Education Bureaucracy in Becoming a Teacher in Ghana, *International Journal of Educational Development*, 22, pp. 353-366. http://dx.doi.org/10.1016/S0738-0593(01)00057-8

Holmes, K. & Crossley, M. (2004) Whose Knowledge, Whose Values? The Contribution of Local Knowledge to Education Policy Processes: a case study of research development intitiatives in the small state of Saint Lucia, *Compare*, 34, pp. 197-214. http://dx.doi.org/10.1080/0305792042000214010

Isegawa, M. (2000) *Abyssinian Chronicles.* London: Picador.

Judge, H. (2000) Comparing Education Professionals: an introductory essay, in R. Alexander, M. Osborn & D. Phillips (Eds) *Learning from Comparing, Volume 2. Policy, Professionals and Development*, pp. 151-160. Oxford: Symposium Books.

Kazamias, A.M. (2001) Reinventing the Historical in Comparative Education: reflections on a protean episteme by a contemporary player, *Comparative Education*, 37, pp. 439-449. http://dx.doi.org/10.1080/03050060120091247

King, K. (1991) *Aid and Education in the Developing World.* Harlow: Longman.

King, K. (1992) North-South Collaborative Research in Education, *International Journal of Educational Development*, 5, pp. 183-191. http://dx.doi.org/10.1016/0738-0593(85)90006-9

Lockheed, M.E. & Verspoor, A.M. (1991) *Improving Primary Education in Developing Countries.* Oxford: Oxford University Press.

Louisy, P. (1997) Dilemmas of Insider Research in a Small-Country Setting: tertiary education in St. Lucia, in M. Crossley & G. Vulliamy (Eds) *Qualitative Educational Research in Developing Countries: current perspectives.* New York: Garland.

Maclure, M. (1993a) Mundane Autobiography: some thoughts on self-talk in research contexts, *British Journal of Sociology of Education,* 14, pp. 373-384.

Maclure, M. (1993b) Arguing for Your Self: identity as an organising principle in teachers' jobs and lives, *British Educational Research Journal,* 19, pp. 311-322.

Munro, P. (1998) *Subject to Fiction: women teachers' life history narratives and the culture of politics resistance.* Milton Keynes: Open University Press.

Mwiria, K. & Wamahiu, S.P. (1995) Introduction, in K. Mwiria & S.P. Wamahiu (Eds) *Issues in Educational Research in Africa,* pp. 1-11. Nairobi: East African Educational Publishers.

Nespor, J. & Barylske, J. (1991) Narrative Discourse and Teacher Knowledge, *American Educational Research Journal,* 28, pp. 805-823.

Ngugi, wa Thiong'o (1977) *Petals of Blood.* Oxford: Heinemann.

Nias, J. (1989) *Primary Teachers Talking: a study of teaching as work.* London: Routledge.

Osborn, M. (2004) New Methodologies for Comparative Research? Establishing 'constants' and 'contexts' in educational experience, *Oxford Review of Education,* 30, pp. 265-285. http://dx.doi.org/10.1080/0305498042000215566

Osler, A. (1997) Teachers' Biographies and Educational Development: a Kenyan case study, *International Journal of Educational Development,* 17, pp. 361-371. http://dx.doi.org/10.1016/S0738-0593(97)00001-1

Palme, M. (1999) Cultural Ambiguity and the Primary School Teacher: lessons from rural Mozambique, in F. Leach & A. Little (Eds) *Education, Culture, and Economics: dilemmas for development,* pp. 261-282. New York: Falmer Press.

Pennycuick, D. (1993) *School Effectiveness in Developing Countries: a summary of the research evidence.* London: Department for International Development.

Rasmussen, S.J. (1999) The Slave Narrative in Life History and Myth, and Problems of Ethnographic Representation of the Tuareg Cultural Predicament, *Ethnohistory,* 46, pp. 67-108.

Riessman, C.K. (1987) When Gender Is Not Enough: women interviewing women, *Gender and Society,* 1, pp. 172-207.

Riessman, C.K. (1993) *Narrative Analysis.* Newbury Park: Sage.

Serpell, R. (1993) *The Significance of Schooling: life-journeys of an African society.* Cambridge: Cambridge University Press.

Shaw, C.C. (1996) The Big Picture: an inquiry into the motivations of African-American teacher education students to be or not to be teachers, *American Educational Research Journal,* 33, pp. 327-354.

Soyinka, W. (1989) *Ìsarà: a voyage around 'Essay'.* London: Methuen.

Stephens, D. (1998) *Girls and Basic Education: a cultural enquiry.* London: Department for International Development.

Stephens, D. (2006) *Culture in Education and Development: principles, practice and policy.* Oxford: Symposium Books.

Tabulawa, R. (1997) Pedagogical Practice and the Social Context: the case of Botswana, *International Journal of Educational Development*, 17, pp. 189-204. http://dx.doi.org/10.1016/S0738-0593(96)00049-1

Tikly, L. (1999) Postcolonialism and Comparative Education, *International Review of Education*, 45, pp. 603-621. http://dx.doi.org/10.1023/A:1003887210695

Tikly, L. (2004) Education and the New Imperialism, *Comparative Education*, 40, pp. 173-198. http://dx.doi.org/10.1080/0305006042000231347

United Nations Education, Scientific and Cultural Organisation (UNESCO) (1998) *World Education Report 1998: teachers and teaching in a changing world.* Paris: UNESCO.

Voluntary Service Overseas (2002) *What Makes Teachers Tick? A Policy Research Report on Teachers' Motivation in Developing Countries.* London: Voluntary Service Overseas.

Vulliamy, G., Lewin, K.M. & Stephens, D. (1990) *Doing Educational Research in Developing Countries.* Basingstoke: Falmer Press.

Welch, A. (1999) The Triumph of Technocracy or the Collapse of Certainty: modernity, postmodernity, and postcolonialism, in R.F. Arnove & C.A. Torres (Eds) *Comparative Education: the dialectic of the global and the local*, pp. 25-49. Lanham: Rowman & Littlefield.

Woods, P. (1996) *Researching the Art of Teaching: ethnography for educational use.* London: Routledge.

World Bank (1995) Priorities and Strategies for Education: a World Bank review. Washington, DC: World Bank.

CHAPTER EIGHT

Curriculum Narratives:
the global dimension compared

GEORGE M.P. BAILEY
Independent Consultant,
Gloucestershire, United Kingdom

Introduction

As globalisation dominates political discourses, particularly those on issues of poverty (Department for International Development, 2000), and governments seek to develop their education systems to cope with rapid changes in technology and business practices, education and the role of the teacher are seen as significant in developing a global dimension in pupils' thinking. Smith (1999) argues that:

> Globalisation could be seen to be as much a master narrative
> as modernisation theory: groups are excluded from processes
> of globalisation; there remains a dominant centre and
> subordinate periphery; socio-economic and political
> differences are defined by reference to a norm
> (interdependence). (Smith, 1999, p. 490)

For most of the world's population, school plays a significant part in developing an understanding of the world in which they live. In the past, the school curriculum in the United Kingdom (UK) was delivered in a world that was only just beginning to see the advantages of the technological revolution and where global issues were not part of a young person's life in the way they are today (Department for Education and Employment, 2000). The Department for Education and Employment (DfEE, renamed the Department for Education and Skills in 2001) set out the UK government's ideas for developing a global dimension to the primary and secondary school curriculum in England and Wales, with the argument that:

> Including a global dimension in teaching means that links can
> be made between local and global issues and that what is
> taught is informed by international and global matters. It also
> means that young people are given opportunities to examine
> their own values and attitudes, to appreciate the similarities
> between peoples everywhere, to understand the global context
> of their local lives, and to develop skills that enable them to
> combat prejudice and discrimination. This in turn gives young
> people the knowledge, skills and understanding to play an
> active role in the global community. (DfEE, 2000, p. 3)

The UK's case for the need to prompt teachers' thinking about the
content of the curriculum is made through the focus on and the use of
concepts such as 'citizenship', 'social justice', 'sustainable development',
'interdependence' and 'human rights', all of which are being given
greater emphasis in the curriculum (DfEE, 2000). The observer might
question whether this new focus on the 'global' means that the
curriculum has to be designed in such a way as to meet particular kinds
of political, economic and social agendas.

However, although one cannot argue with the need to encourage
schoolchildren around the globe to be aware of the above concepts and
what it means to live in a global society, it must be recognised that the
'global dimension' to the curriculum that the UK government is
concerned with is being designed and delivered from a Western
perspective. Thus, it is important to be clear what is meant by the term
'global dimension'. Before providing a definition, the reader should be
aware that I, the author, live and write in a Western society, and
approach this piece of research influenced by narratives associated with
being both an educator and researcher in the UK. My own narratives are
rich with episodes of seeking ways and means of helping individuals to
use their talents and enrich their potential. A number of these episodes
have been very successful, while others have been very frustrating. I am
always keen to ensure individuals understand terminology; thus the
definition of 'global dimension' used in this chapter is that suggested by
Professor Dave Hicks, quoted by Bourn (2002):

> The 'global dimension' refers to the curriculum as a whole,
> while a 'global perspective' is what we want students to
> achieve as a result of having a global dimension in the
> curriculum. (Bourn, 2002, p. 5)

In this examination of teacher narratives, the focus is on the content of
the curriculum in terms of its 'global dimension' and an assessment of
the extent to which such content produces a 'global perspective'. As an
educator myself, now in the higher education sector, I became concerned
about the nature and characteristics of the UK government's emphasis on
a 'global dimension' to the curriculum, and what I saw as the likelihood

of a Western perspective dominating its content and delivery in its schools. Furthermore, I wanted to explore the role of teachers in determining the content of the 'global dimension' and to see the extent to which flexibility for the teacher in choosing content and means of delivery emerged.

Although I was exposed, in an informal way, to narratives from a number of teachers in the Graduate School of Education at the University of Bristol and in my own community outside Bristol, only six were able to give me enough time for my research in this chapter. Of these, three narratives of appropriate depth and breadth in content emerged, and are explored and compared in detail. The first is from a teacher of Social Education and Ethics in a secondary school in Kenya, the second from a Kuwaiti English-language teacher in a school, similar to a UK secondary school, in Kuwait, and the third from a teacher of mathematics in a secondary school in England. Other narratives used as a source for comparison and discussion have their origin in UK government documents and in academic literature.

The aim is to assess similarities and differences, and to identify the nature and characteristics of the 'global dimension' in the narratives. A further aim is to identify possible reasons why the emphasis on the 'global' in the curriculum has become a priority of governments and to focus attention on problems associated with Western cultural perspectives dominating the 'global dimension' to the curriculum.

Narrative Structuring and Analysis

In the attempt to avoid influencing each teacher's thoughts in relation to the 'global dimension', I decided to ask them to tell the story of their curriculum and allow the 'global dimension' to emerge explicitly or implicitly from the narrative without prompting from me. A further consideration was that of 'narrative structure', that is, arranging each text in terms of 'the temporal and social organisation of the text in order to bring out its meaning' (Kvale, 1996, p. 192). Thus, the respondents were asked to relate their curriculum narratives in such a way that they began with the past, went on to the present, and ended with a curriculum narrative of the future. Personal experiences in many forms emerge from the narrative, such as experiences situated in the 'family, or schooling' (Richmond, 2002, p. 2). Each interviewee, therefore, 'by telling his story brings his experiences and bits out of his stock of personal stories into a temporal order to explain how it has developed' (Lucas-Horne & Deppermann, 2000, p. 205).

It is important to recognise, however, that narrative operates at more than one level. Mills (2001), in researching the role of interviewing in educational research, makes the point that:

> Narrative thus operated at two levels, both within and beyond
> the text. Brief stories could be located within each interview;
> subsequent reflection on each interview revealed a larger
> overall narrative. (Mills, 2001, p. 298)

For example, in the narratives that follow, stories operate at the level of the individual, the school and the nation; these stories can be both explicit and implicit. Further, structuring the narrative has the potential to produce more elaborate stories from what appear at first to be simple pieces of text (Kvale, 1996, p. 193). There are, however, significant factors for researchers to take into account in relation to the narrator. (Although later I highlight the situation of two narrators operating in a narrative, I refer to the teacher as narrator and the focus of Szanto's points below, rather than myself as author.) Szanto (1972) highlights two key considerations relating to the reliability of narrators in telling their story. The first concerns how the narrator filters information:

> The narrator cannot always be relied upon to report what is,
> for the filter of their personality can distort his described
> picture, yet he is not being dishonest, for he reports what he
> sees in the way he sees it. (Szanto, 1972, p. 6)

Furthermore, no matter how reliable the narrator or the skill in communicating the story, defining the real nature of the world is beyond the individual:

> The world consists of what is and the manner in which it is
> known. A man is defined by these aspects of the world and his
> memory which he chooses to know and by the manner in
> which he sees them, his descriptions rarely begin to define the
> nature of the world. (Szanto, 1972, p. 12)

Szanto's second point is significant here, as the narratives and individuals originate from diverse societies and cultural backgrounds, where very different ways of seeing the world operate.

Another important factor in narrative structure and analysis is the issue of different types of narrators. According to Mieke (1997) there are two kinds of narrator: the 'character-bound narrator' and the 'external narrator'. In this instance, the 'character-bound narrator' is the teacher, while the 'external narrator' is myself, the author/researcher (Mieke, 1997, p. 22).

A final point, one that has key significance to the comparison of the 'global dimension' in the narratives, is that 'Narrative is a cultural phenomenon, partaking of cultural processes' (Mieke, 1997, p. 9). Therefore, one can expect the emergence of an explicit cultural presence from the curriculum narratives, since 'language, culture and cognition are closely related to each other' (Hui, 2003, p. 340).

Three Case Narratives

The 'case narrative' (or story) is described as an approach that: 'provides descriptive knowledge which must be understood in context' (Richmond, 2002, p. 4). Thus, the teachers were asked to provide curriculum narratives; as the focus here is on the 'global dimension', the extracts provide only a small part of the narratives as they were related during the interviews. At the conclusion of the interviews, confirmation was obtained from participants about the extent to which a 'global dimension' was present in their narratives and the nature and characteristics of that dimension. For example, a confirmation of a 'global dimension' was given when the terms 'international context' and 'world' were used.

The Teacher from Kenya

The first occurence of the 'global dimension' in the Kenyan teacher's narrative is clearly one that intends to instil a sense of value in oneself and others, associated with an individual's behaviour towards other people in the wider world. The Kenyan teacher gives an insight into why students are encouraged to have a global perspective:

> Their development in an international context ... the other peoples ... how to become a worthwhile person in society, to yourself, your country, to the world and so a certain kind of behaviour has got to be taught.

An explanation of why such an emphasis is given to behaviour emerges in the narrative, as the origins of the Social Education and Ethics curriculum are described:

> It started when the government realised that the youth were losing track in terms of respecting elders and people in society ... they found it better to teach them behavioural science where they know how to respect ... so you promote peace ethics in a topic of leisure and work.

After a period of reflection on this teacher's transcript, it was clear to me that beyond the text, a contemporary story of concern for society in Kenya, as well as for others in the world, was emerging from this narrative, one that justified providing students with a global perspective (Bourn, 2002). Furthermore, the narrative signifies a missionary, active, practical and relevant curriculum, rather than one that is passive and irrelevant. It is evident that students in Kenya are asked to compare their behaviour with that of others, both within their own country and in communities and cultures throughout the world in the present, rather than to base their actions on a historical perspective. In the process of comparison, the teacher encourages adoption of practices from other cultures, with the caveat that they must be applicable to Africa:

> We come to what is the family ... the types of family that exist
> ... even types of marriages, the faiths that are there, the African
> way of life ... they are a part of the world ... the west ... we use
> the west as a focal point ... what they do and is it applicable to
> Africa.

As my reflection showed, as well as the extracts here to some extent, there emerges a more elaborate overall narrative (Mills, 2001, p. 298): that of a nation seeking to contribute to, communicate and integrate with other countries and cultures around the globe:

> A country like Kenya has its own working system, it's
> multicultural ... we have Asians, we have Europeans and
> Kenyans ... you have other tribes who are in their communities
> ... their international identities and how do you articulate
> yourself to the environment ... so that's really the core of the
> subject ... how do you relate to the world ... the world is very
> vast ... how do you relate to the system ... you pick something
> from the world and you contribute something to the world.

An indication of the influence of the 'globalisation' master narrative (Smith, 1999, p. 490) is implied by the teacher's reference to a lack of independence:

> The Kenyan nation is not independent from the rest ... it's
> dependent with the globe so you need to have some aspects of
> international consciousness ... I think what it's trying to do is
> enhance your own inter-activeness toward the wider world
> society.

However, in order to maintain the teacher's ability to develop a relevant and contemporary global perspective, the use of technology is paramount. In the following extract we see an emerging story of a Kenyan nation that is lacking in the appropriate resources, skills and time:

> ... because of the technology that is coming in the growth ...
> technological input is more borrowed because there is not time
> to nurture skill from within because of lack of resources and
> lack of money.

As the above extracts show, the nature and characteristics of the 'global dimension' in the Kenyan curriculum indicate that the nation is keen to engage with other communities and cultures and respect differences where they arise. The teacher describes this as tolerance:

> ... tolerance ... we will give the positive side of every religion
> ... negative sides but then we pin down on similarities where
> our religions are meeting.

In the Kenyan teacher's summing up of the future for the curriculum, there emerges a narrative that is characterised by continual change and a quest for new ways of communicating and interacting with other cultures of the globe, and defined by a continual questioning by teachers and students alike in the search for new ways of communicating:

> Because of the dynamism of human nature it will have to go
> on and explore zones because we are continuously becoming
> inter-active with the global culture ... so how do we present
> ourselves ... so how do we articulate our issues?

The Teacher from Kuwait

In contrast to the Kenyan curriculum, the content and structure of the English-language curriculum in Kuwait came from outside the country, with the aim of developing students' ability to use English:

> No, the people who wrote the books ... even the teacher books
> are from England ... Yes it is the ministry of education and
> they have to do some contracts with the university in England.

A further difference is that the 'global dimension' in this teacher's narrative is implied rather than explicit. For example, the teacher does not state explicitly that teaching students to use the English language is developing a global perspective on the use of that language. However, it can be argued that English is a global language, as it is used in a considerable number of cultures and countries as different as Papua New Guinea, the Gambia and Singapore (Crystal, 1995). Thus, the conclusion is that the 'global dimension' is present in the teacher's narrative, as the following example clearly demonstrates:

> The English language curriculum we called present English
> course and it was by the university in England.

The Kuwaiti teacher's narrative highlights a very different student experience of a 'global dimension' to that experienced by students in Kenya and England. Kenyan students, in contrast to students in the other two countries, are exposed to a curriculum that compares other countries and cultures. Kuwaiti students, however, learn a language in isolation from its vast number of diverse users, and thus are not able to compare other countries and cultures in the process. As an educator hearing of such a situation, I felt frustrated for the students, as I believed that they were losing what should be a very rich and beneficial learning experience. For example, another teacher, who was from Italy, told me that when learning about England and the language, she was told that in England the English always, like clockwork, have tea at 4 o'clock, and wondered why we all didn't stop at that time every day to drink tea. While such information in language lessons relating to, for example, the tea habits in England is beneficial to broadening cultural understanding, for students and their teachers to develop a more accurate narrative about a country's customs, the information needs to go beyond a stereotypical view.

Later in the Kuwaiti teacher's narrative, the 'global dimension' began to emerge more explicitly when the teacher was asked to clarify the content of the curriculum:

> The content ... well, it was nothing in particular but it was
> something maybe we called mixed information ... sometimes
> we have topics about England, about tourists, places ...
> sometimes we have topics about animals and how to survive
> the environment and sometimes you have topics about Kuwait
> as well or about other countries in the Gulf.

In response to a query whether the teacher was able to use material from the Internet, the response was:

> Well, we can't do that ... . No, because normal teachers are
> usually supervised by a senior teacher and the senior teacher
> and the head teacher and the deputy have the right to visit you
> any time without any notice ... so you have to be prepared ...
> this preparation have to have strong relationship with the
> teacher book ... shows you the objectives, the procedures, the
> tests that you are going to follow ... so you have to do these
> things.

Once again I was left feeling very frustrated for both the students and the teacher, as the vast range of resources available at the touch of a button was being ignored.

The above response is an example of a subnarrative within the overall narrative; in this instance, it suggests a story where teachers are being monitored in both their teaching methods and the content that they deliver to the students. Although monitoring has to take place, the implication here is that the 'global dimension' is restricted and inflexible in the ability to develop within students a broad global perspective (Bourn, 2002). In comparison, in Scotland, for example, the degree of success of the 'global dimension' in the curriculum is measured by 'the extent to which the main ideas of the global dimension are being consolidated'; these ideas include 'equality, democracy, global citizenship, multiculturalism, peace and conflict resolution and interdependence' (Learning and Teaching Scotland, 2001, p. 34).

A marked difference in emphasis in content of the curriculum in Kuwait and Kenya was evident when the Kuwaiti teacher reached the point in the narrative where assessment was the focus:

> We didn't assess the communication ... we didn't assess anything of the spoken English, nothing! [emphasised this omission very strongly] ... nothing ... and this curriculum is supposed to do with communication and spoken English ... but no assessment ... Of course what is assessed and what is marked is the written English and I am one of those people who admit my writing is better than my spoken English.

For the Kuwaiti teacher, the future narrative for the curriculum was viewed as a repeat of the present. There was a sense that, while there is a story of life teaching in the early part of the twenty-first century for this teacher, the narrative for the curriculum, both for the present and future, is one where little use is made of the Internet or of other cultures and communities around the globe, in order to enable students to apply their learning and develop a wider global perspective. Such a picture gives the impression that the 'global dimension' to the narrative will continue to be implicit rather than explicit, and set within an inflexible restricted framework, which may lead to students having a narrow global perspective. This is in stark contrast to the Kenyan teacher's view of the Social Education and Ethics curriculum, in which the 'global dimension' will remain explicit, broad and flexible and will lead to students having a broad global perspective.

The Teacher from England

Like the Kuwaiti and Kenyan teachers, the teacher from England is presented with a curriculum that originates from the government and is prescribed:

> We have a well-defined scheme of work based on the national curriculum ... As a mathematician we're not really left with a whole lot of choice ... we are prescribed quite heavily by the government what we do.

Although in the next extract there is a sense of the presence of the 'global dimension' through the use of the term 'multicultural', unlike the Kenyan narrative, which seeks to link the student's thinking to other peoples and cultures, the story here is that it is an administrative exercise driving teachers' thinking, which appears to have little to do with developing a sound and broad global perspective in students:

> Okay, the content of each chapter starts off with a little story about Bill and Tanya but of course it's not Bill and Tanya, it is

> Yasmin and Aswaz ... we've got to be seen to be multicultural
> ... we've got all these foreign names in these books.

Emerging beyond the text of the teacher's narrative, there appears a story of a curriculum being delivered in a political climate that insists on the delivery of a 'global dimension' meeting particular characteristics. From this teacher's perspective and experience, the characteristics and process are not seen as a positive experience for all concerned, as the following extract clearly demonstrates:

> Well, it's the old political correctness things really I suppose,
> isn't it ... the pupils have got to be encouraged to see our
> society as multicultural place ... Because we've got a box to
> tick somewhere on the development plan ... do you use
> multicultural resources and there's got to be a tick in that box
> or we will get into trouble.

Listening to this description, from what I can describe as a very committed, pupil-centred teacher, left me feeling sad, frustrated and very concerned on three counts. First, I saw a negative rather than a positive situation: rather than creating a 'global dimension' that exploits the talents of both teachers and students, here was the 'big stick' being waved, creating an environment of austerity, punitive measures and fear that stunted creativity, rather than an environment that developed it. Secondly, these words raised a question in my mind: was this situation a product of the ethos of the school, or did the teacher's perspective get constructed at the point of training and development? If the latter, then one must be very concerned that such perceptions and attitudes may extend beyond this one school. Thirdly, I felt that the teacher was giving the impression that there was a lack of agency to turn the 'global dimension' into something more rich and enlightening for teacher and students, rather than just a mechanical exercise to meet a government administration requirement. It is sad to think that in England we might be removing opportunities to learn about different cultures, societies and nations through the use of a recording process that does little to promote and encourage exploration of a 'global dimension' to the curriculum in a meaningful way. The challenge for policy-makers and curriculum designers is to communicate clearly why such exercises are used and how they help both students and teachers to grow in understanding others around the globe.

In contrast to the Kuwaiti teacher, the teacher from England used the Internet as a means of accessing topics and knowledge for use in the curriculum; in this regard the 'global dimension' is of a historical nature:

> I always do that ... I always start with that bit ... they think I'm
> mad ... why are we learning about this? ... certainly the Greek
> mathematicians absolutely fascinate me because it's so long

ago they developed these amazing theories ... you know it
endlessly fascinates me if I'm introducing something like
Pythagoras ... textbooks are not very good at doing that ... no
they're not ... so I use the Internet a lot for that.

In the above extract we are given a sense of the biographical relating to
the teacher's interests and love of mathematics. Interestingly, it was not
until the tape was switched off that the teacher was aware that the
content relating to the Greeks was similar in nature to that of the 'global
dimension' required by the UK government for teachers of mathematics
to deliver (DfEE, 2000, p. 9). However, unlike the Kenyan teacher, this
narrative showed that the 'global dimension' was restricted to the past,
rather than relating to contemporary Greece or other countries, which is
a desired goal of the government. For example, its guide to 'Head
Teachers, Senior Managers and Local Education Authorities', describes
how a topic in the primary school mathematics curriculum on water
meant that:

Pupils then learnt about the water needs of villagers in Ghana
through a free video. Pupils were involved with data handling,
volume and weight and dimension. (DfEE, 2000, p. 6)

On being asked to clarify why real-world experiences were not being
used in the delivery of the curriculum, unlike the Kuwaiti teacher who
cited lack of time, this teacher cited technical reasons for their omission:

I mean I wouldn't purposely go out of my way to introduce it
... I can't think of an example because the books are all ... it's
getting all technical maths ... they don't really have people's
names in it ... I could be wrong there ... the books in the lower
school tend to have little pictures of people going shopping.

In this last extract we get an indication that as the students get older, the
mathematics curriculum narrative changes. In an earlier extract, we saw
that for younger students, relating the curriculum content to the 'living
world' is done through the use of stories about characters.

Although the narrative from the teacher from England at times gave
the impression of a story that was vague and even negative in places, in
common with the Kenyan and Kuwaiti teachers, this teacher was
passionate about the curriculum, teaching and helping students to
develop and use their talents. However, this teacher did not demonstrate
an interest beyond the Greek mathematicians in exploring issues and
exercises associated with other societies and cultures around the globe.
To me this was puzzling, particularly as, in contrast to Kenya, there is
such a wide range of technology, resources and sources of help available
to teachers in England.

Issues and Conclusions

All the teachers were very clear about their role in delivering the curriculum, and how important it was to develop the students' abilities. The Kenyan narrative demonstrates the need to develop in students self-esteem, respect and a sense of responsibility for themselves as well as others. Thus 'cultural cognition' plays a significant role in shaping and constructing self-perception, whether as an educational institution, an individual or a nation. However, in order to develop a positive and constructive global perspective, the individual must be able to get into the cognition of the culture or society they are studying. Therefore, it is very important that the 'global dimension' of the curriculum is active rather than passive and allows the individual 'hands-on' experience of the different cultures and societies that inhabit the globe.

Although the comparison of the narratives is very valuable as a means to identifying the nature and characteristics of the 'global dimension' to the curriculum, there are a number of issues arising from such an exercise. Akoojee & McGrath (2004), in discussing the further and higher education sectors, give cause for caution at all levels of education where a global perspective is being developed: 'the GATS (General Agreement on Trade and Services) in seeking to remove restrictions thus result in national regulatory mechanisms being overtaken' (p. 35). The thrust of Akoojee & McGrath's argument is that private providers would challenge such policies, 'particularly where governments remain opposed to the marketizing and globalizing narrative' (Akoojee & McGrath, 2004, p. 35). Thus, future curriculum narratives may well be quite different in nature and characteristics to that of, for example, the Kenyan narrative discussed here. For example, a future 'global dimension' to the curriculum might be dominated by economic factors, rather than seeking to combine both human and environmental perspectives, for example. Education International (2000) emphasises that: 'At a national level, decisions on investment in education are increasingly related to national economic imperatives in turn dictated by the changing global economy' (p. 2). Furthermore, Hartley (2003) argues, global economics are driving changes in education, with the aim that:

> Education systems will be enabled to compete globally, not
> within some neutral international economy, but within a
> global capitalist economy. (Hartley, 2003, p. 448)

As emphasised earlier, there is the issue of the influence of the Western perspective on the teacher's own outlook and thinking. This is particularly significant where the teacher has to leave his or her country to gain further education and training, as was the case with the teachers from Kenya and Kuwait. Indeed, the development of critical thinking in teachers is paramount to successful positive global perspectives.

Donnelly (2004), writing on the role of teachers in the construction of the ethos of respect and tolerance, argues that:

> If teachers are not accorded the time and space to develop a critical understanding of their own values and beliefs then there is potential for schools to simply reinforce the psychological barriers which sustain division. (Donnelly, 2004, p. 263)

Smith (2004) raises the issue of non-governmental development organizations (NGDOs), and argues that their development agenda is dominating 'the contemporary manifestation of the potential of global and civil society global citizenship' (p. 70). Smith argues further that 'in the past, the development narrative has been driven by charity to the third world which produces stereotypical perspectives'(Smith, 2004, p. 71). Smith's arguments are a significant reminder of the pitfalls of delivering a 'global dimension' to the curriculum to all teachers, as was exemplified by the teacher from England, expected to teach students the history of mathematics, rather than combining the historical with contemporary developments in the mathematical narrative.

The very act of relating the narratives for the three teachers, and my interpretation of their narratives, are other factors to take into account. For example, Stavans (2003), comparing monolingual Hebrew and English narratives, argues that:

> It is insufficient to characterize the bilingual production as 'all or none' monolingual production. Rather, to look at the bilingual as consisting of a continuum of 'more or less' appropriateness accuracy in one or other language. The adult bilingual narrator with one set of experiences which are subject to expression in either of two linguistic systems, each of which may be constrained by a different storytelling culture. (Stavans, 2003, p. 153)

The issue of cultural difference was apparent when I offered the teacher from Kenya a mug or cup of tea. What people in the UK call a mug was referred to as a 'jug' and other kinds of vessels in Kenya. Thus it is important to recognise that the collection of narratives from non-native English speakers, while being for me as a researcher a very valuable and rich exercise, was also one of constant clarification of both meanings and contexts as the narratives emerged and developed. Understanding how individuals, cultures, societies and nations live and use language in the 21st century is crucial to developing a relevant view of the world that is useful to all individuals and to ensuring effective communication. Such understanding would have a positive effect, for example, on the Kuwaiti student, where the 'global dimension' would be richer and broader in terms of by whom, where and how the English language is used.

141

The goal, therefore, for governments and all those associated with education policy is to ensure that the 'global dimension' to the curriculum produces relevant, contemporary and positive global perspectives. The curriculum narrative has to demonstrate challenge to such ideas as stereotyping, division and inequality. Therefore, it is important to 'understand the ways in which either existing or new stories are mediated and produced' (Smith, 2004, pp. 71-72). Indeed, Dunn (2004), writing about a history curriculum, argues that the big issues and questions for international educators are:

> To figure out how students use their minds to connect their own experience to that of human beings who are dead and gone. Where do students put themselves, if anywhere, in the stream of global time? In my view we should see what answers we get when we free the curriculum from identity politics, hunts for 'our origins,' and telling of cultural success stories. (Dunn, 2004, p. 6)

If teachers and students from around the globe are to develop a wider understanding of their own culture and that of others, the availability of technical resources is paramount. All future curriculum narratives relating to the 'global dimension' should include reference to the use of the Internet. This would enhance the 'global dimension' in both the Kenyan and Kuwaiti curriculum, and indeed in all countries. Further, it has to be recognised that teachers throughout the world do not teach and live in a vacuum; thus, as now, the future curriculum will be subject to the guidelines set down by particular governments. However, rather than the future 'global dimension' in curriculum narrative content, consisting mainly of a passive and narrow global dimension, curriculum planners and policy-makers have an opportunity to take a lead from such definitions as those offered by the 'Global Teacher Project' in the UK, for example:

> Global Education reflects the global nature of our society and responds to the diverse backgrounds and experiences of children in the classroom. Global Education develops skills and attitudes, which enable people to take responsibility for their own lives and the world we live in and become active global citizens. (Global Teacher Project, 2004, p. 1)

Finally, while it is important for all students throughout the world to be aware of the history of societies and cultures, there needs to be greater emphasis on the use of relevant contemporary information and experiences that bring the teacher and student in touch with the issues and concerns of today. This will ensure that future curriculum narratives are rich in examples of students and teachers interacting with other societies and cultures, whether through the use of technology or travel.

Such interaction would increase the opportunity of achieving a future 'global dimension' that is not dominated by a Western perspective, but one that is rich in diverse perspectives from other nations, cultures and societies. That is the challenge for us all.

References

Akoojee, S. & McGrath, S. (2004) Assessing the Impact of Globalization on South African Education and Training: a review of the evidence thus far, *Globalisation, Societies and Education*, 2(1), pp. 1-39. http://dx.doi.org/10.1080/1476772042000177032

Bourn, D. (2002) The Importance of Learning with a Global Perspective, in J. Hemery, S. Hitchens & A. Hill (Eds) *Learning World: citizenship focus.* London: British Council.

Crystal, D. (1995) *The Cambridge Encyclopedia of the English Language.* Cambridge: Cambridge University Press.

Department for Education and Employment (2000) *Developing a Global Dimension in the School Curriculum: guidance, curriculum standards.* DfEE 0115. Nottingham: Department for Education and Employment.

Department for International Development (2000) *Making Globalisation Work for the World's Poor: an introduction to the UK government's White Paper on international development.* London: Department for International Development.

Donnelly, C. (2004) Constructing the Ethos of Tolerance and Respect in an Integrated School: the role of teachers, *British Educational Research Journal*, 30(2), pp. 263-278. http://dx.doi.org/10.1080/0141192042000195254

Dunn, R.E. (2004) Issues in Global Education: contending definitions of world history. Newsletter of the American Forum for Global Education. Available at: http://www.globaled.org/issues/151/a.html

Education International (2000) Education and Technology Stakes and Challenges for the Public Sector: teacher qualifications and mobility. Available at: http://www.ei-ie.org/educ/english/eedhelsinkilennon.html

Global Teacher Project (2004) What Is Global Education? Available at: http://www.globalteacher.org.uk/what_is.htm

Hartley, D. (2003) Education as a Global Positioning Device: some theoretical considerations, *Comparative Education*, 39, pp. 439-450. http://dx.doi.org/10.1080/0305006032000162011

Hui, L. (2003) Journey to English, *The English Teacher*, 6, pp. 335-342.

Kvale, S. (1996) *Interviews: an introduction to qualitative research interviewing.* London: Sage.

Learning and Teaching Scotland (2001) *The Global Dimension in the Curriculum.* Dundee: Learning and Teaching Scotland.

Lucas-Horne, G. & Deppermann, A. (2000) Narrative Identity Empiricized: a dialogical and positioning approach to autobiographical research interviews, *Narrative Inquiry*, 10, pp. 199-222.

Mieke, B. (1997) *Narratology: introduction to the theory of narrative*, 2nd edn. Toronto: University of Toronto Press.

Mills, J. (2001) Self-Construction through Conversation and Narrative in Interviews, *Educational Review*, 5(3).

Richmond, H.J. (2002) Learners' Lives: a narrative analysis, *Qualitative Report*, 7(3). Available at: http://nova.edu/sss/QR/QR7-3/richmond.html

Smith, M.W. (1999) Teaching the 'Third World': unsettling discourses of difference in the school curriculum, *Oxford Review of Education*, 25, pp. 485-499. http://dx.doi.org/10.1080/030549899103946

Smith, M. (2004) Mediating the World: development education and global citizenship, *Globalisation, Societies and Education*, 2(1), pp. 67-81. http://dx.doi.org/10.1080/1476772042000177050

Stavans, A. (2003) Bilinguals as Narrators: a comparison of bilingual and monolingual Hebrew and English narratives, *Narrative Inquiry*, 13, pp. 151-191.

Szanto, G.H. (1972) Narrative Consciousness: structure and perception in the fiction of Kafka, Beckett and Robbe-Grillett. Austin: University of Texas Press.

CHAPTER NINE

Conversations across Cultures: the narrative construction of the primary class teacher in England and Denmark

ELIZABETH McNESS
University of Bristol, United Kingdom

Introduction

In line with a more explicit focus on the role of emotions in teachers' work, educational researchers are recognising the value of narrative methodology in understanding the lives of teachers and illuminating the link between public policy and personal experience (Nias, 1989, 1996; Goodson, 1992; Hargreaves, 1994; Acker, 1999; Helsby, 1999). The capacity of teachers' 'stories' to make connections with more broadly experienced social realities has been referred to by Goodson (1992, p. 6) as the telling of 'a story of action, within the theory of context' and by Behar (1996, p. 14) as personal voice leading the reader, 'not into miniature bubbles of navel-gazing, but into the enormous sea of serious social issues'. This chapter draws on narrative data collected as part of a study of the impact of education policy on the professional lives of four teachers working in two differing European contexts, England and Denmark, to explore these issues in more detail.

The study was prompted by an interest in understanding why teachers in the two countries, despite a congruence of aims and ambitions, seemed to have such different experiences. Having supervised student teachers in primary classrooms in England, as well as having taken student teachers to Denmark to experience an alternative system of schooling, I was left with the impression that, though teachers in both countries had similar expectations of their professional role and priorities for their children, their lived experiences were quite different.

My intention was to find answers to questions concerning the motivations, values, satisfactions and frustrations of teaching in the two countries. What was it about the way that teachers worked in Denmark that helped them appear to be more confident and satisfied with their role? Why were teachers in England experiencing such frustration doing a job that they loved?

A multimethod approach was used to gain a holistic view of the professional lives of four case-study teachers: Jane and Sarah in England, and Anja and Birgith in Denmark. The methodology of this approach has been discussed in more detail elsewhere (McNess, 2004), but what is examined here are their 'stories', which they shared with me as a fellow teacher as they talked candidly about their professional experiences. The narratives describe the powerful influence that national context and local context have in creating the space for teachers to construct their own meaning and understanding of what it is to be a 'teacher'.

National Context

Circumstances within the two countries provided an interesting contrast, not only because of the marked organisational differences in the work of primary class teachers, but also because of recent policy changes in both countries, which had been put in place partly to counteract criticism of poor pupil attainment compared with other industrialised countries.

Historically, teachers in both England and Denmark, particularly of younger children, have been as much committed to their pupils' personal and social development as to their academic progress. Jane, Sarah, Anja and Birgith were each responsible for a class of 10-year-olds, an age group chosen because of the major changes to practice that had resulted from the introduction of the 1988 Education Reform Act in England (Osborn et al, 2000). The Act had imposed a system of national testing (Standard Assessment Tasks [SATs]) at 7, 11 and 14 years, as well as introducing, for the first time in recent history in England, a detailed national curriculum to be followed by all children. These changes had been brought about in an effort to increase accountability and improve teaching quality.

But what about the organisational differences characterised by the work of Jane and Sarah, and their Danish colleagues, Anja and Birgith? Whereas the role of the primary class teacher in England is that of a generalist who teaches most, or all, of the curriculum to a particular class group, usually for one year, the Danish class teacher (*klasselærer*), in contrast, traditionally has a continuing responsibility for a class of children, often for the whole of their primary and lower secondary schooling (from 7 to 16 years old). They also have a more explicit responsibility for the social development of the class group, together with communication with parents. While qualified to teach several of the main curriculum subjects, Danish teachers typically work in a team of four or five other teachers to provide a full spread (McNess, 2001).

The Teachers

Jane, Sarah, Anja and Birgith were approached to take part in the study, having been identified as committed, competent teachers who, to give some spread of experience, were at different stages in their careers and worked in schools with contrasting pupil intakes. Both Jane and Sarah worked within the maintained sector of primary schooling in England. At the time of the study, Jane was in mid-career and was class teacher for a Year 6 class of 10- and 11-year-olds. Her school served an inner-city population where there was a degree of social and financial disadvantage. Sarah, in contrast, had been teaching for over twenty years and was beginning to think of retirement. Like Jane, she was class teacher for a group of Year 6 pupils, who lived in the prosperous suburbs of a medium-sized town situated approximately fifteen miles outside the city in which Jane worked.

Anja and Birgith also worked within the maintained sector in Denmark. They each acted as *klasselærer* for a Grade 3 class of pupils (mostly 10-year-olds), working with a team of other colleagues to provide their pupils' full curriculum needs. Anja, like Jane, was in mid-career and taught in a school that served an inner-city population where there was some social and financial disadvantage. Birgith, in contrast, had been teaching for twenty-five years and taught in a prosperous suburban school situated in a medium-sized town approximately twenty miles from the city in which Anja taught.

All four teachers had their own reasons for taking part in the study. Jane and Sarah were keen to understand why their job, which they both loved and was an integral part of their personal identities, was creating real frustration and leaving them exhausted. Anja and Birgith, on the other hand, had both spent some time teaching in England and the USA, respectively, and were keen to understand a little more about the experiences and working practices of colleagues in other countries. They were both fluent in English and happy to share their experiences in this language.

Jane

When we met, Jane was in her twelfth year of teaching and had been at her inner-city primary school for five years. Jane had not originally intended to be a teacher but a disappointing set of mock 'A' level examinations in her final year at school meant that she could not follow her first intention of combining her languages with a business career. Her initial doubts had been overcome and she was now enjoying her work,

147

which included not only her class teacher duties, but also several school-wide responsibilities. Jane was also studying for a Masters degree in education in her spare time. When asked about the qualities of a 'good teacher', as well as humour, Jane emphasised motivation, assessment skills, subject knowledge and behaviour management:

> Well I think, one, motivation, high expectations. Matching the children to what you're giving them. Being able to use assessment as part of the tool, so it's an ongoing assessment and knowing what comes next. Having the knowledge to be able to impart it to the children, so having quite a broad knowledge and skills yourself. A sense of humour, don't get too stressed, keep smiling even when you want to cry! Oh control, let me say behaviour as well, behaviour management. I think that's quite an important one, a very important one. Not just reprimanding the ones who've been naughty, but reward and praise and so on.

Despite the changes that had brought increasing pressure to perform for both herself and her pupils, Jane considered that she had worked hard to ensure that this had not affected the essential relationship between teacher and pupil:

> I think you try not to make it any different, but I think [pause] no I would hope I wouldn't try and make it any different. I think there is pressure on you to try and say 'Right, now come on, you've got to get this right', and you do do that. But not to make children feel that they aren't liked by me or respected by me just because they're not as good as someone else or because they're under pressure for these tests [SATs] and they're not achieving as well as anyone else.

She considered that this important relationship with her pupils had two distinct but complementary elements, which extended well beyond the school gates and were exemplified in her interaction with pupils on school trips:

> It's like when you go on school trips. Your role as a teacher, although you're still a teacher, you're responsible for these children, they're in your care, the relationship is different because you're outside of the school gates. It's much more relaxed, it's much more of an 'in loco parentis' if you like and much more approachable and friendly way. But still keeping the 'I am the teacher' type of barrier, if you like.

Jane considered that the aims of primary schooling were broad and that her priorities should reflect this. Her emphasis on safety reflected the environment in which the school was situated, but she was also clear that schooling should not be purely about academic achievement. It should include a moral dimension to benefit both the individual and the broader society:

> I think to make them feel safe, give them a safe environment,
> where they feel they can learn. I think that's an essential
> criterion for the school. And then give them the opportunity to
> develop their knowledge and their skills and their
> understanding in all the different subjects. To foster an
> attitude and a moral responsibility, in all these sort of aspects
> that means they are going to be a developing person in
> themselves, an individual and have responsibilities to society
> as well. [pause] So it's a whole package really of not just the
> academic but the pastoral and the developing side as well ... I
> think it's to get the best out of a child in whatever way it
> happens to be.

When talking about the impact of education policy and the 1988 Education Reform Act, Jane had some concerns about less-favoured areas of the curriculum:

> They [the pupils] must be covering more, they must be taking
> more on board. They've probably definitely got a more focused
> curriculum. As for a broader curriculum, well I suppose the
> aim is that it's meant to be a broader curriculum, but the
> things that are missing out are always the things like your
> Music and your Art and your PE [physical education] and
> they're always the first to go because of this pressure to have to
> do your core ones [national curriculum subjects].

Jane considered that this was a particular problem with regard to Art, which was also linked to a celebration of children's work evident in the elaborate classroom wall displays:

> I think the Art, there probably has been less of because you
> haven't got the time. In literacy, for example, everything's so
> much more focused and you can't do your drawings with your
> pictures any more. I'm not saying that's Art, but you know
> there isn't time to do, uhm, things where you're not seen to be
> learning something. And your Art has got to be really focused,
> it's got to be in the time, an hour, so you can't, maybe in the
> afternoon, well we do, but everything's got to be 'houred' and
> timetabled. And you can't go onto maybe, if we were doing
> humorous poetry for example, here I might have previously
> got the children to do some artwork that we wanted to then
> display or something, whereas now ...

Jane was also opposed to the idea of a quasi-specialist model of the primary teacher, which had the potential to further limit any cross-curricular activity. She considered that being a generalist teacher, who covered the whole curriculum for a particular class, was fundamental to the role of a primary teacher. Needing to teach areas which were not familiar acted as a form of professional development for a teacher. However, she valued the informal combination of individual teacher's skills:

> I think maybe primary teachers might get more subject orientated. It'd be a real shame, I hope it doesn't go down that line. I would say the love of being a primary teacher is the fact that you're a 'generalist'. You feel like you can cover everything. And yes there are always going to be areas where you feel like 'Yes I have more knowledge in that than something else' you know. For example, obviously literacy is my thing but not RE [religious education], I don't have the knowledge in my head, it'll just be purely from what I've had to teach the children, it's not anything else. And I have worked in one school where I used to do the PE [physical education] for another Year 2 class and she did the Music for example. And in those situations, if a colleague was much more of an expert at something like Music, then I would welcome it. But, saying that, when I do do things like that, I really enjoy it. I might not be as fantastic as this other teacher, but it'd be a real shame, I think, if I never ever did Music.

This preference for a generalist role was not, for Jane, merely to do with personal and professional development. She saw benefits in the close, ongoing relationship between a primary teacher and his or her class that could contribute positively to the quality of pupils' learning:

> I think it's really good that primary [school] children develop a relationship with one teacher. It makes such a difference to the way children respond. There is that development, that growing, that I think comes from having one teacher. But I think it'd be so like secondary [school], it'd be so impersonal and so like having to move. Everything would be moving around and it [the curriculum] would be even more blocked into time. It's bad enough now just having setting [attainment grouping] where they've got to move from one class to another. I mean it's nice that I get to know more of the Year 6s than I did before. But that's enough – and it's only in maths. If you had to do it with the whole school, for example. So the main thing is from a professional point of view you would lose skills and you would not be stretched in areas that it's quite nice to be stretched in. But from the children's point of view

it's about the relationship that you build up with them that would be damaged if you didn't have them, and see them doing everything.

Jane was also concerned about the effect that such a change would have on an individual teacher's relationship with the parents of pupils. She considered that this relationship had been changing and that parents now felt more able to get involved with their children's learning, which she saw as a positive development, although she was also concerned that there should be reciprocity within this relationship:

I think parents obviously feel like they've got more rights now in schools, which is good that they have a right to know what's going on in their classes and they have a right to know about their child's education – to know what's going on and have what's best for them, if you know what I mean. And I think you do feel like you need to be more accountable to them to make sure they know test results or they know how well their child's doing. But also for them to support their child at home. There's that much more pressure on. You know, we need to make sure there's this relationship both ways, you know. That both of you have got responsibility.

This communication and contact with parents Jane regarded as being as much pastoral as academic. Many of her conversations with parents centred on behaviour and the extent to which pupils were 'happy' at school. This detailed knowledge could be compromised if she were to see her pupils on a purely subject basis only. The contact with parents and thus children's home backgrounds also gave Jane an additional dimension to her teaching, as she explained:

Yes, I think it does have an effect, in that it helps me to understand more about the child's background and find out any issues or problems, whether it's unconsciously, just find out from observations of parents and so on, or knowing what's going on in their lives and who's influencing them in their lives. And having that support from parents on a behaviour level or an academic level I think has to be really important. Knowing they've got those supports if there's an issue can only be beneficial if the parents are seeing it positively. Sometimes you do get parents who get very, very defensive about anything like that. But even then I feel it's my right to talk to the parent about it even if they are going to turn round and blame someone else.

For Jane, this intermingling of the academic and the pastoral played a very important part in her work in schools and, as such, was a central aspect of her professional identity as a teacher. But how is this story

151

reflected in that told by Sarah? To what extent is Jane's story an individual one, and to what extent does it resonate with a wider experience?

Sarah

When I first met Sarah she had been teaching for over twenty years, sixteen of which had been spent in her current school. She had started teaching at the school on a part-time basis after a break to have her family, while waiting for a full-time post to become available. Originally, Sarah had qualified at a teacher training college in a nearby city and, after a brief period teaching in a primary school within the city limits, had left to teach in a British Forces school in Germany. She had married a fellow primary teacher who, at the time of the study, was head of a primary school in a neighbouring county. Sarah, like Jane, had many school-wide responsibilities in addition to her role as a Year 6 class teacher.

When asked what her priorities were in relation to her pupils, Sarah, while recognising the pressures exerted by national curriculum targets, like Jane, considered that her aims must be broader. Her emphasis was on processes rather than product and her aim was to develop the children's independence. She considered that she had a commitment to both her colleagues at the secondary level of schooling and to the pupils themselves in encouraging and developing an independent and organised approach to their schoolwork:

> Well, there's the curriculum and the academic development, but of equal importance I think is the independence and their preparation for secondary school. I think they run parallel really. I mean what drives the curriculum is the fact that we have targets to meet. So I suppose that does drive it. But having said that we always drove them hard before we had the SATs [national testing] really. But the independence is important and the organisation and the preparation for secondary school is very important. And we actually get very good feedback that our children actually cope remarkably well [when they go on to secondary school].

In order to achieve this, she considered that it was important to have clear expectations for her pupils to enable them to develop an understanding of the importance of their own efforts. However, like Jane, she also considered that it was important to build up a personal relationship with them so that she could engage with them in constructive criticism of their work:

> I think work ethic. I think the children need to have a very positive work ethic. And I think a positive learning

environment. But that doesn't mean, I'm not talking about being woolly with them, if they do something and I don't like it, I'll tell them. So it's having clear expectations of what I want them to aim for and helping them define what I would like them to aim for personally, I suppose.

Sarah had experienced an increase in collaborative planning with colleagues since her early days in teaching. She enjoyed this and saw it as a positive development that helped them 'share the load'. But again, like Jane she expresses the pressure and even guilt experienced because of the need to comply with the demands of policy with regard to the national curriculum and testing:

Well, I think maybe the only thing is people are so much feeling the pressure of what they've got to do, where they've got to start and where they've got to get to with their children. This isn't a criticism it's just the way it is. When their children then come to them in September [from a lower class] they have a higher expectation, you know. They're not saying that the previous year hasn't done its job, they're just frustrated that they know how much they have to get through and they want their children to be further on than they are. It [joint planning] does help, but at the end of the day, with the best will in the world, they [the teachers] just run out of time. And it's not anybody's fault. They just run out of time, they haven't covered that bit of work. It's just a sign of the times. [Previously] we would have been much more accepting for them to be where they were. Well that's the pressure, it's a pressure for everybody. Because people feel guilty because they haven't done it.

This could be felt particularly keenly in relation to national testing, which took place for 10- and 11 year-olds each Spring and demanded a great deal of curriculum time for preparation:

Yes, it's a knock-on effect. I mean that happens quite a lot here [in Year 6] because what we lose is virtually a term of work because of SATs [national tests] the way they are. Plus we have to revise *everything* basically. And we go into total panic in September and think 'Oh, these children!'. But that's nobody's fault.

When asked about the role of specialist primary teachers, as opposed to the more traditional generalist class teacher model, Sarah again had mixed feelings, though she saw current curriculum pressures as a concern. She considered that it was not merely a matter of subject knowledge but also one of lack of resources and facilities, especially with regard to the science curriculum:

Really we could do with an ICT [information and
communications technology] teacher and although we get by
with science, to a large extent, for the work you're supposed to
cover you need a science lab to do it properly. You know in
the autumn term we make do with plastic bottles and paper
towels and things to do water experiments, it's ridiculous!
Resources are an issue for science. I mean we're supposed to
be doing a thing with the comprehensive [secondary] school
where they have to do an open-ended investigation. And
we've done it before but we've been cobbling along with
ridiculous resources. Why can't we go up there and do it
properly in a science lab? So yes, that's an issue. I sometimes
think Art, but I don't know. I mean some of the children do
some lovely Art and neither of us [the teacher of a parallel year
group in the school] is particularly artistic, but they take care
and they do some really quite nice Art. So maybe that's not
such a pressing thing, I don't know. I mean at one time I did
think Maths. But I'm not so convinced now about Maths. You
know, even now we come up with things and they ask me
things and I have to say 'Well, I don't know, we will have to
find that out, let's work at it'. [pause] Let's see, I think RE
[religious education] is an issue because I think RE's a difficult
one for people to wrestle with because I think it's very much a
personal thing. And I think being asked to teach RE to the
depth without conveying any particular feeling, one way or
the other, is quite hard so I don't know. We do it but we
dabble a bit.

These pressures of time and the need for the class teacher to cover the
whole of the curriculum also had repercussions with respect to the
affective and pastoral element of Sarah's work. She considered that
learning within the school had been enhanced by a very 'caring' school
ethos. This was partly the result of an inclusive approach to children
with physical disabilities. She had taught blind, deaf and wheelchair-
bound pupils within the school, as well as two Downs' Syndrome
children. She saw this as generating a very caring approach to learning,
which had had a positive effect on the rest of the school population. The
school also had an active and effective programme for personal, social
and health education, but Sarah did perceive tensions with other areas of
the curriculum. She considered that the personal and social needs of the
children could sometimes be pushed aside in order to enable her to meet
other, more academically focused commitments:

Yes, I think there are [tensions] because it's the pace. You
know, at the end of the day we've got to get through the
curriculum. And the number of times that I say to them 'Just

hang on to that one, we'll come back to that one'. I don't know how many times I've said it to them, about 5 or 6 times at least and it's only Wednesday. And I have to try and remember those things. You know, so I do try to come back to these things. Okay, some of them are academic. But some of them are just as important, but they're not academic.

This was a great regret to Sarah because, although her pupils' results in the national tests were very good, she considered that they were missing something very important in their development as individuals and her professional identity as a teacher was being compromised.

These stories, which Jane and Sarah shared with me, clearly articulate the feelings of stress and frustration that they were experiencing. Pressure from national testing and a crowded, subject-orientated curriculum meant that the professional priority to engage with their pupils' social and personal needs was being compromised. What then can the narratives of Anja and Birgith tell us about life as a teacher in Denmark? To what extent can we find differences and similarities in relation to the impact of policy and societal pressures on the role of the class teacher?

Anja

Anja had been teaching for fifteen years when I met her, six of which had been in a *folkeskole* close to the centre of a city in central Denmark. After completing her studies at upper secondary school (*gymnasium*), she traveled to England for six months before returning to Denmark to work as an unqualified supply 'teacher' for a period. Having gained some first-hand experience, Anja then continued her studies by enrolling on the standard four-year training course to become a qualified *folkeskole* teacher. Her mother had been a teacher and Anja had decided on a career in teaching because of her enjoyment of working with children. Anja shared her time between the responsibilities of *klasselærer* for a class of 10-year-olds (Grade 3) with a male teacher called Niels. As well as teaching Danish and Music to her class, she also contributed to another teaching team within the school by teaching three lessons of English each week to a Grade 8 class of 15-year-olds. The rest of her working week (eight lessons) was spent teaching in a regional unit for children with special educational needs, which was attached to the *folkeskole* in which she worked. When asked what she considered to be her general aim in relation to the children in her class, Anja emphasised the personal and social dimension of her work:

They will be 'whole' human beings. That they will be able to manage in society and that they will be able to operate in a democratic world and get on with each other.

155

When asked specifically about her professional responsibility she said that it was primarily to herself and her colleague Niels, as well as to the pupils; not, in the first instance, to the headteacher, the municipality or, more importantly, to national policy. When asked to reflect on her priorities when working with the children, Anja offered the following, which underlined a commitment to a combination of the academic and the affective:

> I want to create whole human beings. I want to make the children able to live in a democratic world – to make them feel responsible. It's important that they are able to distinguish between good and bad norms of behaviour. They need to develop a value system for life. I want to help strengthen everybody's self-confidence – without exception and at nobody's expense. I want to give the children as much academic knowledge as possible to enable them to choose between the various options in further education – technical, commercial, academic, etcetera. Their choice of education and career path should not be determined by a lack of skills and ability [i.e. poor schooling/education] but rather by their interests. I want to give them courage to deal with the authorities and develop a suitably critical attitude to life issues.

Unlike Jane and Sarah, Anja was allocated thirty-five non-teaching hours a year specifically to discharge her duties as *klasselærer*. The collaborative nature of this role was described by Anja:

> The class teacher acts as leader of the team. They are responsible for communicating with the headteacher and for creating an agenda and calling team meetings. It is also the responsibility of the class teacher to communicate with the parents of the students in their class. Every month the class teacher sends home a newsletter, which explains what the children will be doing over the coming month within their class. The back of this newsletter includes a letter from the headteacher with more general information relevant to the whole school.

This professional responsibility to mediate between the needs of the school, the pupils and the parents was further extended with regard to the central role Anja shared, in common with all class teachers, in being knowledgeable about the personal circumstances of their pupils. This role could go far beyond the teaching day and included a responsibility to develop the class as a democratic unit:

> The class teacher is expected to show initiative and to try and solve problems and conflicts within the social group of the

class. It is also their task to contact the parents, if necessary, and to cooperate with the social services when there are social problems for the child or their family. A class teacher must be prepared to meet with parents in the afternoon, after lessons have finished, or even be contacted at home. If one of their students causes trouble in the playground or with another teacher, for example a substitute teacher, it is the responsibility of the class teacher to sort things out.

This concern for the discipline of the class was a shared professional responsibility with the other teachers who worked with the class, and provided a focus for regular discussion:

The team also creates a set of guidelines for discipline within the class. It is important that we all have more or less the same attitude towards the children, that we all stick to the same limits and conditions. It is very important for us to continually evaluate the cooperation between team members and discuss how things might be improved.

The most recent relevant legislation, the Act of the *Folkeskole* (1993), had outlined a curriculum framework within which teachers were required to work. However, Anja considered herself to be relatively free to create the detail and was unencumbered by the demands of national testing. As she explained:

We must discuss and define the curriculum aims, as well as the social and personal objectives for all the students in the class, both individually and for the class as a whole. These must correspond to the aims and objectives laid out in the Act of the *Folkeskole* but there is a great deal of flexibility in the way the Act can be interpreted. The State does not dictate exactly what you must do, only an outline of the content to be covered. In Denmark, pupils do not need to be prepared for external, national examinations until their 9th Grade [16-year-olds].

Twice a year Anja, together with the other teachers in the team, created a curriculum plan, which needed to be approved by their headteacher. The most recent curriculum plan demonstrated the integrated way in which much of the teaching was approached, making use of themes and topics to explore different curriculum areas. As Anja explained:

The teachers within the team also work together to plan the work for the class for the coming year. This plan is shown to the headteacher once a year, when we have our class conference. In this curriculum plan we show when we run an inter-disciplinary topic across subject boundaries, and when

we keep the subjects discrete, for example, courses in reading
or computer skills.

This is a very different story to the ones told by Jane and Sarah. Anja was
not working to a strict set of curriculum criteria and she and her
colleagues had the space to develop connections between different
subject areas in an holistic way reminiscent of that encouraged in
England by the Plowden Report (CACE, 1967). Though a concern with
progression and continuity was a major argument in establishing the
later, more detailed national curriculum in England, this was of less
concern in Denmark, where the majority of pupils not only completed
their primary and lower secondary education in one school but often
remained the responsibility of one teacher for the whole of that time.

Again, Anja's story described a different approach to testing in the
two countries. For Anja, assessment was ongoing and formative in nature
and closely dependent on the detailed knowledge she had of her pupils,
which had been built up over the previous two and a half years, rather
than through a set of national tests. She described a certain amount of
freedom to use her professional judgement in the way she approached
assessment. Anja drew on her knowledge of each individual pupil's
academic, as well as social, development and was not required, at this
stage, to grade the pupils either in relation to each other or by normative
standards. Anja had the space to speak once a term to her pupils
individually about their work, and the length of the meeting would
depend on each child and their particular needs. Meetings were usually
carried out in the room next to their classroom, once she had set the rest
of the class some work to get on with. She agreed that, legally, she was
probably not supposed to leave her class unattended, but her experience
was that the pupils continued to work whether or not she was in the
room. She was probably required to conduct the discussion during break
times or after school, but her headteacher allowed her to use her
professional judgement. Again, this story is free from much of the
tension and pressure surrounding assessment that typified the stories of
Jane and Sarah.

The process of assessment was also considered to be a joint project,
which included not only the teaching team but also the parents:

The team must also decide how they want to evaluate the
progress of their students. Sometimes we talk to the students
individually about their work and twice a year we invite their
parents to come to the school and we talk together with the
parents and their child about how they have been progressing.
Together we then make plans for the coming year. Of course,
these plans are general rather than very detailed. During this
meeting we also focus on the social development of the
student, both inside school and after school. We encourage the

parents to open up their homes to other children from the
class so that we can avoid cliques and create a happy
environment within the class.

This emphasis on the class group can be seen in contrast to the demands
on teachers in England to set individual pupil targets that are linked
closely to academic attainment. It also illustrates the greater emphasis
placed on the role of parents and the home circumstances in pupil
achievement. However, Anja was concerned that society was changing
and that this had brought with it particular problems for the schooling of
children. There was more emphasis on the 'market' and materialism, and
young Danes, brought up under a Conservative government, were more
concerned about individual rights and individual success at the expense
of social cohesion and group working. She also perceived that there was
now more criticism of schools and teachers, both in the press and from
individual parents. Previously, parents would have been more content to
trust the teacher and more concerned with the well-being of the group.
This resonated with what Jane and Sarah told me.

However, in Denmark, such a change was challenging a older,
comprehensive educational ideal. Although Anja was pleased that the
most recent school legislation had removed any 'setting' or ability
grouping within the *folkeskole* system, this was tempered by a concern
that the recent requirement to differentiate teaching in order to tailor it to
the needs of individual children could prove divisive. If teachers were
required to push forward high attainers in the interests of improving the
national skill base, it could open up divisions and make it even more
difficult to create a cohesive class group. How did Anja's story compare
with that of Birgith, who had been teaching for longer?

Birgith

When I met Birgith, she had been teaching for nearly thirty years, fifteen
of which had been in her present *folkeskole*. During her career she had
taught various subjects at different levels in the *folkeskole*, but had
recently returned to the role of *klasselærer* to take responsibility for her
present class. In addition to her class teacher role, Birgith also taught
maths to a parallel Grade 3 class (10-year-olds), taught English, science
and history to a Grade 6 class (13- and 14-year-olds), ran the school
choir, and was a staff representative on the Parent/Teacher Association.
Birgith had taught for some time in the USA and said that she had been
greatly influenced by what she had read about child-centred learning in
England. When asked about the qualities of a 'good' class teacher,
Birgith, like Jane, Sarah and Anja, was clear that, as well as good subject
knowledge, it included an ability to empathise with the children and to
create an environment in which they felt safe and happy:

> I would say that every day we have a good laugh. It is so
> important to laugh together and to feel safe. It is important to
> me that children feel safe with me. Subject knowledge? Oh
> that's important, we should also be smart, good at our work
> and at our subject.

This linked into her general aims for primary education, which she saw
as two-fold, combining good subject knowledge with personal
development, within a secular, communitarian ideology that emphasised
the importance of cooperation and good citizenship:

> Two things – educating them well in all the subjects, that's
> one thing. The other thing is to be in a group, to respect other
> people, all the good human manners. I think that is very
> important and I think the parents can't give the children that.
> It is the school's responsibility. Educating a good human
> being, and a good citizen, good moral code, though not in a
> religious way.

Like Anja, Birgith considered that her first responsibility was to her
pupils and, secondly, to their parents. This was coupled with a
professional confidence that saw her as the 'expert' in the relationship, a
confidence that is perhaps missing from the stories of Jane and Sarah:

> The children! Of course parents too, but first of all the
> children because the parents don't know what my job is. I will
> tell them about it and they can ask me all they want, the door
> is open but I am the one who decides what I am doing because
> that's what I'm good at! When I teach student teachers I say
> never defend yourself as a teacher but tell them what you are
> doing, explain, do not go on the defensive. This is what I am
> doing, explain what and why and then they [parents] will
> understand. I think that is very important.

She talked with more ambiguity in relation to her responsibility to her
headteacher. Rather than a manager or curriculum leader, she saw her
headteacher as an unbiased arbiter when there was disagreement:

> The headteacher? Actually none because – well, perhaps I do.
> She is the person within the school who has ultimate
> responsibility if there is something wrong or I need her help. If
> I am doing something wrong and the parents call her or the
> students go to her, she will ask me what is all this about and I
> will explain. She will say I think we should do this or that. If I
> have a call from the parents and they argue with me I say,
> 'Stop this and we will arrange a meeting with the
> headteacher'. I will say to her I want you to be there as the
> person who is responsible for the whole school and as a third

party, so that you can listen to the parents and to me and listen to what is going on here. In that way, we have responsibility to each other. But I see this as a moral question and mostly I feel responsible to the children. She [the head] is not there to check on me, she is there for the staff, the children and the parents and she has to have a good overview and she is very good at it.

Birgith, like Anja, Jane and Sarah, considered that she had a responsibility for her pupils that went beyond the school gates. In contrast to Jane and Sarah, however, she had more of a sense that this was a joint project. She was part of a community that was responsible for the children's upbringing, which included teachers, parents and pedagogues from the after-school clubs (the School/Freetime Organisation, or SFO):

I feel a responsibility for the children outside school, but it is not only *my* responsibility. I think the child is in the middle and around them are the parents, the school and the teachers, and the pedagogues at the SFO. We are the adults who are taking care of the child. So, I make time to talk with the pupils individually and ask them, 'How are you getting on in school, how are you at home?'. 'Do you have any friends, is there something going on at home that I can help you with? Something you want to talk with me about?' The parents know that, so I consider that we have a responsibility for the child in the whole of their life when we are around them. It is broader than just giving knowledge especially in the early years.

The Danish concept of *dannelse*, which has no direct equivalent in English, encompasses this view of education as a social, as well as cognitive, project. Despite a current national concern with the relatively poor results of Danish pupils in large international surveys, Birgith was convinced of *dannelse*'s continuing relevance in today's society:

Dannelse is about how to behave when you are in a group, what language it is appropriate to use. But it is also broader than that. When we compare our children with other nationalities we are not, maybe, such good readers and writers and mathematicians, but we have a lot of knowledge about the whole world and I think it is very good. To concentrate and to go deeper and deeper into some areas of debate, to find out. I think it is important that they learn to be responsible for pollution, etcetera, to have an opinion about it. It is about being a good person, a good human being, a good citizen, a good parent, a good co-worker, and so on.

Two Different Constructs of the Teacher

Despite the differences in initial training, length of service and position on a career path, the narrative which Jane and Sarah provided was surprisingly consistent. Both teachers were supportive of the generalist model of the primary class teacher, which contained elements of both the academic and the social development of their pupils. However, both considered themselves to be under pressure from government policy to focus more directly on levels of attainment, as expressed by national testing, and conceded that this could lead to a form of teacher specialisation that they would regret. Both could see a benefit in some level of primary specialist teaching in order to 'share the load' required by a prescriptive curriculum, which left little space for flexibility or creativity. A disappointment was expressed that a culture of 'performance', for both themselves and their pupils, had created workload pressures that restricted their ability to concentrate on individual pupils' concerns and build the type of close personal relationships with their pupils which they saw as a prerequisite for effective teaching and learning. However, there was some evidence that Sarah especially, who had qualified earlier and taught before the introduction of the 1988 Education Reform Act, could remember a less pressured and more creative model of the primary class teacher, which facilitated a degree of professional discretion. Jane and Sarah both felt remote from government policy-making, which appeared to have undermined a professional identity that perceived the social and personal development of their pupils to be as important as academic attainment. In fact, they saw these two aspects of teaching and learning as being inextricably linked and necessary to enable pupils to develop as mature, independent learners.

In the case of Anja and Birgith, again, the narratives which they provided were surprisingly consistent. Both teachers were committed to an holistic approach to the curriculum, which included joint teaching, project work and the inclusion of topics that had a relevance to their pupils' lives. They also laid great emphasis on the personal and social development of their pupils, who they considered needed to learn to work together in preparation for active citizenship. Anja and Birgith were also keen to ensure good communications with the parents of their pupils and the other community and professional colleagues with whom they shared responsibility. Unlike Jane and Sarah, however, they talked with more confidence about their role in this shared responsibility. Their approach to these relationships was influenced by a confident professionalism, which saw themselves as having an expert voice with regard to the process of teaching and learning. Though they appreciated that changing social circumstances were affecting their work, unlike Jane and Sarah, they remained confident that change would not be imposed from outside but would be strongly influenced by their professional judgement.

Conclusion

These data reveal the everyday experiences of four experienced and dedicated teachers working in two contrasting national contexts. Their stories illustrate the differences that national context can have on the concept of the class teacher (Broadfoot et al, 1993, Alexander, 2000). This suggests that theories of a deep-rooted cultural identity (Mallinson, 1975; Archer, 1984; Hedetoft, 1999) based around the outward signs of a nation-state, for example a common language and a common history, continue to influence current policy and practice. Within the English education system, the role expectations placed on primary class teachers have been influenced by a concern with discipline, a belief in innate differences in individual ability, and a clearly delineated hierarchy of knowledge. In contrast, the Danish *klasselærer* is the result of role expectations that include an emphasis in Danish society on social cohesion, the collaborative nature of learning, and an encyclopaedic view of knowledge which allows everyone to have access. This has allowed for a more even balance between the demand for high academic achievement and the development of personal and social skills. Despite earlier widespread professional support within England for a more holistic 'Plowdenesque' approach to the work of the primary class teacher (CACE, 1967), evidence from Jane and Sarah suggests that current government policy is again emphasising issues of discipline, summative assessment and a concentration on the formal teaching of basic literacy and numeracy skills.

In contrast, the collective nature of Danish society continues to give prominence to the need for close, ongoing relationships between pupils and their teachers, further extended to the parents of pupils, who remain closely involved with the class group (Ravn, 1994). Although Jane, Sarah, Anja and Birgith had common concerns focused on changing social patterns, which have created new pressures for schools, the opportunity that they had to address them was mediated by differences in national policy and school organisation, which in turn gave rise to two different sets of role expectations.

However, the globalisation of education policy has meant that in the few years since Jane, Sarah, Anja and Birgith were interviewed, national policy has changed. Within Denmark, emphasis is shifting towards a more prescribed curriculum and proposals for more national testing. Meanwhile, in England, there has been a renewed emphasis on formative teacher assessment to replace some aspects of national testing and a relaxation of the national curriculum in some areas. The question is, to what extent will these policy changes affect the stories that classroom teachers tell us? Will teachers in England have more confidence in their expert knowledge and gain more time to get to know about the lives of their pupils outside school? Will teachers in Denmark begin to feel the pressure of 'performance', both for themselves and for their pupils, restricting their ability to use their professional judgement in decisions to do with the curriculum and assessment? The strength of using narrative in comparative research to understand the impact of national policy, as these stories show, is that it can throw light on unintended consequences, which appear in the gap between rhetoric and reality.

References

Acker, S. (1999) *The Realities of Teachers' Work: never a dull moment.* London: Cassell.

Alexander, R. (2000) *Culture and Pedagogy: international comparisons in primary education.* Oxford: Blackwell.

Archer, M. (1984) *Social Origins of Educational Systems.* London: Sage.

Behar, R. (1996) *The Vulnerable Observer: anthropology that breaks your heart.* Boston: Beacon.

Broadfoot, P., Osborn, M., Gilly, M. & Bûcher, A. (1993) *Perceptions of Teaching: primary school teachers in England and France.* London: Cassell.

Central Advisory Council for Education (England) (CACE) (1967) *Children and Their Primary Schools.* The Plowden Report. London: HMSO.

Goodson, I. (Ed.) (1992) *Studying Teachers' Lives.* London: Routledge.

Hargreaves, A. (1994) *Changing Teachers, Changing Times.* London: Cassell.

Hedetoft, U. (1999) The Nation-State Meets the World: national identities in the context of transnationality and cultural globalization, *European Journal of Social Theory,* 2, pp. 71-94. http://dx.doi.org/10.1177/13684319922224310

Helsby, G. (1999) *Changing Teachers' Work.* Buckingham: Open University Press.

Mallinson, V. (1975) *An Introduction to the Study of Comparative Education,* 4th edn. London: Heinemann.

McNess, E. (2001) The School Teacher: a universal construct? in C. Day & D. van Veen (Eds) *Educational Research in Europe Yearbook 2001.* Leuven: Garant.

McNess, E. (2004) Culture, Context and the Quality of Education: evidence from a small-scale extended case study in England and Denmark, *Compare,* 34, pp. 315-327. http://dx.doi.org/10.1080/0305792042000257158

Nias, J. (1989) *Primary Teachers Talking: a study of teaching as work.* London: Routledge.

Nias, J. (1996) Thinking about Feeling: the emotions of teaching, *Cambridge Journal of Education,* 26, pp. 293-306.

Osborn, M., McNess, E. & Broadfoot, P., with Pollard, A. & Triggs, P. (2000) *What Teachers Do: changing policy and practice in primary education.* London: Continuum.

Ravn, B. (1994) Expectations about Parents in Education in Scandinavian Countries, in A. Macbeth & B. Ravn (Eds) *Expectations about Parents in Education: European perspectives.* Glasgow: University of Glasgow Press.

CHAPTER TEN

Embedded Narratives, Negotiated Identities and the Complexity of Learning Landscapes in Upper Primary Classrooms in Scotland and Jamaica

BETH CROSS
University of Edinburgh, United Kingdom

In a fractured age, when cynicism is god, here is a possible heresy: we live by stories, we also live in them. One way or another we are living the stories planted in us early or along the way, or we are also living the stories we planted – knowingly or unknowingly – in ourselves. We live stories that either give our lives meaning or negate it with meaninglessness. If we change the stories we live by, quite possibly we change our lives. (Okri, 1997, p. 46)

Introduction

This chapter examines teachers' classroom interaction and the underlying narrative assumptions that do much to structure the learning culture with their pupils. Two contrasting contexts in Scotland and Jamaica are explored, where there are tensions between local community languages and the recognised language of the global marketplace. Following Wertsch & Smolka (1993), I argue that it is often in very subtle ways that teachers either encourage or restrict the amount of dialogue and exchange there can be in their classroom, often drawing on unspoken yet powerfully present embedded narratives to do so. Informal exchanges within the classroom can be vital for children to work through their own strategies for navigating their multilingual contexts. This chapter draws on the metaphor of fractals derived from complexity sciences (WolframResearch, 2003) to develop a more sensitive and appropriate framework for discourse analysis.

Access and inclusion have gained prominence in many education and social development agendas, following trends set by global leaders at recent international conferences. Although many different language policies address different facets of inclusion and access in differing contexts, some of the most crucial dynamics that make school communication either inclusive, engaging and rewarding, or exclusive, inhibiting and ultimately discouraging, are not mentioned at all in policy documents or are only vaguely alluded to in phrases about school 'culture'. Similarly, these same factors defy quantification and therefore remain difficult to detect in large-scale research methods that are inherently reliant on predefined categories of response, and therefore unsuitable for examining individual interpretation and adaptation to local practice.

Yet an understanding of these communication dynamics is vital to pursue. Narrative analysis provides a means to do so. This chapter extends the practice of narrative analysis to include an exploration of the narrative environment of a school. This understanding begins by recognising that communication happens through three related but distinctly different spheres:

- *Inbuilt communication*: the built infrastructure of a school and its relation to both the natural environment and the larger built network communicate messages about how the pupils themselves are to relate to the larger network of society.
- *Embodied communication*: the embodied physical routines, forms of discipline, and sanctioned forms of play communicate very strongly messages about who and how a learner is allowed to be. Many para-linguistic features, such as gesture, tone and stance, that are banished from consideration by some models of discourse and conversation analysis are an indispensable facet of this sphere of communication.
- *Articulated communication*: it is only with reference to, and very much shaped by, these forms of communication that the third form of communication – that of language, textual and spoken – conveys its message.

The classroom teacher has a very complex role orchestrating and navigating the relationships that these messages form. Narrative plays a key role in this process, both the unspoken private narratives that are an ongoing part of a teacher's stream of consciousness, as well as the explicit, deliberate ones used in communication with the class. Together, internalised and externalised communication and the narratives threaded through both create the classroom culture and do much to determine what the learner's school experience will be. Often, in very subtle ways teachers signal their attitudes about this mixture of messages: which message is to be stressed and how they are to be interpreted. These subtle but crucial signals do much to indicate to learners how they can view their own place in the flow of communication. Teachers at these moments can either serve as bridge-builders or conversely, they can build rigid walls and act as wardens patrolling the borders. Narrative and allusion to narrative play pivotal roles in this definitive interchange.

I would go so far as to assert that narrative, as it is normatively conceived and studied, is not in the form that it functions most powerfully. It is the half-submerged narratives, conveyed by a gesture or phrase, that are actually most powerfully present in how both teachers and learners make sense of their interaction with each other. This awareness is captured in Dubose-Brunner's definition of narrative, which I use throughout this chapter:

> Expressed uncertainty, representation, telling of events, ordering of one's life 'story', knowing or imaginative play, making sense of the fictive world and thus vicariously of the lived world, all of these and none of them capture in its entirety the sense of complexity and a range of boundless possibilities within narrative. Narratives are not fixed, neither are our readings, they grow fluctuate, shuttle back and forth recursively, the way we tend to live our lives. (Dubose-Brunner, 1994, p. 17)

This definition of narrative highlights how inextricably bound up narrative is with discourse and communication as a whole, making the distinction between discourse and narrative analysis one of emphasis rather than discrete categories. Embedded narratives, in complex and indirect ways, are always present in communication choices.

To understand teachers' roles as either bridge-builders or gatekeepers is to understand their communication choices in relation to the choices children make. These choices take place in both the immediate context of school and within cultural dynamics on a larger scale (Alexander, 2000). A word needs to be said about both the immediate and wider context before particular instances of teachers' choices in Scotland and Jamaica are examined in detail, and the paradigm of complexity brought to bear on an analysis of the narrative landscape they create.

Narrative Choices in the Globalisation Context

Much has been written about what different forms of communication can mean or accomplish. The differences between 'oral' and 'literate' cultures have been thoroughly contested and deconstructed (Serpell, 1993; Gee, 1994). Yet there is a third component, that of the increasing importance of reading and organising visual images, which also needs to be taken into consideration. Video imaging is becoming centrally important in children's culture and forms a central part of their communication awareness and expertise. Grossberg's (1994) point that pop culture has been usurped by game culture is important to consider. What this means is that the predominant form through which cultural messages are conveyed is no longer that of a linear narrative or song lyric but of multiple, and to varying degrees interchangeable potential scenarios or strategy fragments. Children are becoming much more adept at playing and thinking in the latter mode. Not surprisingly, at the same time technology has made the transition from linear sequential storing of information to the more compressed and compact configuring of images or information made up of component clusters or bitmaps.

Children's narrative activities demonstrate that they are not only social agents but also cultural producers. The boundaries between consuming, recycling and producing culture are very permeable and fluid, and take on different meanings in differing contexts. The impediments or constraints that children overcome, as well as the various forms of encouragement or inspiration they receive from various forms of adult culture, all shape their own cultural creations. The explosion of visual media across information technologies means that school literacy is not the same window on the world that it could once claim to be (Rushkoff, 1996; Broadfoot, 2000). What children are already competent at when they come to school, what competencies they can gain at school and how the interface between these competencies is to be negotiated is changing (Buckingham, 2000; Lankshear & Knobel, 2003). The interface as it exists is not understood as well as it should be, and grows ever more complex.

Yet within globalised popular culture there is much to cause concern. The powerful forces of globalisation can also be seen as a serious drain on resources, democratic, economic and cultural, from localities that are already disadvantaged. As Louisy (2001) comments:

> The fears that the tentacles of cultural globalisation will entrap the soul of the Caribbean people, especially the young, and make of them a new flood of cultural refugees seem well founded, unless the region makes a concerted effort to locate its culture, and its contributions as differentiated elements in the globalized environment. (p. 433)

A sense of local cultural production is closely tied to that of classroom practice. Teachers' attitudes towards their own narrative creativity and their students' are a fundamental gateway to processes of local cultural production, or else a dismissal of them.

Contrasting Communication:
policy statements and classroom practice

The Scots Pairlament (*sic*) Cross Pairty Group on the Scots Language published on 19 March 2003 a document entitled 'Scots: a statement o principles', recommending 'that Scots shuid be an essential pairt o the educational curriculum in Scotland at aw levels' and arguing that:

> Gin we in Scotland dinna staun up for the guid o the Scots
> language an its future at a time when we see the diversity o the
> warld's tongues unner threat, it will add ane mair leid tae the
> leet o language extinction an gar anither rich an distinctive
> idiom gang oot o the warld. Let us mak shair that the people o
> Scotland aye has the choice tae uise the Scots language. Juist
> as we seek tae gaird the earth's bio-diversity, sae we need tae
> gaird linguistic diversity. (p. 15)

Similarly, across the Caribbean communities have had to struggle with the legacy of having their local community languages beaten out of them and the standard language of the imperial power drummed in. By 1993 the Standing Committee of Ministers Responsible for Education and Culture in the Caribbean was able to agree:

> To recognise all the languages in each society as equally valid
> and to see multilingualism and multi-dialectalism as positive
> attributes. (Bryan, 2000, p. 6)

This committee set as a goal for secondary school graduates the ability to 'use and understand a linguistically valid script for representing the creole-related vernaculars of their communities' (Bryan, 2000, p. 6).

Nevertheless, whether this concern to protect or validate local languages translates into actual practice in classrooms is questionable (Ministry of Education and Culture, Jamaica, 2000). Addison (2001) characterises the treatment of Scots dialect in schools as a 'Tartan gesture'. This gesture, usually made around the anniversary of Scotland's national bard, Robert Burns, is closely tied to images that the tourist industry seeks to project of Scotland, much as Jamaican schools make selective use of Patwa in the form of poems by 'Miss Lou' (Bennet, 1966) to commemorate National Heroes' Day in concert with the Jamaican Tourist Board's cultural development aims. Addison reports in confirmation of McClure (1980) that:

> many classroom teachers, if they use Scots in literary terms do
> so in a way which is confined to the past and is
> unrecognisable for people living in modern urban
> communities. (Addison, 2001, p. 158)

Addison found that the working-class Scots with whom he worked characterised their everyday speech as 'just slang', not Scots, just as many Jamaicans would characterise their speech as 'patter chat', or 'chattin bad'. If the language in which narratives flow within a community is constrained, so too are the narratives. Some examples from two years of ethnographic fieldwork in both settings illustrate the day-to-day nuances in which language is used to either affirm or negate local community narratives.

The Scottish Context

Scots was permitted as the subject of lessons some weeks before Robert Burns' birthday in the two Scottish schools where ethnographic research was conducted. However, a closer look at the teachers' own language use on a regular basis revealed that they drew on distinctly different narratives, which reinforced very different messages about how the Robert Burns lessons should be seen in relation to the curriculum as a whole.

Reciting Lines at Braeview

In the school I will refer to as Braeview, the teaching culture had a fortress mentality. Both the headteacher and senior teacher emphasised to me several times in the course of research that their task was to keep the norms and practices of the surrounding community at bay, and provide a markedly different culture within the school's boundaries. The school culture could be characterised by strict discipline and sharply defined roles for teachers and learners. This culture was maintained by one teacher, Mr Ruhl, in his composite primary Year 6/7 class predominantly through linguistical means. Throughout the day Mr Ruhl provided a running narrative of what the class had achieved, what they should achieve now and what rewards this would lead to by the end of the day. This use of narrative effectively suppressed alternative interpretations pupils might have about their school day, what was to be achieved, and what value or meaning this may have in comparison to what they knew about life and the challenges it held beyond the school walls. Behaviour that deviated from this script was often censored by use of the past conditional verb tense: 'I would not have expected that of you', conveying the sense the act was unthinkable. I never heard children adopt this verb construction themselves. In fact this verb construction contrasted quite sharply with their standard Scots verb construction, 'I wouldnae'.

In the weeks preceding Robert Burns's birthday Scots was officially allowed into the classroom and taught in the same manner as all subjects. This excerpt comes from a lesson where Mr Ruhl is commenting on a student's performance of a poem in Scots:

Mr Ruhl: How does she pronounce tomorrow? [met with blank stares] How would she pronounce it on the playground?
Jackie: Th' morn?
Mr Ruhl: That's right, very good, the morn. [Many students are inattentive. One is reading *Our Willie*, which the teacher suddenly notices.]
Mr Ruhl: Ian McNiel, I am surprised at you reading that, you put it away so you are not tempted!

Ian was often the focus of Mr Ruhl's censure. Often the use of Scots played a key role in their confrontations, which routinely took the form of Ian being made to stand at his place at the table and receive a telling-off punctuated by rhetorical questions. Each question was designed to elicit from Ian compliance that implicated him in his own punishment. He was to agree that his behaviour was unacceptable. However, each question also offered a small opportunity to resist, one that was sometimes too tempting to pass up. Sometimes he offered his assent not in standard English but in Scots, saying 'Aye'. This was immediately met by Mr Ruhl's raised, offended tone, 'What did you say?!', effectively daring Ian to be more overt in his resistance, at which point, more often than not, he tactically retreated into English. Both participants in the interaction, perhaps intuitively drawing on several centuries of history to enact their roles, knew the use of Scots was definitely not viewed as a welcome part of the school culture. It should be noted that during these confrontations the other children in the class seemed to be listening at their most attentive, particularly in the pauses before Ian decided to answer either 'Aye' or 'Yes'. It is particularly ironic that *Our Willie*, a longstanding staple of Scots identity, should draw censure, as it could be interpreted as embracing and putting into practical application the very cultural dimension the lesson was addressing.

Sporting Colours at Forest Hill

Scots has a very different place in a nearby school, which I will call Forest Hill. Children's home culture is seen as less of a threat and is therefore permitted much more widely throughout the school day. One teacher, Mr Irvine, very mindful of his own working-class roots, draws upon this to form a politicised conception of his motivation for teaching. He uses Scots consistently throughout his teaching day. He has a reputation among students as a very demanding teacher, but is also often described, particularly by the boys, after a moment of thought and a shrug of the shoulders, as 'well, cool'. Often I heard him berate his class for not thinking or being their best, but never by setting himself apart by using a distinctly complex verb form, as Mr Ruhl and many other teachers do. Over the course of eight months' research, never once did I hear him tell his students they should do something because they should submit to the authority of their teacher. It was not about conforming to his expectations but about living up to their abilities. This in itself meant that a fundamentally different narrative underwrote his teaching. His appeal was always to their own intelligence, the need to sharpen their wits and figure things out for themselves.

Although his class is pushed quite hard to complete assignments and progress through the curriculum ahead of schedule, there is a constant use of humour in the class, all of it thoroughly unapologetically in working-class Scots, and much of it centring upon many of the boys' support for a rival football team to that of the teacher. This ongoing 'slagging match' played out across all three spheres of communication. Boys wore their team's colours on their trainers, or under their uniform. They decorated the pencil-holders they made for the tabletops as a class project with team insignia. These symbols, worked into the infrastructure of the day, were then alluded to in asides by the teacher. These barely audible quips encouraged a playful opposition and gave it a limited space for expression. They also relied on a working knowledge of current football dynamics, with each match containing narratives of loss, betrayal, endurance or superiority, and each player's fitness supplying a series of attendant narratives. It is these narratives that teacher and pupils alluded to and used to spar with each other. Paradoxically, building rapport and a camaraderie within the class provided boys with an impetus to imagine a 'cool' role and narrative for themselves in which they could stay involved and included in the classroom and thereby access a range of skills, foremost among them information technology skills, which they might otherwise have not take up so keenly. Although the 'slagging match' was not part of the school's policy, and could be seen as contrary to the stated aims of positive regard for everyone, it actually brought into the school arena children's expertise and interests, which female teachers can react to as foreign and threatening, and often act to exclude, albeit without ever directly criticising them.

It is important to note that through this use of male culture, Mr Irvine did not make all boys equally welcome. It is only one kind of masculine identity among others (Mac an Ghaill, 1994). There are important differences in how each of these male primary teachers approaches gender dynamics in the classroom. Each chooses a different way of being masculine and asserting masculine authority and thereby presents a different set of choices to which pupils make their gendered responses or accommodations. It is also interesting to note that in these two Scottish settings the girls were often positioned as a passive audience to displays of male authority and resistance.

These observations illustrate that it is not so much in the stated outcomes of a lesson plan, which may look very similar, but in the more engrained everyday patterns of teacher-student interaction that different school cultures are created, either ones that prohibit children's home language, carrier of their home culture, or are receptive to it. Similar contrasts can be drawn from the Jamaican context.

The Jamaican Context

In Jamaica there was a more prevalent, ingrained, adept use of oral culture within the wider community. In a number of ways, there was encouragement for children to see themselves as legitimate, accomplished producers of culture in the Jamaican context (Cross, 2003), whereas in Scotland this encouragement was more often absent or constrained, largely because of how children are positioned as socio-economic consumers of culture.

Yet, for a formidable host of reasons, many classrooms in Jamaica rely on rote, repetitive lessons, often with the aid of a belt (Evans, 2001). In this kind of lesson, the language curriculum does not draw upon oral and physical performance skills; rather, curriculum exchanges require a lack of sophistication, and a blanket acceptance of received texts, regardless of relevance or meaning.[1] In these conditions children's cultural expertise is not drawn upon to interpret the curriculum content.

Though the situation described above may be the case too often, there are teachers who, against tremendous odds, find room for a different kind of pedagogy. I found this to be the case at the school I will refer to as Caledonia Heights, situated in a rural highland Jamaican community within commuting distance of two of Jamaica's urban centres. Like Mr Irvine, Mr Lewis pushed his class to stay ahead of the curriculum. All the blackboards were usually full of assignments, which children stayed into the lunch hour and after school to copy. However, he found time within the school day to literally take the children outside the echoing confines of the building. He did this routinely to listen to them read and for religious education lessons, a strong component of the Jamaican curriculum. It was in these lessons that Mr Lewis drew on local, salient cultural practices and values, thereby signalling to students that they could and should re-examine and contextualise information, as the example below illustrates:

> Mr Lewis accepts girls' performance of the song 'Jesus Is a Friend' in response to his question, 'What kind of a person was Jesus?'. While the girls sing, the boys beat a steady rhythm on their Bibles. As the song concludes with 'Amens', Mr Lewis pushes the critical thinking possibilities of the topic further: 'How do you know that Jesus was born on Christmas?'
>
> The girls' reaction is confusion. Mr Lewis continues, suggesting in a hypothetical narrative how they might think about this topic. In other words he invites them to play out in their imagination a possible experience they could have at Sunday School. He does so knowing he is suggesting a

provocative event worthy of a tale: 'Have you ever posed the question at Sunday School?' He looks to see their reaction. 'So why you don't do that?' He explains in narrative form what this process of inquiry might mean: 'You go to Adventists, maybe Adventists have one view, maybe Leah's church have another view. I'm not claiming to be an authority. I have my views, which may be different from others. So, Nicholas, you're going to ask whosoever is knowledgeable when he was born. We want some feedback next Monday.'

Someone pipes up: 'Sir, we can't.' Another person claims: 'Sir, mi naw go to church.' But this is countered: 'He go to church.' Meanwhile, Mr Lewis continues building a possible narrative that the students' exploration can join: 'Some say he was born in September cause it took that long for the wise men to get there. Don't ask lickle people, ask the elders.'

Leah: 'Sir, you ask them if he was born at Christmas, they say yes, you must ask them how they know?'

Mr Lewis: 'There's one school of thought. Some believe he wasn't born while shepherds watched their flocks by night. Shepherds couldn't be out in field in winter. Some that they could have a fire.'

A discussion about time and different ways of measuring it begins to surface. One girl reports to Mr Lewis that 'Sir, Nicholas say the months start at April.' That different points of the globe might have different ways of orienting their measurement of time to suit the agricultural seasons pulls powerfully away from the reinforcement of the imperial centre that the language texts present.

Ruth is saying to her neighbour in a quiet voice: 'If you watch the news they are fighting over Jerusalem and Palestine, both claim it as their capital. They're at war over that lickle piece of land.' A boy breaks in: 'It's Israel's!'

Ruth: 'You chat too much, you listen!'

This side conversation is overlaid by Mr Lewis's continued encouragement, which I record imperfectly as 'We've talked about this, you can learn everyting ...'

Another girl raises her hand, still unsure of the permissible boundaries that Mr Lewis is suggesting: 'Sir, suppose Nicholas came with a different answer to Sarah?'

Mr Lewis: 'That's what we want, so we can draw our own conclusions.'

I record another nearby girl, Esther, being a little more confident in switching to this different discourse style: 'Yes, you see!' Mr Lewis continues explaining: 'When you grow up and go to high school or if you go to university, you can't go to one book; you have to look at four or five books.'

There are several things to notice about this. Some of the most confident girls in the class had difficulty believing they could collect different valid answers to the same question, an indication that they had difficulty believing such an activity could be allowed within school discourse. However, one was quite willing to believe it.

Throughout the class discussion Mr Lewis switched between a complex command of Standard English and, at key points of encouragement, Patwa pronunciation. He used narrative to encourage the inclusion of students' experiences and thoughts and was rewarded by a diversity of engagement. When students' responses indicated some thought on their part he responded, often including some use of Patwa to signal his acceptance. When students responded by using strategies that belong to the rote drill of the classroom, he deftly discouraged this by simply ignoring them and waiting for a more engaged response. He modelled code switching and strategy switching and at the same time gave students the space to practice doing so themselves. It is my estimation that these are the most crucial communication skills a child in Jamaica needs.

Analysis of Teachers' Complex Choices in Complex Contexts

The starting point for analysis of these excerpts is to highlight how the teachers themselves across all settings pointed out that teacher training had not prepared them to help children make important communication transitions or to deal with other language issues that the teachers themselves described as crucial to their work. Were these issues not covered, or were they presented in such a way as to be unrecognisable or seem irrelevant? Storytelling as an educational tool is barely covered in Scottish settings, let alone the deeper consideration of the different forms and roles narrative plays in structuring identities, strategies and cultural norms in a classroom. In Jamaica the teacher education situation is more diverse. Storytelling is encouraged and its value recognised, a nationwide cultural competition providing a structure for its inclusion in the curricular year. Mr Lewis's education at the University of West Indies included consideration of local cultural production in a deeper sense, and it may be no coincidence that he evidences the most skilled interactional use of it.

Narrative as illustrated above plays crucial roles and works within the classroom in complex ways at many different levels. It is narrative that operates in all three spheres of communication, building either bridges that enable translation and participation, or walls that prohibit it. The teacher's narrative styles do much to characterise the culture of the classroom, which enables very different forms of literacy: engaged literacy, in which forms are learned and integrated into children's purposeful use of language, and alienated literacy (Cambourne, 1988), in which the forms are dutifully learned but not applied to ongoing life tasks or choices. However, as these excerpts also show, the narrative traffic is not one-way. There are many other factors that contribute to the climate or ecology of the classroom: children's disposition toward school, the similarity of their home language style to standard styles, the overall community culture and its similarities to or differences from the school's culture, the existence of other sites of literacy within the community and their involvement with them, and most importantly, their own agency and imagination.

This point can be encapsulated in a diagram or map in the sense of social cartography. According to Paulston, social maps should be offered:

> as a method of illustrating our vigorous social milieu
> composed of a profusion of narratives. This is done with an
> emphasis on layered or imbricated fields of perception and
> intertextual space, an approach which draws in part upon the
> technique of chorography, that is, the mapping of domains or
> regions, and the ideas of Arjun Apadurai concerning
> disjunctures in the links among space, place, citizenship and
> nationhood. (Paulston, 1997, p. 140)

Paulston's invitation to imagine classrooms as narrative terrains can be facilitated by recourse to the imaging possibilities of complexity science. In particular narratives interaction can be represented in terms of the richness of fractal reiteration.

Classrooms as Seedbeds of Fractals

Fractals are the building blocks of some of the most complex structures we see around us, from trees to clouds, to the bronchial tubing in our lungs and the network of signals in the brain taking place as this text is read. The mathematics that generate fractals contain a process analogous to conversation, which makes fractals a compelling metaphor in discourse analysis. Equations that generate fractals are non-linear; that is, they do not have one discrete answer. The relationship between variables is such that in the process of solving for y, a new value for x is generated, which yields a new starting point for another iteration of the equation. Thus the equation when mapped results in, not a simple closed shape, but an open, increasingly complex one, as shown in Figure 1.

In this way non-linear equations parallel the process of hermeneutics and serve as a visual representation of it. Each narrative exchange, like each iteration of the equation, enables more nuanced, detailed understandings, incorporating elements from each other into the overall shape of communication. Absent or limited iterations can also serve to represent the lack of narrative exchange in classrooms.

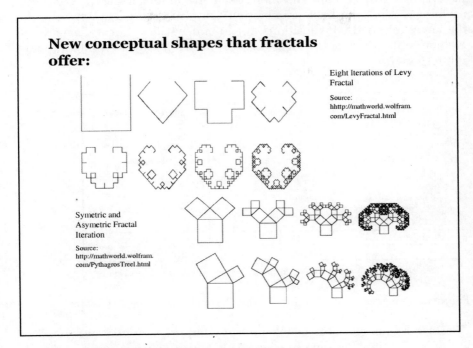

Figure 1. Complex shapes resulting from iteration of fractals.

In Figure 2 the shape of the first iteration of a fractal equation is used to represent Mr Ruhl's discourse at Braeview, standing apart from and above the dispersed elements of his pupils' discourse, which is disallowed. The shape generated by eight iterations of the same equation is used to represent the richer interaction of the classrooms at Forest Hill and Caledonia Heights. As the dialogue continues the understanding of each other's position, concepts, and perspectives grows more intricate. Each exchange can be visualised as a further iteration of the fractal equation. Thus, the third and fourth iterations of fractal equations quickly come to correspond to the intricacy of real-life shapes. Just as a computer follows a program to reconfigure units of information (i.e. pixels) rather than tracking sequentially each individual unit, I suggest that this method of mapping how narratives are juxtaposed against each other yields a much more detailed picture of the dynamics and issues than conventional linear models of analysis.

If only the teacher's voice or discourse is allowed, as in Mr Ruhl's class, the components of fractal reiteration remain separate and do not integrate into a pattern. When both teacher and student voices can engage with each other (Edwards & Mercer, 1987; Chouliaraki, 1998), the exchange can be represented as fractal components coming together in a pattern that grows richer and more detailed the longer the interaction is sustained. What the fractal reiteration can also be used to depict is the tendency for good conversations not to end but to bifurcate, generating further side discussions that form a network of interpretation and reinterpretation.

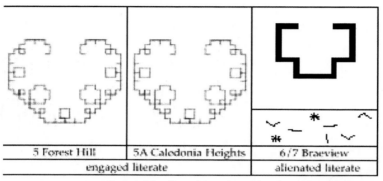

5 Forest Hill	5A Caledonia Heights	6/7 Braeview
engaged literate		alienated literate

Source: Lévy Fractal from http://mathworld.wolfram.com

Figure 2. Conversation possibilities in the classroom depicted as fractals.

The classrooms can also be likened to complex adaptive systems. The study of complex systems has revealed that in a system where there is either too much order or too much chaos, very little that is adaptive or innovative happens. The in-between, flexible state of complexity, though not predictable, is the one capable of creating transformation, in a process known as emergence. Emergence is the capacity for some systems to build order out of disorder in a seemingly disordered process, thus creating change. However, there are also systems in which emergence creates the ability to resist change. When threatened with dissipative factors they reorganise themselves, showing a marked resilience toward change. It is important to keep both eventualities in mind, as well as others, when drawing analogies to society.

To reconsider educational metaphors in light of complexity is to substantially amend mechanistic understandings of organisations to incorporate the lessons of fractal scaling, non-linear fluid dynamics, and complex adaptive systems. Our capacity for and the validity of interpretation and interaction is enhanced by a complexity research stance. It is crucial to understand the relations between terms within the same level of interaction *and* across levels of interaction. The more interactive the variables are, the greater the likelihood that their feedback between each other can amplify or strengthen their effect, be that to throw the system into chaos, or conversely to stabilise and make it resilient to change. Non-linear fluid systems are capable of doing either (Eve, 1997, p. 278).

Teachers' resistance to change, the resilience of school culture, the transformative moment when a child appears to take a quantum leap forward in learning: all of these defy mechanistic analysis, yet they are the very sort of experiences or situations that educators must grapple with most vigorously. Drawing on this complexity model, I would liken Mr Ruhl's class at Braeview to a system where there is too much order for emergence, whereas Mr Lewis' class in Jamaica, and in a limited way Mr Irvine's class at Forest Hill, is like a border situation between chaos and order where complexity becomes active, and where a tolerance for random or unpredictable narrative activity generates new learning and communication possibilities.

In many ways education can be said to be an increasingly complex arena, responding to complex dynamics and agendas. Often this can seem daunting, bewildering even. Through a closer look at the scientific concept of complexity some questions can be opened up that make the prospect of complexity less daunting and more intriguing. From this brief insight into classroom cultures and the narratives within them, we can ask: how might an increased appreciation of narratives as mapped in terms of complexity help teachers better respond to their classroom context? Can it empower or encourage them to view 'chaos' as potential creativity? Can it increase their sensitivity to the complexity children bring to the classroom? Can it help them develop an 'education for uncertainty' (King, quoted in Louisy, 2001, p. 426) that will better help their students cope with the globalisation era?

As many educationalists have pointed out, Giroux (1992) perhaps foremost among them, the classroom can be a site of critical engagement with cultural forms, rather than simply a site of their transmission. Henry, citing Glissant (1997), suggests this very possibility:

> a project of creolization [is] one in which intellectual workers
> would re-enter the long-concealed areas of our imagination
> and undo the binary oppositions and negative evaluations that
> block African and European elements from creatively coming
> together. These subterranean voyagers should strive to open
> blocked arteries and channels. (Henry, 2000, p. 88)

When Mr Lewis asks his class when in the year they think Jesus was born, I believe he is opening up a space for them to do precisely what Glissant envisions as necessary, and no less. Initially it seems a very simple or even absurd question, yet there are deeper carnival (Bakhtin, 1984) dimensions to it. He is asking an open question, not a rhetorical one; a question that invites narrative theorising and imagining; a question that has answers from more than one perspective, each carrying its own particular political, historical and existential meanings to enrich the discussion. He asks a question that can generate a multilinear fractal discussion with the potential to simultaneously deepen understanding about both local and global issues, in such a way as to build a bridge between them with many of the strengths of fractal structures.

As this exploration of the two contexts has illustrated, the role of embedded narratives within communication choices in classrooms, like fractals, becomes more intricate and full of possibility the closer one looks. The absence as well as the presence of interaction are indicative of cultural patterns that are replicated across scales of interaction. This brief glimpse at different classroom cultures in comparative research also illustrates how reconceptualising narrative and discourse analysis within a fractal framework opens up a richer exploration of what can be meant by learning landscapes.

Note

[1] Despite attempts by the Ministry of Education and Culture to produce a Caribbean-based curriculum, many teachers prefer to use older textbooks, the *First Aid in English* series (McIver, 1983), which they see as the 'gold standard'. First published during the colonial era, they reinforce Jamaica's peripheral status and the United Kingdom's pre-eminence. These textbooks enjoy regular reprints - in Glasgow, Scotland.

References

Addison, A. (2001) Using Scots Literacy in Family Literacy Work, in J. Crowther, M. Hamilton & L. Tett (Eds) *Powerful Literacies*, pp. 155-165. Leicester: National Institute for Adult Continuing Education.

Alexander, R. (2000) *Culture and Pedagogy: international comparisons in primary education.* Oxford: Blackwell.

Bakhtin, M.M. (1984) *Rabelais and His World.* Bloomington: Indiana University Press.

Bennet, L. (1966) *Jamaican Labrish.* Kingston: Sangster Book Stores.

Broadfoot, P. (2000) Comparative Education for the 21st Century: retrospect and prospect, *Comparative Education,* 36(3), pp. 357-371. http://dx.doi.org/10.1080/03050060050129036

Bryan, B. (2000) Language Education in the Caribbean: histories, policies and practice. Paper presented at the 13th biennial conference of the Society for Caribbean Linguistics, Kingston, Jamaica.

Buckingham, D. (2000) *After the Death of Childhood: growing up in the age of electronic media.* Cambridge: Polity Press.

Cambourne, B. (1988) *The Whole Story.* Sydney: Ashton Scholastic.

Chouliaraki, L. (1998) Regulation in 'Progressivist' Pedagogic Discourse: individualized teacher-pupil talk, *Discourse and Society,* 9(1), pp. 5-32.

Cross, B. (2003) 'Watch Mi Eyes': the predicament of visual and scribal literacy choices, as explored with rural Jamaican adolescent boys, *Compare,* 33(1), pp. 65-83. http://dx.doi.org/10.1080/03057920302603

Dubose-Brunner, D. (1994) *Inquiry and Reflection: framing narrative practice in education.* Albany: State University of New York Press.

Edwards, D. & Mercer, N. (1987) *Common Knowledge: the development of understanding in the classroom.* London: Routledge.

Evans, H. (2001) *Inside Jamaican Schools.* Kingston: University of West Indies Press.

Eve, R. (1997) Afterword: so where are we now? A final word, in R. Eve, S. Horsfall & M.E. Lee (Eds), *Chaos, Complexity and Sociology: myths, models, and theories,* pp. 269-278. London: Sage.

Gee, J. (1994) Orality and Literacy: form the savage mind to ways with words, in J. Maybin (Ed.) *Language and Literacy in Social Practice.* Clevedon: Multilingual Matters/Open University Press.

Giroux, H. (1992) *Border Crossings: cultural works and the politics of education.* London: Routledge.

Glissant, E. (1997) *Poetics of Relation,* trans. B. Wing. Ann Arbor: University of Michigan Press.

Grossberg, L. (1994) Is Anybody Listening? Does Anybody Care?: on the 'State of Rock', in A. Ross & T. Rose (Eds) *Microphone Fiends: youth music and youth culture,* pp. 41-58. London: Routledge.

Henry, P. (2000) *Caliban's Reason: introducing Afro-Caribbean philosophy.* London: Routledge.

Lankshear, C. & Knobel, M. (2003) *New Literacies.* Buckingham: Open University Press.

Louisy, P. (2001) Globalisation and Comparative Education: a Caribbean perspective, *Comparative Education,* 37(4), pp. 425-438. http://dx.doi.org/10.1080/03050060120091238

Mac an Ghaill, M. (1994) *The Making of Men: masculinities, sexualities and schooling.* Buckingham: Open University Press.

McClure, D.J. (1980) *Why Scots Matters.* Edinburgh: Saltire Society.

McIver, A. (1983) *First Aid In English,* revised edn. Glasgow: Robert Gibson.

Ministry of Education and Culture, Jamaica (2000) Education: the way upward. A Green Paper for the Year 2000. Available at: http://www.educateja.ed.jm/Papers?Greenpaper2k.htm

Okri, B. (1997) *A Way of Being Free.* London: Phoenix.

Paulston, R. (1997) Mapping Visual Culture in Comparative Education Discourse, *Compare,* 27(2), pp. 117-152.

Rushkoff, D. (1996) *Children of Chaos.* London: HarperCollins.

Serpell, R. (1993) *The Significance of Schooling.* Cambridge: Cambridge University Press.

Beth Cross

Scots Pairlament Cross Pairty Group on the Scots Language (2003) Scots: a statement o principles. Available at: www.scottish.parliament.uk/msps/cpg/cpg-scots.html

Wertsch, J.V. & Smolka, A.L.B. (1993) Continuing the Dialogue: Vygotsky, Bakhtin, Lotman, in H. Daniels (Ed.) *Charting the Agenda: educational activity after Vygotsky*, pp. 69-92. London: Routledge.

WolframResearch (2003) http://mathworld.wolfram.com

CHAPTER ELEVEN

'In Fact I Can't Really Lose': Laure's struggle to become an academic writer in a British university

RICHARD KIELY
University of Bristol, United Kingdom

Introduction

This chapter explores the story of an undergraduate student in a British university becoming an academic writer. Laure, an undergraduate student from a French university spending a year in a British university as part of her degree, took an English for Academic Purposes (EAP) programme.[1] The chapter explores her narrative in order to better understand learning in this particular context. The analysis focuses on two aspects of Laure's learning experience:

- The social dimension of her participation in the programme; and
- Writing an assessed essay, the title of which had to be negotiated with the teacher.

The thesis of this chapter is that these two facets of Laure's learning experience help us understand key aspects of developing skills in EAP. They inform on social, collaborative learning on the one hand, and the more isolated experience of writing for assessment on the other. The use of interpretive research methodologies – ethnography and narrative – to explore these aspects of Laure's experience illustrates the discontinuities in the curricular experience, and the personal accounts of the researched and the researcher as they make sense of experiences and observations.

English for Academic Purposes

English for Academic Purposes programmes focus on learning in two ways. They can take a skills approach, developing in students an awareness of the genre and style of academic texts, and the linguistic and textual skills involved in producing these (Jordan, 2002). Alternatively, programmes can take a more critical perspective, focusing on meanings, positions and identities (Benesch, 2001). Although this approach does not marginalise the role of linguistic expression, it posits that the key elements of academic writing are the clarification of the message and the direction of the argument, which derive from the voice of the writer. Lea & Street (1998), looking at the development of such courses over time, outline three stages to the development of academic writing skills in higher education:

> 1. Study skills: a 'fix-it' approach to student deficit areas
> defined as atomised skills, and surface language features such
> as grammar and spelling.
> 2. Academic socialisation: acculturation of students into
> academic discourse, through a focus on orientation to learning
> and interpretation of learning tasks.
> 3. Academic literacies: student's negotiation of conflicting
> literacy practices, at the level of epistemologies and identities
> in institutions that are sites of and constituted in discourses
> and power. (Lea & Street, 1998, p. 172)

Approach 1 corresponds to the skills focus outlined above, whereas 2 and 3 represent variants on critical EAP. While *socialisation* assumes a value-free induction or apprenticeship, the *literacies* approach is more critical, investing more in the examination of power distribution in academic discourses. The three approaches, however, are not discrete or mutually exclusive:

> we would like to think that each model successfully
> encapsulates the other, so that the academic socialisation
> perspective takes account of study skills but includes them in
> the broader context of the acculturation processes ... and
> likewise the academic literacies approach encapsulates the
> academic socialisation model, building on the insights
> developed there as well as the study skills view. (Lea & Street,
> 1998, p. 158)

The EAP programme in this chapter represents such encapsulations: the programme as specified by the institution corresponds in many ways to Approach 1, the teacher's introduction in the first session emphasises Approach 2, and the activities in the classroom, and the particular perspective of the teacher on these, have the critical element of Approach 3 (Kiely, 2004). Laure's particular narrative of learning derives in large part from her navigation of these different strands of the programme. Because her learning experience is shaped by these different dynamics, the research orientation deriving from both ethnography and narrative methodology is particularly useful in understanding her experience.

I adopted an ethnographic approach to tell the story of this programme, which involved one three-hour class per week over twelve weeks. I wanted to document the complex weave of voices and events that shaped the programme, as well as identifying themes that linked classroom phenomena with the wider institutional programme management enterprise. The research strategy involved participant observation in all twelve sessions; collection of all teaching materials, handouts and programme documents, such as the course outline, guidelines for independent study, and details of assessment; and interviews with the teacher and the students. These ethnographic data, telling the story of the programme as a whole, also provide an opportunity for a narrative analysis of the learning experience of Laure, and a similar perspective on my own experience as a reflexive researcher. The next section explores the complementarity of ethnographic and narrative approaches.

Narratives in Ethnography

Ethnography in applied linguistics is a research tool to explore the cultures of communities of practice. This can involve a focus on small cultures (Holliday, 1999) and interactions in classrooms and workplaces (van Lier, 1988; Roberts et al, 1992; Toohey, 2000), as well as the linguistic and cultural practices of larger communities and groups (Heath, 1983; Canagarajah, 1999; Holliday, 2003). A key resource in ethnographic enquiry is the observed behaviour of and detailed information on this from individual informants: such accounts are analyzed to inform on the values and practices that have meaning in the researched community. Narrative enquiry builds on this same resource, although typically the sense-making focuses on understanding the chains of causation that frame the experience of the individual, rather than understanding this experience as part of a cultural phenomenon. Bell (2002) notes that ethnographers in language education, such as Heath, Canagarajah and Toohey, 'produce powerful narratives that have helped inform the understanding of language use' (p. 208). Bell (2002, pp. 209-210) outlines three contributions of narrative methodology to understand language learning, which are particularly resonant in this case:

1. In understanding experience, 'people's lives matter', 'not the outcomes', but the experience itself, 'the impact of the learning struggle'. In the analysis of Laure's experience, the social dimensions

of learning, and the struggle involved in her writing of the essay, provide a perspective not captured in the outcomes of the programme.

2. 'Narrative lets researchers get at information that people do not consciously know about themselves'. In this case, it provides an opportunity for Laure to reflect on her initial responses, and for me as researcher to examine the provenance and direction of my analytical process.

3. 'Narrative illuminates the temporal notion of experience', capturing 'shifting interpretations and changing notions' through the period of the research. In this case the scrutiny of the whole programme, and engagement with Laure throughout, provides an opportunity to engage with the complexities of language learning.

Laure

Laure was a student majoring in English and British Area Studies (Spanish was her minor subject), on exchange from her French university for one year. She was one of nine students on this particular programme; the other eight were international students, from business, health science and computing undergraduate programmes. As part of her languages programme, she was taking courses in Law and Economics as an introduction to the European context of language use. These courses required engagement with discourses in the social sciences in a British context, which contrasted with the arts and humanities focus of her language studies in the French university system. The focus of the English for Academic Purposes class resonated strongly with her sense of what she needed to achieve in her studies, and how these needs might be realised:

> *Laure*: I chose this course because ... academic writing is the
> most interesting to really improve my English, and what I
> really like in that module is that we will learn how to make a
> good essay, to learn the link words and how to illustrate and
> everything.
> *Int.*: The activities in the class yesterday, did you think they
> were appropriate for you?
> *Laure*: Yes, because as we are working in groups, it allows me
> to know the other students in the group, to exchange our ideas,
> to speak in English and to participate. Sometimes in a module,
> in Law for example, or in economics you only have to write,
> and in fact you stay alone during those classes, but in this kind
> of lecture you can meet other people. No, it was great.
> (Interview, Week 2)

These glimpses of Laure's thinking at an early stage of the programme show the importance for her of the two dimensions explored here: the social dimension of the programme, and essay writing.

The focus on Laure for this study has both conceptual and methodological rationales. First, she attended the programme regularly – for eleven out of twelve sessions – and found the learning activities broadly relevant. Thus, from the perspective of participation, she might be considered a student who would benefit from the programme. Secondly, she provided me with a volume of research data:

- classroom observation data, because she attended so regularly;
- recorded small-group discussion data;
- approximately six hours of interview data, including one hour of joint interview with Ina, her friend on the programme;
- a written self-evaluation and evaluation of the programme, which I requested after the formal evaluation event in Week 5.

Laure was a keen and enthusiastic interviewee, who felt she benefited from the experience. At the end of interviews I frequently asked her if she found it useful to talk to me about her learning on the programme, and her responses were consistently positive. She seemed to see the interviews as providing opportunities for learning in much the same way as programme input did. Her focus on the programme was on the process in the classroom, rather than any outcome which might be related to learning. These perceptions are especially evident in the first two interviews:

> *Int.*: Do you like talking about your learning? Is it useful for you to talk about the problems you have in your study?
> *Laure*: Yes. It helps me to further improve, not to do the same mistakes again. (Interview, Week 2)

> *Int.*: Have these interviews changed the way you see the course? This is the second time I am asking you about these activities. Has it changed the way you think about this module?
> *Laure*: No, I don't think so, because last week I told you that I like this module and this week it was the same, because I really love this text [on the ethnic conflicts in the Balkans]. I really like that we are speaking with some other students to speak with them about these ethnic problems. (Interview, Week 3)

Later, Laure is even more specific about the benefits of the interviews to the specific learning focus of the classroom activities:

> *Int.*: One last question, Laure, these interviews that I have with
> you during the module, are they helping you in any way with
> your academic English course?
> *Laure*: Yes, because of the effort to remember what we did in
> the class, so in fact, I can't really lose, I can't really forget it, so
> yes, it's OK. (Interview, Week 9)

> *Int.*: OK, one last question, then. Talking to me during this
> module, Laure, you have talked to me a number of times, have
> these interviews had any effect of your own perceptions of
> learning?
> *Laure*: Oh, I don't know, it is true that, for example when I was
> speaking with you, for example one topic, sometimes I didn't
> really pay any attention to these things, because I thought it
> was not important, and when you were underlining that to me,
> as you were speaking about that, then I paid attention to that,
> and perhaps I wanted to read the text a bit more, perhaps to
> know it a bit better, but I don't really know. (Interview,
> Week 12)

These excerpts from interviews illustrate, in addition to Laure's views of the programme, ways in which she contributed to the ethnographic and narratological orientation of the interviews: as I tried to probe certain aspects of her experience, she would talk fluently about this topic, or after touching on it fleetingly, would go on into other areas. She thus provided a rich account of her perspective on the programme, the values and cultural norms which informed this, and the ways in which she made sense of the learning challenges and her responses to them.

The Social Dimensions of Learning

Laure joined the programme in Week 2; she chose it as an 'option' module, after discussions with friends who had done it with the same teacher in the preceding semester. There are two dimensions to her rationale for this choice, which might be labelled product and process reasons, as are evident in her comments at the start of the first interview above. The product dimension of the rationale is evident in her interest in 'making a good essay', 'link words' and 'grammar', while the process element is represented by 'working in groups', 'knowing other students in the group', 'exchanging ideas, speaking in English' and 'participating'. The former is what she envisages taking from the programme, knowledge which can be consciously transferred to other study areas, while the latter connects with a more personal learning agenda: enhanced skills in English for communication purposes. Knowledge is associated with effort and hard work, traditional elements of study, while the skills element is associated with social, more enjoyable activities.

The social aspect of classroom activities overlaps with life beyond the classroom for Laure. Overseas students in universities are often socially isolated (Lewins, 1990; Ackers, 1997; Furnham, 1997), and see the programme and classroom as a key opportunity to make friends. Laure was strikingly enterprising here: in the previous semester she had become friends with Matti, a Spanish student (who attended the first session of the programme in question), and through her came to know the three male Mexican students on the module. She explains:

> *Laure*: For example, when you know people, sometimes you don't really know what to say but when you have them in your class, after that you can discuss about the lectures, you have many oral presentations and so on to do at home and you can do that two or three, and it gives us also conversation, but not a basic conversation about ... the weather or something like that, something more interesting.
> *Int.*: So you know the Mexican students ...
> *Laure*: Yes, you know, before I know them because my friend Matti is friends with them, but I only speak with them, 'How are you?', 'Are you fine?', 'That's OK'. But now that I am with them in the lectures we are speaking about the lectures and we are walking together and I think it helps us to have a better conversation. (Interview, Week 2)

The 'better conversation' included help with using email to stay in touch with friends in other universities (though she stated later that the Mexicans did not know much more about email than she did). She got to know Della, and invited her to her birthday party in Week 9 of the programme. She had a conversation with Annie on a bus. She advised Helen on cheap ways of getting to France for a weekend, and in turn received from Helen used telephone cards for her brother's collection. More than any other student interviewed, Laure tended to know classmates' names, and various details about them, such as their main study areas, and where they lived.

Bochner et al (1977), in a seminal study of overseas students' friendship patterns at the University of Hawaii, identified three social networks in overseas students' lives:

i) A primary monocultural network, consisting of close friendships with other sojourning compatriots;
ii) A secondary bi-cultural network consisting of bonds between the overseas student and significant host nationals such as academics, students, advisors and officials;
iii) A third multi-cultural network of friends and acquaintances, of which the main function is to provide companionship for recreational, and non-task oriented

activities. (Bochner et al, 1977, p. 292, cited in Furnham, 1997, p. 19)

Laure eschewed a reliance on the first type of network, on the grounds that she had not come to Britain to be with French people. However, as the programme developed, she became closer to both Helen and Arnie, the other French students. The bi-cultural network included her landlady, with whom she became very friendly, and possibly myself, but not the EAP teacher, of whom Laure always remained somewhat in awe. The multicultural network was particularly important for Laure: she had a natural affinity with Spanish-speaking students because of her Spanish studies and her interest in maintaining her fluency in that language. She also associated more easily with all the European students in the class than with the Asian students, whose English she found difficult to understand.

The social reality of the programme had an important status element for Laure: she rated herself against the students in the class whom she considered 'strong', using classroom activities and episodes to inform this social dimension of the programme. She categorised her vocabulary learning in terms of what she and strong students like Sue and Della did not know, and what she knew but Sue and Della did not (Kiely, 2001). For Laure, the learning activities and their relevance to her particular needs were realised socially in the classroom, as she worked out who was doing well and who was having problems, and how these phenomena located her on the classroom ladder.

The twin elements of the programme for Laure – process and product – represent separate discourses. The social process is tangible, lived experience, blending classroom activities with life beyond, prioritising communication and people over linguistic and academic competencies. The product is an aspirational state of knowing, of being able to write academic English, enthusiastically represented as about to be realised, but in reality remaining remote. The next section examines Laure's experience of one dimension of this product: writing an essay as part of the assessment for the programme. Both the nature of the task – writing – and the purpose – assessment – contributed to the isolating, monastic dimensions of Laure's experience.

Writing the Essay

As part of the coursework assessment on the programme, students had to negotiate a title with the teacher for an essay and a related oral presentation. This process is presented in Table I, which shows how Laure's experience did not follow the pattern of the majority of students. Laure provided a number of reasons for not following the pattern:

Laure: The problem is that my title is not really clear at the moment, in my head ...
I needed to leave at 12 o'clock, and I didn't have time to speak before ...
When it was my turn, I thought I will do it later ...
I am quite afraid that my essay will be perhaps too general ...
So I am not sure about what my topic will be ...
I prefer when the teacher give us a subject of an assessment.
(Interview, Week 6)

Week	Activity
1	Assessment tasks pointed out in the introduction to the module, with students referred to Module Guide for details
5	Teacher reminds students that titles must be negotiated by Week 6
6 (last session before two-week Easter break)	Teacher briefly negotiates essay titles with all students except Laure: Mat, Joe, Tigi, Jamie, Sona, Sara, Sue, Mari and Rata at the start of the session while students are arriving; and Helen, Sao, Niki, Arnie, Della and Ina during the break
7	During break teacher negotiates title with Laure and Annie (absent in Week 6)
8	Jamie gets extension; essay due (Friday)
11 and 12	Oral presentation based on essay

Table I. Schedule for coursework assessment.

In the following session (three weeks later because of the Easter break) she spoke to Anna, the teacher, and agreed on a topic and title. She explained in interview after this discussion:

Laure: I am doing something about education. In the introduction I will speak about the history of the education, for example, the Education Act, I will speak about the Education Act of 1944, about the budget of the state, about the percentage of children who come to the private school, and afterwards I speak about the education, the necessity to be educated, to find a job, and also for our own, to know something, to know foreign languages, to be literate, but my second part of it, there are some difficulties, so now I am blocked.
Int.: But you have negotiated a title with the teacher?

> *Laure*: Yes, yes, yes. First I wanted to speak about the
> education, the necessity to be educated, and about the
> education, and she told me that first it would be great perhaps
> to make differences between the education now and education
> in the past, to notice for example, she give me this example, in
> the past, in the farm, for example, the son used to have the
> farm, to exploit the farm as his father, but now, even if your
> father is a farmer, you have to go to a special school, to have a
> special diploma, to be able to do the accountancy, and to
> negotiate, and to know everything about the cultivation and
> everything, I tried also making arguments about that and for
> conserving the integrity of the education, but now, I'm
> blocked, of my second part, but I think that it will work,
> because, I wanted to, in my first part, to give all the arguments
> for education, and in the second part, against education, and I
> make also, a comparison with the education in France, in a
> short paragraph, but I have nearly a thousand words, and we
> have to write 1200 or 1500, so I think I will reach that for sure,
> but in the second part I don't have many arguments.

Laure describes here the type of iterative process many students
experience when working on an independent piece of work (Clark &
Ivanic, 1991). The concern about having enough to say to reach the word
limit is especially resonant. What becomes clear at the end is that she has
not quite agreed a title with Anna: she has spoken about education as a
topic, Anna has tried to focus this interest with a practical example, but
Laure is still struggling with how these disparate ideas – her own
thoughts, Anna's comments, and issues from the literature – might fit
together. She completes the essay on time, but is not happy with it:

> *Int.*: Tell me about your written assignment.
> *Laure*: Yes, I wrote something about education, and it was
> quite difficult in fact, I regretted in fact, that I took this subject,
> because it's so wide, and I wanted to speak about everything,
> but the problem that perhaps I spoke about too many things,
> perhaps she will be quite confused.
> *Int.*: Did you find in the activities and the guidelines you've
> had in the EAP module useful when you were writing this
> assignment?
> *Laure*: The problem is that I wrote my essay without any notes,
> only helping me with the books and the dictionary, that I
> wanted to put the definition of education, but yes, when I
> typed it, I took the piece of paper about the link words to
> change, to really make, for example, as an introduction, I will
> say, or we, I think I used we, we will say, and as a conclusion,
> to really make a difference between introduction, conclusion,

in the first part we will speak, firstly, secondly, or I said at first or at the beginning, and then I said moreover, and finally, and the same in the second part, I tried to organise my work, I tried, but I don't know if it is really, really good, because education is quite vast, and I wanted also to speak about, I spoke mainly about universities, but I also wanted to speak about nursery school and primary school, so I spoke quickly about that in the introduction, but then I did more my essay about education, but at the university. (Interview, Week 9)

Laure got a mark of 42% for her essay. She did better in the oral presentation – 56% – and brought her aggregate mark for the programme up to 56% by getting 63% in the examination.

This episode is telling in three ways. First, Laure did not succeed in developing the writing skills that were part of her motivation for taking the course. This seems to be due in part to a lack of articulation – a strategic link – between underlying knowledge and operational skills with regard to academic writing. At a deeper level, the social dimension of the programme and her learning, which she valued, were not transformative or developmental in terms of her academic voice, in shaping her academic identity, such that she felt at ease setting out a position and constructing arguments to clarify and defend it.

Secondly, when Laure was aware of a difficulty she seemed reluctant to engage with it openly. Her strategy for dealing with the problem was to avoid being labelled with it. She wanted to be seen by teacher and classmates alike as a successful student, and this socially-driven perspective proved ultimately the more important consideration for her.

Thirdly, Laure was not overwhelmed by the difficulties she has with the essay. She remained positive about the programme and the range of learning opportunities it offered her. Skills development approaches in EAP might see this as denial, and conclude that unless she is brought to confront the demons of her unfocused thinking, there can be no real progress. This, however, might leave her a depressed and alienated student who is not coping very well, as opposed to one who is bouncy in adversity. It is optimism for a purpose: the purpose of keeping her engaged, of sustaining her construction of a beneficial programme. She did not drop out, as some students do, and being one of those who got through gave her an opportunity to continue her studies and feel part of the university community: representational evidence of socialisation into an academic community, even if the substance was still not in place.

The story of Laure's learning on the programme illustrates the complexities of learning and serves as a reminder that programmes do not necessarily work for students as institutions and teachers assume. In the fields of programme design and evaluation, we need to be mindful of the diverse ways in which students make sense of the learning opportunities we provide, and the different routes to success. This is particularly important as programmes increasingly emphasise collaborative and social aspects of learning, while continuing to rely on traditional individual-oriented assessments. Teachers' tacit understanding of language learning and the effect of classroom activities derives in large part from familiarity with narratives such as Laure's (Woods, 1996; Borg, 2003). Although such knowing may be beneficial to practice, and contribute to a research agenda, it is important that there is careful assessment and validation of the epistemological and analytical processes underpinning the enquiry. The next section examines this issue in relation to narrative methodology and ethnography, both of which emphasise reflexivity and data analysis as researcher learning.

A Note on Analysis: ethnography and narrative

The narrative of learning presented here builds on two accounts, Laure's and mine. It is my own construction of Laure's experience that I wish to explore in this section. In piecing together this narrative from the multitude of references to Laure in the data, I am both a researcher with an ethnographic orientation, and a teacher who has an interest in evaluation as a sense-making activity. The reflexes of the teacher and the ethnographer are diametrically opposed in one respect: the teacher draws conclusions quickly and intuitively in real time, and although there may be subsequent reflection and accommodation of evidence that alters the initial view, the initial position often stands, and indeed becomes a filter through which later phenomena are perceived. My classroom notes record the first required individual performance by Laure in Week 3, when the teacher was asking students to comment on a text about ethnic problems in the former Soviet Union and former Yugoslavia.

> *Teacher:* I caught your eye.
> *Laure stands up and talks about the problem in Yugoslavia between Serbs and Muslims, and how it is now an issue thanks to the international community. She gets increasingly nervous and flustered.*
> *Teacher:* [helping out] What is the problem? What is the conflict about? [Addressing whole class] Later in writing that is what you will need to address, what you will need to analyze.
> *The teacher seems to shift from Laure, who is not getting anywhere, to a requirement for the whole group. Is this because she seems so flustered, not getting anywhere?*
> (Classroom notes, Week 3)

The teacher had selected the text for the specific purpose of getting students to take a fresh look at their own countries:

Teacher: ... one of the areas that was universal is the question of ethnic conflict, it occurred to me that everyone has some knowledge and experience of ethnic conflict in every country on earth so it is a suitable topic. Here was a quite thoughtful article related to real situations. (Interview with teacher, Week 4)

Laure did not see it like this: she commented on Bosnia rather than on her own country, France:

Int.: When you were speaking afterward, you did not speak about France?
Laure: No. Because I thought we could speak about any problem in the world, so I spoke about the ethnic problem in Yugoslavia ... but if I knew that I will speak about the suburbs in Paris, between Parisian people and the immigrants, that there are still some problems between them. Because in [name of town] where I live we don't have many problems, there are not many immigrant people there, so if there are some problems it is not really important in comparison with Paris. (Interview, Week 3)

Despite the activity not working out successfully for her in terms of the oral performance, or in relation to the teachers's planned objectives, Laure commented positively on the activity:

Laure: ... but here I found it quite interesting that people could express themselves and say their own point of view about that. I really like this module for that.
Int.: Did you find the teacher's comments helpful?
Laure: Yes. Because she tried to in fact to tell us that, we have to develop more our ideas, how to structure, for example, I don't remember what she said to me, but for example, for Helen she said she should organise her ideas to say, for example, the beginning of the problem, to explain the problem, and at the end to try to say conclusion and to give her point of view. That's the same with the Spanish girl, Sona, that she should organise more, to say each idea, not to mix everything, in fact.

My construction of this episode as a researcher derives in five ways from my teacher identity. First, I perceive Laure's performance – nervous and flustered – in a teacherly, judgemental way. Secondly, I account for the teacher's response to what I see as the breakdown in Laure's performance in a teaching frame – using the instance as an opportunity to make a point generally relevant to the class – what Bailey labels 'sharing the wealth' (1996, p. 24), while at the same time tactfully taking attention from Laure. Thirdly, I share the teacher's thinking on this kind of task, the pedagogic logic of getting students to read of one situation and relate to another situation with which they are familiar, a feature of this programme examined in detail in Kiely (2004). Thus, I note Laure's *not* talking about such problems in France as significant, and ask her about it in interview.

Fourthly, I assume that the episode is as salient for the teacher as it is for me, and that it represents a defining moment in how she sees Laure: as a 'weak' student who has a lot of learning to develop the kind of academic voice that is the goal of the programme. Fifthly, I hypothesise that Laure herself is aware that she has represented herself in this episode as a 'weak' student, but avoids a rerun of this part of the episode in the interview the following day by focusing on the teacher's feedback to other students. The data do not confirm these two last points: neither Laure nor the teacher explicitly support these hypotheses in interview. Key methodological principles in ethnography and narrative methodology, however, can provide support for the legitimacy of such inferences. One such principle in ethnography is reflexivity: the inclusion in analysis of the insight, perspective and assumptions of the researcher. Thus, I bring to the analysis my own sense of the significance of the interaction. Ethnography also develops understanding of communities of practice; the research into language classrooms points to such interactional decision-making (Bailey, 1996) or reflection-in-action (Schön, 1983; Wallace, 1991) as ways in which teachers manage the social and interpersonal demands of teaching.

Whereas ethnography emphasises understanding at cultural and communal levels, narrative enquiry provides a basis for sense-making as an individual, personal enterprise, and therefore using both offers possibilities for research in a multicultural context. Thus in the case of Laure, we can connect the classroom episode in Week 3 with her appreciation of the social dimensions of learning in this programme, her engagement with meaning rather than textual conventions, and her overarching positive orientation to learning, helping her to overcome difficult moments such as the oral presentation and the challenges of essay-writing. Her narrative allows us to connect evaluative accounts of separate tasks and activities in the programme, and understand how they construct the learning experience as a whole.

These methodological considerations are relevant to professional development for teachers, to language programme evaluation, and particularly to understanding social and interpersonal dimensions of learning in such programmes. The study of Laure's experience illustrates some of the complexities of learning strategies, perseverance, and development of identity within language learning programmes. Her narrative, as explored in this chapter, illustrates how, despite problems of pedagogic engagement, the programme was a success for her. There may be a kind of poetic justice in the struggle she has with the assessed essay, and the low mark she got for it: it shows the coherence of the programme construct, with its emphasis on academic literacies, rather than a set of discrete, mechanical moves. The main point of Laure's experience is that she stayed with it, continuously engaged in the process, even though on the surface it might be seen as not working for her. Her own words, *In fact I can't really lose,* proved ultimately as sound a truth as any other.

Note

[1] Laure, as with all names of people in this chapter, is not the actual name of the student.

References

Ackers, J. (1997) Evaluating UK Courses: the perspective of the overseas student, in D. McNamara & R. Harris (Eds) *Overseas Students in Higher Education,* pp. 107-200. London: Routledge.

Bailey, K.M. (1996) The Best Laid Plans, in K.M. Bailey & D. Nunan (Eds) *Voices from the Language Classroom,* pp. 15-40. Cambridge: Cambridge University Press.

Bell, J.S. (2002) Narrative Research in TESOL, *TESOL Quarterly,* 36, pp. 207-212.

Benesch, S. (2001) *Critical English for academic purposes: theory, politics, and practice.* Mahwah: Lawrence Erlbaum.

Bochner, S., McLeod, B. & Lin, A. (1977) Friendship Patterns in Overseas Students: a functional model, *International Journal of Psychology,* 12, pp. 277-299.

Borg, S. (2003) Teacher Cognition in Language Teaching: a review of research on what language teachers think, know, believe and do, *Language Teaching,* 36, pp. 81-109. http://dx.doi.org/10.1017/S0261444803001903

Canagarajah, A.S. (1999) *Resisting Linguistic Imperialism in English Teaching.* Oxford: Oxford University Press.

Clark, R. & Ivanic, R. (1991) Consciousness-Raising about the Writing Process, in C. James & P. Garnett (Eds) *Language Awareness in the Classroom,* pp. 168-185. Harlow: Longman.

Furnham, A. (1997) The Experience of Being an Overseas Student, in D. McNamara & R. Harris (Eds) *Overseas Students in Higher Education,* pp. 13-30. London: Routledge.

Heath, S.B. (1983) *Ways with Words: language, life and work in communities and classrooms.* Cambridge: Cambridge University Press.

Holliday, A. (1999) Small Cultures, *Applied Linguistics,* 20, pp. 237-264. http://dx.doi.org/10.1093/applin/20.2.237

Holliday, A. (2003) *Doing and Writing Qualitative Research.* London: Sage.

Jordan, R.R. (2002) The Growth of EAP in Britain, *Journal of English for Academic Purposes*, 1, pp. 69-78. http://dx.doi.org/10.1016/S1475-1585(02)00004-8

Kiely, R. (2001) Classroom Evaluation: values, interests and teacher development, *Language Teaching Research*, 5, pp. 241-261. http://dx.doi.org/10.1191/136216801680223434

Kiely, R. (2004) Learning to Critique in EAP, *Journal of English for Academic Purposes*, 3, pp. 211-227. http://dx.doi.org/10.1016/j.jeap.2003.11.004

Lea, M.R. & Street, B. (1998) Student Writing in Higher Education: an academic literacies approach, *Studies in Higher Education*, 23, pp. 157-172. http://dx.doi.org/10.1080/03075079812331380364

Lewins, H. (1990) Living Needs, in M. Kinnell (Ed.) *The Learning Experiences of Overseas Students*, pp. 82-106. Buckingham: Society for Research into Higher Education/Open University Press.

Roberts, C., Davies, E. & Jupp, T. (1992) *Language and Discrimination*. Harlow: Longman.

Schön, D.A. (1983) *The Reflective Practitioner*. Aldershot: Arena.

Toohey, K. (2000) *Learning English at School: identity, social relations, and classroom practice*. Clevedon: Multilingual Matters.

Van Lier, L. (1988) *The Classroom and the Language Learner*. Harlow: Longman.

Wallace, M.J. (1991) *Training Foreign Language Teachers*. Cambridge: Cambridge University Press.

Woods, D. (1996) *Teacher Cognition in Language Teaching*. Cambridge: Cambridge University Press.

CHAPTER TWELVE

A Part of the Landscape: the practitioner researcher as narrative inquirer in an international higher education community

SHEILA TRAHAR
University of Bristol, United Kingdom

Introduction

The Organisation for Economic Cooperation and Development suggests that the internationalisation of higher education is a response to the impact of globalisation, that 'internationalisation and globalisation are different but dynamically linked concepts' (OECD, 1999, p. 14). Indeed, Marginson & Mollis (2001) suggest that one characteristic of globalisation is a greater movement of people for study purposes, with the 'internationalisation' of higher education providing ideal opportunities for people to participate in an increasingly globalised world. Very little attention has been paid to how this greater movement of international students to the United Kingdom (UK) can 'internationalise' the experience of British students and staff, with no articulation of the ways in which a planned process of internationalisation might benefit higher education (Merrick, 2000).[1] If internationalisation 'is taken to mean that the curriculum, teaching staff, language of instruction, orientation of research or quality assurance arrangements have been changed specifically to expose the British student population which stays at home to an "international dimension"', then UK higher education has *not* been internationalised (Elliott, 1998, p. 38).

It is my experience that although there is much rhetoric about the benefits of internationalisation and its contribution to greater understanding of local cultures, there is very little research conducted into the complex, grass-roots experiences of students and staff in international higher education communities. International students are often spoken of and even defined as a homogeneous group, both in the policy documents of the institution and at a more local level in departments. It is difficult to conceive of another term; the use of this term is certainly preferable to 'overseas students' or 'foreign students', but what is more troubling is the assumption underlying its use, that international students are a homogeneous group when they are not. I am particularly concerned that internationalisation may be a 'cover for creeping Westernisation' (Merrick, 2000, p. xii) especially as, in my teaching and learning approach, I am striving to move away from 'teaching as assimilation ... a kind of colonial phase' (Biggs, 2003, p. 125), a practice that 'stresses adjustment to the dominant culture' (Ofori-Dankwa & Lane, 2000, p. 498). Such a practice denies and ignores the differences between people and between groups of people and allows the privileged groups to ignore their own group specificity.

I have written elsewhere (Trahar, 2002) of the discomfort I experienced when I first worked with groups of international students, illustrating how it contributed to the development of my PhD proposal. The dis-ease I felt then at involving myself in a form of cultural imperialism continues to unsettle me and provokes me to explore ways in which I might unwittingly continue to transfer my own attitudes and practices of teaching and learning, developed and grounded in particular Western cultures, to working with people who bring very different traditions and values. Issues of colonisation implicit in the 'transfer of skills and knowledge from the university sector to the broader community' when 'this broader community is in Asia, Africa or the Middle East' (Cadman, 2000, p. 476) echo Crossley's (1984, 2000) identification of the potential problems arising from the uncritical transfer of educational policies and innovations across international boundaries. Recognition of such issues calls for a greater respect for 'local' knowledge traditions that reflect the social and cultural diversity of modern higher education systems, together with a radical consideration of teaching, learning and assessment practices. This chapter draws on my experience as a practitioner researcher engaged in narrative inquiry to investigate experiences of the multicultural landscape of a UK university. I aim to show how narrative inquiry as methodology can address some of the complexities of engaging in cross-cultural research and in researching one's own practice, crystallising how my own ethnic and cultural background and my 'whiteness' are an intrinsic part of the research site.

Positioning the Research

Much of the research that *is* conducted into the experiences of students and staff in international higher education communities leans towards a comparison of one cultural group with another, usually the 'host' culture. There are very few studies that consider the complexities inherent in groups where the participants are drawn from several countries and cultures. In my own context, the learning groups may consist of students from countries that may be in conflict with each other, such as Taiwan and China; from former British colonies, such as Kenya, Uganda, Tanzania and the small states of the Caribbean; from the Middle East; and from other countries of the European Union, the USA and the UK. The layers that are added by such a range of cultural backgrounds in a group are rarely peeled back to expose the complexities. The 'students' are grouped together and defined as 'international' and 'home'; the former's perspectives and experiences may be called upon as valuable contributors to discussion, but their construction of their own identities as learners is rarely investigated. Even less common is any recognition of how the ethnicities and cultural affiliations of the 'home' students and staff construct their identities as learners and teachers. My research has emerged from my experiences as a white, British higher education practitioner, from recognition of my own dilemmas in navigating the complex landscape in which my students, colleagues and I are all participants. It is fuelled by a desire to advance theoretical understanding of the cross-cultural complexities encountered in higher education and to develop more culturally sensitive learning dialogues and approaches to teaching and learning, which focus on the exchange, reshaping and critical appreciation of the range of different knowledges and practices encountered.

Why Narrative Inquiry?

I am interested in what happens in my 'classroom', but I am also interested in the meaning of what happens for those of us involved in the 'events' and how that meaning is influenced by the ways in which we connect together past and present, self and other. Narrative research focuses on the qualitative experiences of the participants and the meanings given by them to those experiences. It also advocates 'pluralism, relativism and subjectivity' (Lieblich et al, 1998, p. 2). Narratives are '*social products* produced by people within the context of specific social, historical and cultural locations. They are *interpretative* devices, through which people *represent* themselves, both to themselves and others' (Lawler, 2002, p. 242, my emphasis); thus research that explores the narratives people produce will necessarily be *interpretivist* in nature, working from the premise that individuals and groups interpret the social world and their place within it. The question is less 'What happened?' than 'What is the significance of this event?'

> People make sense of what has happened and is happening to
> them by attempting to assemble or in some way to integrate

> these happenings within one or more narratives ... people are
> guided to act in certain ways, and not others, on the basis of
> the projections, expectations and memories derived from a
> multiplicity but ultimately linked repertoire of available
> social, public and cultural narratives. (Somers & Gibson, 1994,
> pp. 38-39)

It follows, then, that the way we all 'act' *in* and our 'projections and expectations' *of* this multicultural learning environment will be influenced by our 'memories' of learning in other contexts. As a practitioner researcher I was also 'persuaded that social science texts needed to construct a different relationship between researchers and subjects and between authors and readers ... the narrative text refuses the impulse to abstract and explain, stressing the journey over the destination' (Ellis & Bochner, 2000, pp. 744-745). I am already in a relationship with my participants; I was and am in the field, 'a member of the landscape ... in the midst' (Clandinin & Connelly, 2000, p. 63) navigating the personal, social and cultural dimensions of that landscape. I therefore offer personal accounts of my own experiences of being in a multicultural learning community, as a 'narrative inquirer', stressing the journey, as well as the accounts of the experiences of a number of postgraduate students.

I am aware that in focusing on the complexities engendered by the multicultural landscape of this community, I might be seen to be ignoring other complex differences between us. I am not neglecting those other differences, but it was cultural difference that so affected me in my early encounters with international students and so it is that curiosity that I have chosen to explore. In addition there is a dearth of work that examines the meaning of cultural difference in higher education in the UK, and the 'containment of cultural difference will persist ... unless we as practitioners are willing to engage in debate ... and challenge the whiteness [of the academy]' (Clegg et al, 2003, p. 166).

'Narratively Composed, Embodied in People, Expressed in Practice'[2]

> Narrative inquirers tend to begin with experience as lived and
> told stories ... Narrative inquiry characteristically begins with
> the researcher's autobiographically oriented narrative
> associated with the research puzzle (called by some the
> research problem or research question). (Clandinin &
> Connelly, 2000, p. 40)

The first story of this narrative inquiry is of an encounter with a group of international students one miserable night in November 1999; as my research progressed I made connections with my own learning stories associated with the research puzzle. I grew up in a town in the north of England in the 1950s. The cotton industry that had led to the town's development had long since declined, but it still bore the scars of the Industrial Revolution. One of my grandmothers was a mill-worker and I often muse on accidents of birth: had I been born some years earlier I too would have been a mill girl, but instead I was the first person in my family to go to a grammar school and on to higher education. I recall the social dislocation that I felt as a working-class girl at a grammar school. Those feelings of social dislocation remain with me today as I continue to feel an outsider, an impostor in the academic institution in which I am very much a part of the landscape, yet am not sure whether I fit or even whether I want to fit. Is it these feelings of being an outsider, an 'other' that attract me to those 'others' who come here and are themselves outsiders? Part of the research puzzle for me has been to explore and contest such positionings and identities.

Polkinghorne (1995) suggests that in the narrative story, causal linkage of events is often known only retrospectively in the context of the total episode. The significance and contribution of particular happenings and actions are not finally evident until its denouement. So in the context of the total episode (my research), the contribution of the stories and my understanding of them help me to understand the new episode (my experiences as a practitioner researcher in my current environment). I recognised some time ago that this story or stories may well not have a settled ending, a denouement that 'leaves the mind at rest' (Trinh, 1989, p. 142), and I am not sure of the beginnings of many of the stories. The journey, which is the process of the narrative inquiry, becomes inseparable from the gathering of the data. One of my family narratives is that as a child I was always writing stories. Mrs Jackson, my teacher, used to take these stories home to show to her husband. I cannot remember the content of those stories but I can remember the 'action', 'the 'happenings' and the 'significance' of them in my family and my subsequent lifelong love of stories, reading them, listening to them and now writing them again.

Methods and Narrative Inquiry

Stories or at least specific stories one can catch hold of like nuggets, though not unimportant, can play a relatively minor role as the narrative inquirer writes field notes about life in its broadest sense on the landscape. The narrative inquirer may note stories but more often records actions, doings and happenings, all of which are narrative expressions. (Clandinin & Connelly, 2000, p. 79)

The narrative inquirer may use a range of research methods, including the maintenance of a research diary recording actions, doings and happenings, students' own writing about their experiences, the involvement of observers in the classroom, sharing work in progress to explore other meanings and tape-recorded conversations. Clandinin & Connelly (2000, p. 91) suggest that 'lively conversations ... just happen'. I had an idealistic view about engaging in such naturally occurring conversations, but accepted that most of the time I was curious and my participants kindly reacted to that curiosity. I have been seeking to hear stories through conversations and have also been sharing the ways in which those stories resonate with me, using 'sameness and difference ... each to interrogate the other, constantly moving between them' (Marginson & Mollis, 2001, p. 588), striving to ensure that one knowledge or experience is not privileged over another. In many of the tape-recorded conversations I share information about learning experiences of my own, which I am reminded of by the participant's story. I invite perceptions on remembered incidents that I have noted in my journal, being curious about others' perceptions or how they experienced those moments. They, too, remembered these incidents, but it was I who did the recalling; it was rare for them to recall an incident and to invite me to reflect on it. 'Capturing the nuances of this living in field texts is complex and filled with ambiguity' (Clandinin & Connelly, 2000, p. 91); I *have* found the capturing of the nuances of this living in field texts complex and *have* experienced much ambiguity through that process.

> Field texts ... are not clearly differentiated from one another.
> Stories slip into autobiographical writing, autobiographical
> writing fades into journals and so forth. (Clandinin &
> Connelly, 2000, p. 116)

It is impossible to differentiate the so-called field texts from the narrative interviews, as they all merge together. I realised that I was 'analyzing' the conversations a year or more after they had taken place and after another year full of stories, including many informal conversations with colleagues and other students. I was aware from previous experience of the difficulties of working through qualitative data, but what I had not experienced before was my own constant interaction with it and my continuous memories of the relationships. My move from field texts to research texts is layered in complexity as I have not had one gathering of the field texts, one sorting through and analyzing them. I have come to realise the enormity of what I have gathered and so I return to them again and again, bringing my own storied life as the inquirer, new research puzzles and ways of re-searching the texts (Clandinin & Connelly, 2000, p. 133), finding different meanings each time.

Researching across Cultures

Researching across any 'difference' is 'messy work' (Gunaratnam, 2003, p. 79) and there can be an assumption that when conducting cross-cultural research the encounter is characterised by:

> Distance and estrangement between the researcher and the research participants which the researcher needs to overcome … The distance of difference needs to be closed or bridged by practices – be they methodological, linguistic and/or imaginative – that bring the researcher closer to the research participant and through this proximity can render the difference knowable. (Gunaratnam, 2003, p. 80)

As my research has developed I have been seeking to find ways of closing that methodological and linguistic distance, but there can then be a danger of implying that difference between individuals cannot be of value in examining and learning from research encounters (Gunaratnam, 2003). By problematising my own 'whiteness', that 'set of cultural practices that are usually unmarked and unnamed' (Frankenberg, 1993, p. 1), and forcing it 'to be displaced from its central unmarked and undefined position' (Watson & Scraton, 2001, p. 273), I am seeking to make transparent not only the problems but also the potential of such cross-cultural activity. hooks (1989) suggests that it is not that white researchers should not write about or attempt to know the experience of minority group students, but that their interpretation of that experience should not be taken to be the most authoritative. Minority group students have insights about and interpretations of their experiences that are likely to be different from those generated by white academics. By reflexively examining my own social and cultural location, not just that of those people whose experiences I am gathering, I am striving to ensure that my own voice does not become the most authoritative.

In seeking to make myself transparent through reflexivity, however, I risk making myself more central to the discourse, pushing other 'narrators' out to the edge. Reflexivity, although it positions itself as a way of uncovering and making visible the social and cultural positioning of researcher and participants, is not sufficient to understand all of the complexities of difference. Gunaratnam (2003) challenges the use of reflexivity to address white privilege in the research process, suggesting that its use can persist in reflecting the complexity of the processes of racialisation. Researchers across cultures cannot ever know the extent to which their understandings of their research participants may be any less partial or complete than their understandings of those participants who share their own cultural background, so we can only 'explicate the processes and positions we are aware of being caught up in. Some of the influences arising from aspects of social identity remain beyond the reflexive grasp' (Reay, 1996, p. 443).

Nonetheless, being brought up against my own whiteness through this reflexivity is a strong theme that permeates this research. I wanted to hear about my participants' background and how it might have influenced their current learning experiences, as well as how they experienced me as a white female British tutor, but in conversations with white British people we rarely discussed our own culture or the influences on learning that it might have had. I realise that at times I have assumed that because a participant is Chinese-speaking or black African that this is a reason for a position, a response and behaviour, whereas I did not make the same assumptions of my white British participants. I have therefore sought to confront my own whiteness through the inquiry, through the narrative analysis and through my unravelling of the epistemological and ontological assumptions underlying research methodologies.

Watson & Scraton (2001), in positioning themselves as white female researchers, share my dis-ease at the obfuscating way that many complex epistemological and methodological questions are presented, and share too my experience that these questions only 'come alive' (Watson & Scraton, 2001, p. 266) when explored through detailed research. Like me they recognise that there is a danger of difference being reinforced if it is only explored through the dynamics of the white researcher versus the black or 'other' respondent position. I now acknowledge that although I set out to achieve a greater understanding of difference, I did not ask the white people in my research about their whiteness or discuss the apparent similarity of our ethnicity. It was through listening to our conversations and reading the transcripts that I recognised how we were positioning ourselves in relation to the 'others', assuming similarity between ourselves and not at all interrogating our own whiteness. This questioning of my own whiteness began to occur in other places, such as everyday conversations with colleagues, friends and family, and has now become an unavoidable and intrinsic part of the inquiry.

Teaching and Learning Practices

It has been suggested that a weakness of much comparative education is its neglect of what is 'arguably the most important part of the educational terrain, the practice of teaching and learning, and what is *possibly the most elusive theme of all, how such practice relates to the context of culture, structure and policy in which it is embedded'* (Alexander, 2000, p. 3, my emphasis). Alexander uses this statement to support his proposition that 'neither culture nor language can be given the status of mere "factors" but must be handled as central and pervasive' (Alexander, 2000, p. 5). Once I started to consider how my own practice had developed, I reflected on the contexts within which I had been both learner and teacher and the cultural and social influences that had spawned the development of the philosophical and theoretical principles on which I claimed that my practice was based.

The experiential methods that I favour were, and still are, predominant in counselling training in the UK, in which I have been involved for a number of years. As I have moved into other areas of teaching with different student populations, I have remained attached to the view that it is through a more participative approach to learning, where their own needs are articulated and respected, that people experience learning as a much deeper and personal process, one that moves beyond the transmission of knowledge to the transformation of lives. Such approaches to teaching and learning are firmly grounded in Knowles' (1990) student-centred principles of adult learning, and owe much to Freire's (1972) politicising of education and his concept of teaching and learning as two internally related processes, and to Mezirow's (1991) notion of perspective transformation. I considered these to be sound principles, advocating that learning is most effective when each person feels valued and respected for the experience that she or he brings to the learning environment. Such perspectives are imbued, however, with an emphasis on psychological rather than social explanations for educational phenomena and behaviours (Pepin, 1998, cited by Malcolm & Zukas, 2001), privileging individual traits and styles and neglecting the learner as a social and cultural being.

The following are some illustrations of the ways in which I have used narrative inquiry to explore the meanings that a few of us in a multicultural higher education environment have attributed to our experiences.

A Story from Cheng-tsung: searching out and valuing complexity

Cheng-tsung is a Taiwanese man in his mid-thirties who left behind a wife and young son in Taiwan to come to the UK to study in 2002-2003. He wanted to be named so that others might read his stories and know about him. Within his Chinese culture this was a very courageous step to take. Cheng-tsung had decided to use his MEd dissertation to investigate how some Taiwanese students had experienced being learners in Bristol. His own learning experiences were to be very much a part of his narrative inquiry. During the summer of 2003 I had read Cheng-tsung's dissertation in draft form and been intensely affected by it: by the power of the writing, by the sadness of some of the stories, and also by the way in which he was emerging from the nightmares he described. He had given his permission for me to use any material from our conversations together, but I asked him if I could also use parts of his own writing. He said he was 'honoured' by this request. The following words are some of those that provoked particularly powerful responses in me:

> I still remember the first time I saw my personal tutor in class,
> a warm, mild and middle age white woman. As soon as I saw
> her, half of my uneasiness was cast away because I felt that she
> is the person I could communicate with. Her speed of
> speaking, the attitude of willing to understand and sincerity
> made me feel that *I could be myself*. I never expected that a
> learning experience could be so different. I like to be respected
> as a learner; I thought to myself that if I had been taught this
> way all along then what would have been different? It seemed
> not bad to me that the 'ground' impression was inspiring.

I have written Cheng-tsung's words exactly as he wrote them. Have I
chosen them because they seem to show me in a good light; because they
reveal how he has been able to use his experiences in an environment
that I have mediated to learn to be himself? I leave it to you to decide,
but in selecting those words and continuing to write about their
resonances for me, I find it hard not to retain my centrality.

I found it difficult to read the words 'mild, middle age white
woman'. I am white, I am a woman and I am middle-aged, but 'mild' was
not a word that I would use to describe myself. Because this word leapt
off the page as somehow not quite accurate from my perspective, I was
consumed by a need to understand the meaning that Cheng-tsung
attributed to it. We had had many conversations about the differences
between Mandarin and English and he had told me of his struggle to find
the 'right' English word to explain what he wanted to say. I asked Cheng-
tsung about his use of the word 'mild':

> *Cheng-tsung*: I use my own understanding. I don't know
> exactly the word mild means, meaning of mild for me is very
> gentle, I don't have to worry my pace, I don't have to adjust
> my pace to someone else's pace.
> *Sheila*: Pace of speaking?
> *Cheng-tsung*: Not really. I use the word 'channel'; we are in the
> same 'channel'.
> *Sheila*: So we're on the same wavelength – do you know that
> expression?
> *Cheng-tsung*: No.
> *Sheila*: It means, how can I best explain it? You know when
> you're listening to a radio and it starts to crackle if it's not on
> the right station, the right wavelength? So, we have this
> expression that if two people think in similar ways, we say
> that they are on the same wavelength.
> *Cheng-tsung*: Yes, that's what I feel, there's no crackle. I'm a
> mild person. The wavelengths are the same.

Writing this now I feel acutely aware of how dismissive I am of another
word that he uses, the word 'channel'. In a similar way to not wanting to

accept 'mild' as one of his definitions of me, I seem to want to coerce him into using a word, 'wavelength', that I have chosen. In these few lines of our conversation I seem to be colonising his use of language and, although another reading might be that we are both grappling with understanding the other, it is I who question his use of particular words, assuming that unless we use the same word we might not understand each other.

Our conversation then focuses briefly on his use of the word 'white':

> *Sheila*: Right. Cos when I read it was a very interesting ... it
> was really interesting for me to read it.
> *Cheng-tsung*: Why? [laughter]
> Sheila: Well because you know it's very interesting to read a
> description of yourself written ... particularly when you say
> 'white'. I mean you know of course I *am* white ...
> *Cheng-tsung*: Okay.
> *Sheila*: ... but to see it ... and in the context of the kind of
> research I'm trying to do. You know there is ... I talked to you
> about this before ... there's a lot of stuff written about whether
> it's possible or ethical to do research with people you know
> from different cultural backgrounds, particularly being white.

The conversation moves away from my focus on being white. I do not pursue this with him and so I lose an opportunity to explore how he and I experience my whiteness. I regret losing that opportunity but my relationship with Cheng-tsung continues, even though he has returned to Taiwan. This continuing relationship will enable me to ask him about this, my whiteness that has now become so visible, and is an example of how stories that I have gathered slip into autobiographical writing (Clandinin & Connelly, 2000).

In my conversations with Cheng-tsung, as with my other research participants, I have striven to use a dialogic style so that when knowledge and experience are not shared we grapple with the differences. I am also aware that I can listen to the recorded conversations and can feel great warmth towards Cheng-tsung in hearing his voice and marvelling at how similar our sense of humour is, and smugly congratulate myself how as we become closer he becomes much braver and more critical of his experiences in the UK. I can claim that because of my counselling background I have an ability to empathise with him. Empathy, criticised as 'romantic illusion' by Gunaratnam (2003, p. 102), is one of the Rogerian (Rogers, 1951) core conditions of humanistic philosophy, and is further contested by Caruth & Keenan (1995) when they suggest, 'Empathy is about sameness ... Something is not confronted there, when you think you're understanding or empathising in a certain way' (Caruth & Keenan, 1995, pp. 264-269). For me empathy is not about sameness: it is about striving to see another's world in the way that they themselves see it. This does not mean that I understand or know it, rather that through trying to see their perspective I am more able to question my own.

> Rather than ... erase the complexities of difference and powered relations in the interview, there is much to be achieved by distrusting any neatness, and actively searching out and valuing the complexity and richness that comes with the mess. (Gunaratnam, 2003, p. 104)

In the earlier example the conversation was triggered by my curiosity about Cheng-tsung's use of certain words. One of my readings of that conversation now is that I was colonising his use of language, perhaps seeking neatness. Yet, for him, being 'mild' was a similarity between us. In that conversation we uncovered a connection and as a result I was better able to understand how he had positioned me. This process of 'uncovering and discovering' could be interpreted as a 'getting closer to' position, but connection is:

> not based on a merging with or swallowing up of difference through imposed and contrived versions of commonality ... In this sense points of connection in the research interaction are not assumed to be pre-established and guaranteed by levelling commonalities of 'race', ethnicity, religion and/or language; rather connection is worked for, with and through difference – even when apparent points of commonality are present. (Gunaratnam, 2003, p. 102)

In spite of my apparent desire for a 'levelling commonality of language' there are several resonances with each other and we explore these resonances. Such exploration occasionally leads Cheng-tsung and me to connection. We are not becoming the same but we are pursuing and making connections. Such a process is important if we are to understand another's experience, or at least understand it sufficiently to move forward in the quest to peel back some of the layers in this multicultural environment. I believe that Cheng-tsung and I are finding points of alignment and orientation between us as part of the research encounter. I am actively searching out and valuing the complexity and have come to distrust the apparent neatness of my conversations with those of similar ethnic and cultural backgrounds, recognising now that those conversations are just as complex and in many ways more complex because of the apparently similar backgrounds.

Some Stories from Philippa and Rebecca

Two participants in my research who have apparently similar backgrounds to me are Philippa and Rebecca, both white and British. I have included, with their permission, extracts from their stories in this chapter for several reasons. First, 'there is hardly any mention in the literature of the significance of local students' attitudes and behaviours on inter-cultural contact' (Volet & Ang, 1998, p. 8) Secondly, in listening to my conversations with Philippa I often hear both of us refer to the 'others' with very little questioning of how we came to hold 'our' perspectives, and thus with no distrust of our apparent neatness. Finally, Rebecca's perspectives are included because I identify her retelling of her rather negative experiences as one of the points at which I began to reflect on and make more visible my own whiteness.

I met Philippa when she joined the course I was teaching, Guidance and Counselling in Education, a course that runs for twenty weeks. Philippa is a British student who is studying part-time for her MEd. In her early forties, Philippa describes herself as being of mixed heritage, a reference to her Spanish ancestry. The following is a part of a conversation where she recalls how she felt at the first meeting of the course:

> *Philippa*: And their reaction was ... it was almost like saying well they're just importing people to get the funding. And I thought 'Oh well you know that attitude really undermines the value and the sort of status. By holding that attitude, by that opinion, what you're saying is "Well it's a no good course and they're having to import lots of people to make up the funding".' And I sort of thought about that and thought 'No no no, I don't think that's the reason at all'. And as the course has unfolded it's just been really valuable. Because we've had a real cultural mix, haven't we ... I think it was a course in which a massive amount of learning went on for everybody. I think there was a widening of horizons generally. Or that's the feeling I got, that it wasn't just me that was having revelations [laughter]. I think for a lot of people it was really making us sit down and look at the sort of fundamentals that we adopt and look at them in relation to different cultures.
>
> *Sheila*: So through the relationships that you made with people in the group, those relationships sort of extended outside of the sessions, you've made a real shift or you know started to kind of change your own thinking about some things?
>
> *Philippa*: Yes, I think what I've done is I've revisited places that I've been in the past when I was younger and didn't have any responsibilities or commitments, when I had a more

ideological lifestyle. Through my contact with people and things that we've discussed ... not just the people, the actual content of the course, things that we've discussed, issues that we've addressed ... it sort of made me realise that I can actually regain those and develop them.

In my many conversations with Philippa and through our relationship, I came to learn that she was a challenge to the stereotype of the home student, reluctant to move from her or his comfort zone to make successful relationships with international students (Volet & Ang, 1998; Wright & Lander, 2003).

In contrast to Philippa, Rebecca had a very different experience. Rebecca is also in her early forties, white and British. She came to see me in the middle of the first term of Guidance and Counselling in Education to express a number of concerns. Her main one was that there were too many 'international students' and that she felt less challenged by the course than she had anticipated. Rebecca enjoyed writing and so we agreed that keeping a journal to note down her reflections each week would be a way of participating in my research and be valuable for her in understanding her reactions, which were uncomfortable for her. The following is an extract from her own writing, in which she shares some of this discomfort:

I was concerned that my reaction might also be racist. For this reason I made mince pies for the last session before Christmas. This was a kind of atonement. I know that I often use food in this way (particularly with my stepchildren) to atone for behaviour of which I am not proud. I also deliberately chose a kind of food which was emblematic of Britishness as I worried that the foreign students would think that my unwelcoming behaviour was typical of British people in general.

Language Is Never Innocent

Some of the difficulties in communication between those who speak English as their first language and those for whom it is an additional language are well-known and recorded in the literature (e.g. Wright & Lander, 2003). English as additional language speakers claim that the former speak too quickly and use jargon, making them feel excluded from conversations, while those who have English as their first language can feel that they have to use a particular vocabulary and spend too much time explaining technical terms. One of the participants in Hellsten & Prescott's (2004) study, when asked how she felt in the classroom, responded that she was spoken to in the diminutive voice. Many narratives that I have collected support this statement. Wan Yi, from Taiwan, recognised that those students whose first language was

English were trying to help her by waiting for her to reply. She felt that they assumed this was putting added pressure on her and so would move quickly on to the next point for discussion. She found this experience diminishing. Mei, another student from Taiwan, commented, 'They assume that Chinese people don't have opinions.' The way that such students spoke English was also very important to Rebecca, and in one of my conversations with her after the course had ended we turned to talking about the first meeting of the group in October 2003:

> *Rebecca*: I think it was a combination of the fact that as they weren't native English speakers I didn't feel that they would be confident enough I suppose to ... I don't know, confident to take part? ... I suppose partly I was overawed by the fact that they could do that course in a language that wasn't their own, but how ... I suppose the other thing was that they wouldn't have any of the kinds of idioms or ... that lack of a common language in a sense.
> *Sheila*: So you would have to be careful about the kinds of words that you used?
> *Rebecca*: Yes.

The following is an extract from her writing where she recalls the earlier part of the course:

> As the course went on, I found myself becoming more impatient. One point early on in the course stands out as influencing my attitude. We were discussing Freud, and I realised that some of the non-native speakers were unable to pronounce the name correctly, pronouncing the letter 'r' as an 'l'. This flicked a switch in my brain. I was brought up in the Midlands [an English region], but my father was fanatical about what he perceived as 'proper' English and drummed out of my speech the slightest hint of a regional accent until he was happy with my neutral, sub-received pronunciation speech ... All this meant that the moment I heard one of the non-home students say 'Floyd' rather than 'Freud' I was lost. I think that my reaction was a combination of two things. Firstly, my childhood-imbued intolerance of 'wrong' pronunciation. Secondly, a process of completely specious reasoning that went something like this 'If they can't even pronounce Freud's name properly, how are they going to be able to grasp the concept of psychodynamic therapy?' Intellectually I know that these reactions are utterly indefensible. They did, however, affect the way I perceived the group ... There was a sense in which my frustrations at being part of the group were like material for these stories [told to friends and family about her experiences of the course]. The

> danger, of which I was very conscious, was that I then started
> to perceive the stories as reality, which then informed my
> actions in the group.

This extract from Rebecca's writing provoked a number of responses in me. I was disappointed to learn of her negative feelings towards some of the students because the way that they spoke English differed from the way she spoke it herself. Her reaction led her to make assumptions about their intellectual capacity to grapple with the theoretical concepts that were being explored. These assumptions of Rebecca's cause me to reflect on the extent to which 'language barriers are often constructed in our minds ... as social barriers which are then used to define cultural differences' (Watson & Scraton, 2001, p. 270). Reading Rebecca's words in the light of my commentary on the extracts from my conversations with Cheng-tsung earlier in this chapter, I now speculate on whether I was seeking to overcome a language barrier in *my* mind (his use of the word 'mild') rather than accepting his use of that word as his way of speaking English.

Continuing to follow this train of thought, to what extent did Rebecca make judgments about my intellect based on my way of pronouncing English with a regional accent? Was this a language barrier used to define social and cultural difference between two people who shared the same first language? Finally, I was embarrassed that what I experienced as a rich learning community had become the source of stories that she told to amuse her friends and family.

Another extract from Rebecca's writing signals further frustration with one of my teaching and learning practices:

> I did in fact find the reading for the course and the process of
> assignment writing very stimulating but the weekly meetings
> quickly became frustrating. A major source of frustration was
> the time that we had to spend at the beginning of each session
> going over that week's reading.

My experiences of working in an international learning community and of hearing stories of how this community is experienced by students have led to my making a number of changes to my teaching and learning practice. For example, the majority of students value my encouragement of their work together in groups on set tasks outside the sessions. Such activities have lessened the feelings of homesickness to which many of them are very understandably prone (Volet & Ang, 1998), and also enable them to feel sufficiently prepared for the following session and more confident to express opinions. I have learned that providing students with questions to accompany prescribed readings can help them to identify the salient points, make links between concepts and feel more confident to participate in discussion. Such activities were frustrating for Rebecca, who experienced them as a rather tedious 'going over that week's reading'. I acknowledge that frustration, but as a practitioner I need to balance her frustration with my own desire to facilitate an environment that is inclusive and cognisant of diverse values and where discriminatory behaviour is not acceptable.

In other conversations with Rebecca she told me about some of the difficulties in her life, which had perhaps contributed to her own stated resistance to being in such a diverse group. Hearing of these personal difficulties reminded me that as a tutor I can never be completely aware of the 'expectations, projections and memories' (Somers & Gibson, 1994, pp. 38-39) that people bring into the learning context. I can only seek to uncover some of the meanings, remembering their influence on the 'ultimately linked repertoire of available social, public and cultural narratives' (Somers & Gibson, 1994) that is the landscape of a higher education learning community.

Conclusion

The dialogue emerging from this narrative inquiry is becoming embedded in my teaching, learning and assessment approaches. My research grew out of my experiences as a practitioner, and the process of being in the midst of my research raises questions for my practice. Taking those questions into my practice leads to other research puzzles that I seek to explore; truly an iterative process. I have become aware of the importance of recognising the experiences that international students bring with them and ways in which I can learn from them. I believe that I have a responsibility to bring about climates within which all people feel that they want to make relationships with each other, learn from each other and be explicit about the complexities that we all encounter in an international learning community. Being a part of this landscape of different cultural backgrounds, educational experiences, views of knowledge and academic traditions, I am coming to believe that it is only through dialogue about difference and similarity that we can learn from and about each other. Some people may need to be encouraged and supported to engage in this dialogue, but without it we miss valuable opportunities, not only for learning about others, but for learning about ourselves, crucial dimensions of comparative and international research in education. Storying research through narrative inquiry offers such opportunities.

Note

[1] Throughout this chapter the term 'international students' is used to refer to those students from outside the UK and the term 'home students' to those resident in the UK. These terms are not intended as signifiers of homogeneous groups; I have merely used them for ease of description.

[2] Clandinin & Connelly, 2000, p. 124.

References

Alexander, R. (2000) *Culture and Pedagogy: international comparisons in primary education.* Oxford: Blackwell.

Biggs, J. (2003) *Teaching for Quality Learning at University,* 2nd edn. Buckingham: Society for Research into Higher Education/Open University Press.

Cadman, K. (2000) 'Voices in the Air': evaluations of the learning experiences of international postgraduates and their supervisors, *Teaching in Higher Education,* 5, pp. 475-491.

Caruth, C. & Keenan, T. (1995) The Aids Crisis Is Not Over: a conversation with Gregg Borodowitz, Douglas Crimp and Laura Insky, in C. Caruth (Ed.) *Trauma: explorations in memory.* Baltimore: Johns Hopkins University Press.

Clandinin, D.J. & Connelly, F.M. (2000) *Narrative Inquiry: experience and story in qualitative research.* San Francisco: Jossey-Bass.

Clegg, S., Parr, S. & Wan, S. (2003) Racialising Discourses in Higher Education, *Teaching in Higher Education,* 8, pp. 155-168. http://dx.doi.org/10.1080/1356251032000052410

Crossley, M. (1984) Strategies for Curriculum Change and the Question of International Transfer, *Journal of Curriculum Studies,* 16, pp. 75-88.

Crossley, M. (2000) Bridging Cultures and Traditions in the Reconceptualisation of Comparative and International Education, *Comparative Education,* 36, pp. 319-332.

Elliott, D. (1998) Internationalizing British Higher Education: policy perspectives, in P. Scott (Ed.) *The Globalization of Higher Education.* Buckingham: Society for Research into Higher Education/Open University Press.

Ellis, C. & Bochner, A. (2000) Autoethnography, Personal Narrative, Reflexivity: researcher as subject, in N. Denzin & Y. Lincoln (Eds) *Handbook of Qualitative Research,* 2nd edn. Thousand Oaks: Sage.

Frankenberg, R. (1993) *White Women, Race Matters: the social construction of white women.* London: Routledge.

Freire, P. (1972) *Pedagogy of the Oppressed.* Harmondsworth: Penguin.

Gunaratnam, Y. (2003) *Researching 'Race' and Ethnicity.* London: Sage.

Hellsten, M. & Prescott, A. (2004) Learning at University: the international student experience, *International Education Journal,* 5, pp. 344-351.

hooks, b. (1989) *Talking Back: thinking feminist, thinking black.* Boston: South End.

Knowles, M. (1990) *The Adult Learner: a neglected species,* 4th edn. London: Gulf.

Lawler, S. (2002) Narrative in Social Research, in T. May (Ed.) *Qualitative Research in Action*. London: Sage.

Lieblich, A., Tuval-Mashiach, R. & Zilber, T. (1998) *Narrative Research: reading, analysis and interpretation*. Thousand Oaks, CA: Sage.

Malcolm, J. & Zukas, M. (2001) Bridging Pedagogic Gaps: conceptual discontinuities in higher education, *Teaching in Higher Education*, 6, pp. 33-32. http://dx.doi.org/10.1080/13562510020029581

Marginson, S. & Mollis, M. (2001) 'The Door Opens and the Tiger Leaps': theories and reflexivities of comparative education for a global millennium, *Comparative Education Review*, 45, pp. 581-615. http://dx.doi.org/10.1086/447693

Merrick, B. (2000) Foreword, in B. Hudson & M.J. Todd (Eds) *Internationalising the Curriculum in Higher Education: reflecting on practice*. Sheffield: Sheffield Hallam University Press.

Mezirow, J. (1991) *Transformative Dimensions of Adult Learning*. San Francisco: Jossey-Bass.

Ofori-Dankwa, J. & Lane, R.W. (2000) Four Approaches to Cultural Diversity: implications for teaching at institutions of higher education, *Teaching in Higher Education*, 5, pp. 493-499.

Organisation for Economic Co-operation and Development (OECD) (1999) *Quality and Internationalisation in Higher Education*. Paris: OECD.

Polkinghorne, D.E. (1995) Narrative configuration in qualitative analysis, in J.A. Hatch & R. Wisniewski (Eds) *Life History and Narrative*. London: Falmer.

Reay, D. (1996) Dealing with Difficult Difference: reflexivity and social class in feminist research, *Feminism and Psychology*, 6, pp. 443-456

Rogers, C. (1951) *Client-centered Therapy*. Boston: Houghton Mifflin.

Somers, M.R. & Gibson, G.D. (1994) Reclaiming the Epistemological 'Other': narrative and the social construction of identity, in C. Calhoun (Ed.) *Social Theory and the Politics of Identity*. Cambridge, MA: Blackwell.

Trahar, S. (2002) Towards Cultural Synergy in Higher Education. Paper presented at the Second Symposium on Teaching and Learning in Higher Education, National University of Singapore.

Trinh, T.M. (1989) *Woman, Native, Other: writing postcoloniality and feminism*. Bloomington: Indiana University Press.

Volet, S.E. & Ang, G. (1998) Culturally Mixed Groups on International Campuses: an opportunity for inter-cultural learning, *Higher Education Research & Development*, 17, pp. 5-23.

Watson, B. & Scraton, S. (2001) Confronting Whiteness? Researching the Leisure Lives of South Asian Mothers, *Journal of Gender Studies*, 10, pp. 265-276. http://dx.doi.org/10.1080/09589230120086476

Wright, S. & Lander, D. (2003) Collaborative Group Interactions of Students from Two Ethnic Backgrounds, *Higher Education Research and Development*, 22, pp. 237-252. http://dx.doi.org/10.1080/0729436032000145121

CHAPTER THIRTEEN

Learning from Elsewhere: ethical issues in a planned piece of narrative research in New Zealand

SUE WEBB
Massey University, New Zealand

Introduction

This chapter is based around some research I am planning. Normally when researchers write about ethics, they do so with hindsight, profiting from the numerous benefits that accompany this. However, this is not how ethical dilemmas are actually lived and nor is it the point at which researchers need to grapple with discerning and addressing ethical issues in their work. Hindsight accounts are useful, in that they offer the benefit of experiential learning to other researchers, but they cannot represent the imagined experience of what is to come. Nor do they tend to describe the reality of opening attempts to predict and manage ethical issues, or the often messy and emotional experience of grappling with these in conjunction with other issues, such as cross-cultural dimensions, as they arise in the course of the research.

As counsellor, counsellor trainer, counselling supervisor, professional association ethics committee member, health consumer, eager participant in other people's investigations and member of the general public, some of my experiences outside my own research activity are relevant to this project and inevitably inform my stance as researcher as I begin. In counselling empathy is a highly valued quality, richly discussed. Empathy plays an important part in research ethics too, in that it can enable the researcher to put herself or himself 'as if' in the skin of the other, in order to ensure that participants' interests are predicted as far as possible, and appropriately attended to. These are essential components in comparative and international research, as other chapters in this book indicate.

Sue Webb

My past experience as a researcher and research supervisor is also highly relevant. Unfortunately in the field of ethics, the best learning appears to come from mistakes either made or only narrowly avoided. For the most part these are not envisaged in the planning stages, but once encountered are unlikely to be forgotten in subsequent research activity.

Making Friends with Ethics

If research activity tends to operate within something of a context of induced paranoia, addressing its ethical aspects risks being an extreme example of this. 'Ethics' can appear a frightening topic, somehow belonging to experts and not linked, as it should be, to everyday relationships and commonsense care for the welfare of others (Selwyn, 2002). Given that narrative research, more than most approaches, requires on-the-spot decision-making between participants and researcher, a strong sense of ongoing responsibility and the competency to put it into practice are vital.

My aim, therefore, is to provide an account of the envisaging of possible ethical dilemmas, with a view to providing an untidier, unfinished and less certain account, in the hope that this will provide more opportunity for reader identification and imaginings. It also requires me, as researcher, to put myself out there for scrutiny, a reflexive feature of narrative research itself.

First I shall write about the context and intended content of my research, before addressing the various ethical dilemmas I have thought about so far. Throughout, I intend to position myself in this story as researcher, research participant, supervisor of research and teacher, with a focus on my personal experience of ethics. An ethics of responsibility must draw on experiences in these other roles.

My Research Task

My aim is to examine the counselling process. As a counsellor trainer, counsellor and feminist, I am interested in how a woman counsellor and woman client construct themselves and each other through the time of their engagement and how these 'selves', as found in the texts of their sessions together and their accounts of these afterwards, change over time. To this end I wish to use video recordings of the counselling sessions, diaries kept by participants during the counselling and email interviews with each participant after counselling has concluded.

Is This Really What You Want to Read About?

After agreeing to write this chapter, I was concerned about whether what I was intending to do was actually 'narrative' research. I suspect it is

222

quite common, at the outset of a research task, to be unsure about precisely how to name the approach one is taking. Added to this were worries about how my perspective might contribute to the comparative nature of the book and also its focus on education.

The question of what sort of research this is highlights an important ethical dilemma. Ethical issues have to be envisaged and addressed at a time when the research design itself may be fluid, a situation common to much qualitative research (Birch et al, 2002). Qualitative research tends to be about exploring rather than defining, to want to take into account participant perspectives as it develops and to engage actively in relationships that will shape the research process. It tends to shift in the doing. This means that ethical management needs to be an ongoing process, rather than mainly an early stage linked to the development of design.

This highlights the importance of Bond's perspective (2004) that it is trust, rather than informed consent, that sits at the centre of ethical research practice, just as it does at the centre of the counselling process. The relationship between participants and researcher is given primacy in narrative research, rather than the processes used in the research that have been agreed upon at the beginning. Clearly participants being as well-informed as possible before the research begins, and being kept informed as it develops, are important aspects of the trusting relationship, but not the only component.

As a research participant I was involved in a colleague's study of a small group of counselling trainers. Individual interviews were followed by focus group discussions of some of the key topics. Some of the more significant discussions moved into areas that risked causing considerable tensions to ongoing professional relationships. Checking, correcting and adding to transcripts proved a time-consuming process, beyond what I had envisaged. The research took a different turn in the later stages and I think the transcripts were never used. I was left with some disappointment and a sense of waste. Ethically, while I benefited professionally from the discussions we had, the task to which I thought I had given my time did not come to fruition. More involvement, as a participant, in the process of the research, and information about the changing focus, would have left me less hurt.

Counselling has a long history of arguing for its close relationship with education (see Rogers, 1980, for example), either as valuable adjunct or key site of learning. In many countries, including New Zealand, counselling training programmes sit within schools and faculties of education and maintain close links with teacher training and education consultancy and research. However, the dilemmas in research with humans relate not to the discipline within which the research operates but to its processes.

A comparative perspective seems to demand the identification of engaging differences. As a former colony with a defining treaty dating from the mid-nineteenth century between settlers and indigenous Maori, a pioneering history in welfare provision, an unusual number of women in positions of political power and, of course, a beautiful landscape, New Zealand is often seen as a little crucible for experimentation and a model of innovation and can-do resourcefulness. However, its research traditions are firmly allied to those of Europe, in particular the United Kingdom, and North America; moreover, the 'global village's' academic inhabitants communicate – and travel – extensively. Any excitement may prove to be more about sameness than difference, an element I also notice in Bond & Mifsud's chapter in this volume. The colonial legacy, however, brings anxiety about having anything useful to add and a fear of being 'behind the times'. From an ethical standpoint, my fears are a mixed blessing. They may make me appropriately cautious in my preparations; they may also lead me to preoccupation with some matters, to the detriment of others of potential ethical importance.

I remember discussing at a seminar overseas a video I had just shown of some counselling work in New Zealand. To some of those present New Zealand was a far-away place with a special position on bi-cultural relations and particular expertise in the use of Narrative Therapy. My video was of two well-educated white middle-class women, one of them using a Gestalt approach in working with the other. It would have been tempting, but not honest, to try to present my interests in a way that profited from New Zealand's glowing reputation in other areas.

Taking Culture into Account

New Zealand's attention to bi-culturalism, however, does bring a useful perspective. Cultural awareness, sensitivity and respect underpin all aspects of ethical functioning in research. Culture means more, however, than ethnicity, and is multifaceted and multilayered. I am defined by being a Pakeha (a white European New Zealander), but also by my educational background, profession, gender, sexual orientation, provincial town residency, post-war birth, religious affiliation and family memberships. Each of these, with varying degrees of importance, plays a part in my perceptions of self and my ways of relating to others. The interplay of my cultural affiliations is forever shifting according to context. At different times power relations will alter, according to which cultural identifications are most evident. I weave a tapestry of cultural difference and similarity with each participant, of which I need to be reflexively aware. Problems that are well-known and documented in relation to cross-cultural (usually meaning cross-ethnic) research (Cram, 1997) exist to some extent in all research. Difference may lead to insensitivity to needs, disrespect, misunderstanding and, at its worst, cultural abuse. Similarity may create false illusions of shared perspective, which may persuade participants to make themselves unduly vulnerable. It may also blind the researcher to key aspects in the field of study.

A research student undertook a study about a particular cultural minority of which she was a member. Her membership gave her access to volatile information confided in her by the participants. When they were shown a draft paper from her study and read what they had said in the context of the literature and the student's own perspective, they were incensed, demanded that large portions of the interview data be removed and threatened legal action if any of the study were ever published.

How is one to address this? It is helpful to be aware of one's own cultural affiliations, and how that mix is working for and against the research, to take into account the cultural expectations of participants and to pay attention to power relationships, regardless of a sense of closeness and identification with participants.

Doing 'Good' Research

The obligation to undertake 'good' research is often a neglected area in considerations of ethics. By good research, I mean research that is useful; in this case, relevant to the work of counsellors; of sufficient import to be worth participants contributing; and trustworthy (David & Sutton, 2004) in providing readers with something they can understand and set in the context of their own experience. Such matters are addressed within the positivist paradigm by considerations of reliability and validity, as well as the research being situated as a significant and logical development in a field of knowledge. Qualitative methods originally struggled with attempting to create systems for asserting their own versions of reliability and validity. However, more recently the underlying principles of trustworthiness, relevance and honesty have proven more useful.

Getting Permission

Institutional procedures, such as applications to ethics committees, risk working against an understanding of the organic nature of the narrative process, given that the exploratory nature of such work tends to lead to a fluid research design (Pugsley & Welland, 2002). Ethics committees often set an agenda that requires all procedures to be 'tied down' and documented before the research ever begins. The risk is also that the researcher, having treated the committee as an obstacle to be hurdled, then regards ethical issues as largely resolved, with no need to address them again as necessary.

On the other hand, committees can provide useful templates of consent forms and information sheets, checklists of things to address and an outsider's weather eye on process, not hindered either by intimate involvement in the task or by a passionate, and at times blinkered, interest in the topic. At their best such committees can provide ongoing mentoring that draws on multiple experiences of other research, a clearing-house for solutions to problems new to the individual researcher and a connection to other researchers with similar issues.

Politics and Accountabilities

Linked to ethics vetting procedures are the problems to be found in getting permission from organisations where narrative approaches to research may not be well understood and there may be vested interests in other types of research. These may include funding sources, research sites and approval bodies. Often these groups express their concerns in terms of ethics, in particular focusing on the ethical importance of doing 'good research' (Crano & Brewer, 2002), enabling them to take the research design to task. At times the politics of competing disciplines may intervene.

As a member of a multidisciplinary working party on guidelines for the treatment of a mental illness, I experienced powerful elements in the group arguing to dismiss all research that did not include large samples and control groups, thus excluding small-scale qualitative studies. There remained a preponderance of medical studies of prescription drugs to guide our deliberations. From an ethical standpoint, this potentially severely limited the final guidelines and patient access to a variety of sources of assistance.

A Double Focus for Ethics

A problem I have is how to manage two sets of agendas, the counselling itself and the research relationships, if their needs come into conflict. This applies to any research that considers a process or a relationship that has its own purpose and accompanying ethics. Counselling and teaching both work within professional codes, which must be taken into account if they are to be studied. Both counselling and qualitative research methodologies have struggled with attempting to introduce equality between parties in a relationship that is essentially unequal. Clients, learners and research participants cannot easily gauge the value or appropriateness of their engagement, but must rely on the fiduciary responsibility of the counsellor, teacher or researcher. So the researcher must 'take care of' the research participants, the research relationship and the activity that the participants are engaged in (Edwards & Mauthner, 2002). In my case, the needs of the counselling must come before those of the research.

Co-construction

Narrative research tells stories and stories are co-constructed (May, 1997), whether in counselling, education or research. My task therefore involves a layering of co-construction. There are, in the beginning, the stories that a client envisages telling a counsellor, based in part upon the ways in which the client has already construed, elsewhere, the events about which he or she wishes to speak. Then there are the stories that are actually shared in counselling, which take into account the counsellor's influence upon the construction. This is in turn influenced by the stories, of theory or professional practice for example, that the counsellor brings to the relationship. Next there are the stories each of them tells me, as researcher, about the counselling afterwards. Finally there are the stories that I produce, based on my perceptions of these other stories and linked as best I can to the accounts in the literature that appear to have relevance to my stories. This is complex and it leads to an ethical need to pay attention to the accurate representation and naming of different voices in the stories, and an awareness of where power differences may give some stories precedence over others. This is not exclusive to counselling research; the same co-construction issues occur at each stage of communicating during a research process and is a key awareness in feminist approaches (Edwards & Mauthner, 2002).

My experience of academic writing gives me an awareness of how hard I can find it to do justice to what others have said, and conversely how hard it can be to maintain my own voice through this. The final story needs to be clearly mine, but also transparent in its use of other people's stories along the way. A further requirement is that the final product be accessible – and acceptable – to the reading audience.

I have in mind numerous experiences of trying to help research students use quotations from interview data in ways that create elegant sentences, while leaving it clear where words come from. Trials with fonts, italics, indents, different sides of the page, struggles with sentence structures that aim to incorporate their words and ours ... Sometimes there is a startled realisation that what is now on the page bears little relation to what happened in the interview. Words flow and relate in complicated cross-referencing ways to each other.

The answer is to keep up the struggle to find ways to represent matters accurately while making it easy for the reader to follow the sense. To be avoided are 'cute' approaches, which may distract, and complexity, which can mislead.

Co-researchers

Co-construction goes hand in hand with changes in how participants are perceived, owing much, according to Punch (1994), to the influence of feminist research approaches. Those once known as 'subjects', a depersonalising and distancing term that implies passive and minimally informed contributions, have become 'participants', who have an active, more informed role, and then 'co-researchers' (May, 1997), which stresses both the importance of the relationship and the acknowledgement of expertise. With this changed positioning of those engaging with researchers come changed ethical responsibilities. The research needs to make sense to all involved, it has to have some evident usefulness to them, even if the main beneficiary will be the eventual readership, and everyone needs thorough information through all stages of the process.

I appear in Kim Etherington's chapter earlier in this book. I enjoyed the process of the two interviews. Partly it was the anticipated pleasure of another stimulating talk, partly the enjoyment of Kim's company. Most of all, however, it was the sense that the interview process furthered and clarified my thinking in a way that benefited my own development as a researcher. A key contribution to this was the extent to which Kim shared her own ideas and experiences in the interview. In more traditional research frameworks this would have been regarded as undue influence upon the data. Instead it served to challenge and deepen my initial responses, while conveying a strong sense of empathy and respect.

The Influence of Research on the Process

Research cannot help but have an impact on the process it studies (May, 1997). This has methodological implications; how useful can the findings be, for example, given the artificiality of this particular working relationship? More worrisome, however, are the potential ethical difficulties. What if the two participants are unable to set aside, as they work together, the awareness that sessions are being videoed for research purposes? Will each feel able to withdraw part of the way through, if the research feels intrusive? What if the client finds herself delving into areas of her life she never expected to disclose when she agreed to the research? Might the two be unaware that the research is negatively affecting their work together? Might the client only agree to participate because she imagines the counsellor wants her to? What shall I do as researcher if I experience the counsellor as functioning unethically? These concerns could equally relate to teaching process research.

Although there are strategies for alleviating risk in relation to all of the above, the core protection is the quality of the relationships between all the parties involved and the commitment to open communication throughout. Counselling codes in recent years have advocated the founding of ethical functioning on virtues such as trustworthiness, honesty and respect (see, for example, the ethical framework of the British Association for Counselling and Psychotherapy, 2002, and that of the New Zealand Association of Counsellors, 2002). Within the research, these must underpin both the strategies developed in the initial stage for addressing possible dilemmas and the ongoing revisiting of these.

To counter the negative perspective above, I should also stress that involvement offers participants an opportunity to explore their experience in a different way and to have a detailed record of its progress that may be useful long after the work is finished. Overall the focus needs to be on responsibility. Although participants may need some protection in relation to aspects of the research they do not know about or have not fully understood the implications of, responsibility sets up a respectful alliance between the parties engaged in the research.

The Research Triangle

A further dynamic is that the research 'system' contains several subsystems or relationships. All possible combinations of relationship need to be considered from an ethical perspective. Three-way relationships can become problematic in that they tend towards the creation of pairs, with an externalised third.

As already indicated, the needs of the process, in my case the counsellor/client relationship, should take precedence over any research relationships. Because I, as researcher, am also a counsellor, there is a risk that we counsellors together do not perceive the needs of the client. Similarly, I may respond to the client from the role of counsellor, when I am in fact the researcher, thus intruding on the real counselling relationship. The counsellor and client might together experience the research as uncomfortable and without realising it, behave in ways that hinder my progress. These sorts of difficulties are less likely to arise if parameters are carefully set at the beginning (Berg, 2004), discussed fully with all parties and participants encouraged to voice any concerns as these arise. In addition, good clinical supervision as well as research supervision may provide an outside eye on the processes.

The Effect of Relationship

My focus is to look for discourses within the counselling sessions, diaries and email interviews. In thinking about these sources of data it is important that I keep in mind that all narratives are designed to communicate and thus take into account likely observers, listeners and readers, not just those present at the time. No researcher can be 'outside' the relationship that shapes the narrative, however unknown they may be to the participant. Ethically this requires a responsibility in terms of relationship with the text and an awareness that one is present to the speaker or writer, even if unknown. It also requires a constant monitoring of what influence the researcher's presence has had upon the construction of the text.

As a participant in some social policy research about couples' finances, I was surprised to discover I did not like the person I appeared as, in the transcript. The researchers were feminist sociologists and I may have intended to display my financial independence, know-how and determination not to be taken advantage of. In print my account looked selfish, calculating, middle-class and mean. I felt ashamed but said nothing, leaving the transcript unchanged. I never asked to see the final research report, nor could I face checking if I was identifiable. How might this have been different? Perhaps more discussion of the transcript would have enabled me to express my reaction. Sensitivity to my non-verbal behaviour could have helped, as could a question about my emotional response to the transcript, and to the interview itself.

Interpretation

One of the key dilemmas in my research is to take into account the feelings and views of participants about whatever interpretive stance I take in relation to their narratives. Discourse analysis is interested in what is not explicit and explores this in terms of power relations. Such interpretation presents problems for feminist research, which values equal relations (Weatherall et al, 2002). 'Interpretation' also occupies a conflicted place in the culture of counselling, which is now wary of its tendency to label, often negatively, to silence and to undermine. However, from a narrative perspective, every response by one party to another's disclosure of self brings with it a perspective on the speaker's story, the co-construction in action. Interpretation can be helpful in enabling a story to be seen in a new way, but risks hurt if it imposes a storyline that is unwanted or negative. Power relations are inevitable and implicit in counselling, learning and researching relationships, regardless of approach. 'Interpretation' therefore is unavoidable, but needs to be managed with care and sensitivity.

A woman in one of the earliest pieces of research I undertook, on anorexia, was interested in women's mental health and well-read. However, she seemed oddly reluctant to receive any feedback about the overall findings of the project or the sense I had made of her experience. With hindsight, she was probably fearful of hurt if she saw her story shaped in terms of the anorexia literature of the period. She may also not have wanted to be reminded of her experiences yet again.

Changing the Context of the Words

When stories are collected in one form, such as audiotaped interviews, and handed back in another, such as written transcripts, the changed medium, as well as the re-engagement, can be a shock. Most participants are taken aback to discover how their speech reads. Grammar can seem chaotic and ideas often less clearly expressed than they remember. Tact in the handling of transcript material is helpful, as indicated before. Participants often seem to want to rush or even ignore the transcript process; the emotional resonance is no longer there, time is short and aspects of the experience embarrassing. Busy researchers may be tempted to acquiesce; a wiser and more ethical approach is to encourage more discussion.

A further shock can occur when segments of what was said are placed in relation to other text, for example, information from other participants, from the literature or from the researcher's own perspective (Cohen et al, 2000). While it may be illuminating to encounter one's personal story in another way, it is risky and not the actual purpose of research. Because participants may have been quite unaware this might happen, it needs care, trustworthiness and a careful monitoring that what one writes is respectful (Johnson et al, 2001).

Being Recognised

The nature of narrative research, the detailed exposition of people's stories, challenges traditional notions of how to keep the identity of participants confidential (Berg, 2004; David & Sutton, 2004). Participants' uniqueness, explored in rich detail, sits at the centre of the research task. Protection from recognition can never be guaranteed when phrases and sentences are used directly from the data collected, where individuals' opinions are reported or where a series of pieces of information are used at different points but clearly relate to the same participant. Unfortunately it is often the most interesting, vivid and useful data that is most likely to identify the participant.

Whatever the size of the communities in which we reside, we play out our lives in a series of small villages: work settings, leisure pursuits, social groups, learning situations, professional activities. In New Zealand this is particularly obvious; just three or four pieces of information about a school can narrow it down to a mere handful of possibilities. The geographical location of the researcher provides an extra clue. It is important for participants as part of the informed consent process to be aware that recognition may be likely by those who know them well, and that they have a chance to revisit later the decisions they have made about what to share and how. In delicate circumstances a final view of what will actually be used and in what context may be necessary. Decisions need to include discussion of the various risks, without expecting participants to discern these for themselves.

The notion of the co-constructing expert may lead narrative researchers to see the problem of recognition as somewhat irrelevant. Participants may indeed be proud to be recognised; however, this needs approaching with caution. Identification of one person may lead to others being identified. These others may not have given permission and may be harmed by being recognised. From the perspective of individual rights it might seem acceptable to take no responsibility for those not directly involved, but a more communal sense of responsibility would include the needs of these people too.

A woman participating in a narrative study on sexual abuse was keen to be named in the research and to use her abuser's name too. She saw this as part of her own healing process by challenging the abuser's original secrecy. The abuser was dead and there appeared to be no obvious legal risk to her. However, the man had children and grandchildren. After considerable discussion of the conflicting needs and rights, and of how the data would actually be presented, we did not use either name. The woman instead chose names that had special significance to her and went some way toward meeting her need.

Sometimes some participants want to be named or recognised and others do not. This poses particular problems if these people form a cohort where identification of some will automatically make it easier to identify others too. The needs of the whole group should be taken into account, with special attention to those with less power (Cohen et al, 2000).

A student interviewed families, each of which had a child with a particular learning difficulty. A parent in each family sat on a national lobbying committee, so families were well-known to each other, as well as to others within the same network. A number of the adults, but not all, were keen to be named, seeing this as contributing to their political task. In one family, all members wanted to be named, except for the child with the difficulty. In the end no real names were used, but families were made aware of the ways in which they would be able to recognise each other and adjusted their transcripts accordingly. Each family was shown a copy of the final report before it was submitted, with the option to withdraw any of their data that they did not want included. We remained anxious about whether the confidentiality needs of the children had been adequately addressed.

A third recognition problem occurs when a group process, for example a classroom interaction, a support group or a counselling relationship, is researched using individual narratives. Participants may speak about each other in ways that could risk causing hurt, if disclosed, and which may harm the continuing process. Some participants may not be concerned about this and others may not be aware of how what they have said might be received by others, or used by the researcher. The commitment not to do harm to the participants or the context under study requires the researcher to think very carefully about what may be used and how, by relating it to each of the individuals or situations that might be affected and by checking back with participants.

Getting Blinkered by Excitement

In the process of collecting information and beginning to work out how to use it, it is easy for excitement to blind the researcher to ethical difficulties that may be emerging. At times research can seem a lonely and turgid task. It can also be frightening when nothing interesting or useful seems to be emerging. Those heady moments, when at last something novel leaps out, have a special risk to them. Away from participants it may be hard to keep their vulnerabilities in mind, with the desire to make use of what has emerged blinding the researcher to its ramifications. Strategies to address design issues that were carefully managed earlier become ignored in the heat of the moment.

Any changes to design need careful rethinking and discussion, taking into account the interests of participants. I find imagined conversations, as well as real ones, may help to regain empathy. Reflecting on my own feelings, needs and interests may also clarify what I am doing.

During a difficult piece of research, a student and I became excited about an interview disclosure hinting at a problematic issue. It related to boundary mismanagement, a particular interest in the research. With a lamentable lack of awareness as to how we were mirroring boundary problems, we decided the student should seek more information. In the event none could be used as it went well beyond the informed consent given; several participants took fright and removed themselves from the study altogether; and the student was left with some severed relationships in his professional network.

Facing Up to Hypocrisy

The process of communicating in depth and at length with participants creates a bond. This can lead to the disclosure of information or attitudes that, in other circumstances, participants would not choose to share. Communication is specific to the situation; speakers do not monitor what they say according to what might be done with it, but on their sense of the relationship they are in, in the moment.

Researchers set about establishing good relationships with participants in order to collect rich and interesting data for their research (Smith & Wincup, 2002), but participants share information because they like the person in front of them, relish the chance to express something that is often not listened to and trust the listener to see it from their point of view. They certainly do not have in mind the readers who might eventually access their words, even if able to gauge who these might be.

To a certain extent the hypocrisy created is unavoidable, linking back to the layers of cultural affiliation discussed earlier. The best chance to address this is to monitor it throughout the research process. To feel uncomfortable about what I have heard or how I can use it means I need to unpack what is troubling me. The checking and revising of transcripts provides an opportunity for rethinking, with participants having delicate information drawn to their attention.

Messy and Emotional

Although ethics committee approval processes and examples in books often convey the impression that ethics is merely a matter of careful right-mindedness and sound logic, the lived experience (Cohen et al, 2000) is more likely to feel messy, terrifying and/or infuriating at times. Seeing the right thing to do and then accepting it is not straightforward. Sometimes it takes a while to realise there is an ethical dilemma at all. A participant who suddenly wishes to withdraw, a piece of key information that cannot be used, a sudden realisation that the identity of a participant may have been exposed, a conflict of interest between one participant's needs and another's: these are developments that can lead to much misery and loss of sleep. Participants and the narratives they have provided are especially precious because of the richness, depth, detail and sheer hard work involved. The very nature of narrative research makes the stories personal and exposing, the participants' rights complex and therefore the management in the field of ethical matters more fraught.

A colleague was begged by a potential participant to conduct a research interview about her school. From their brief conversation it was clear that this person's story of her school's attitudes would be ideal to include. The school principal, whose permission was required and who was only too aware of what she might say, refused to allow participation. The teacher was distraught, having seen the research as a chance to voice her difficulties, experience a sense of community and make a useful contribution to a field she cared about. Despite the researcher's sympathy for the teacher's situation and the temptations of her excellent information, the teacher could not be included and was hurt and angry. The researcher continued to meet the teacher in professional development contexts, where the teacher's exclusion from the research had been discussed but not well understood.

To address these sorts of difficulties it is important to notice discomfort, dwell upon it and discuss it with others. The emotional experience deserves to be acknowledged and addressed, in order to respond ethically. The careful processes often needed to unpick difficulties can only occur if emotions are not still clamouring for attention. Talking with colleagues, supervisors and mentors can help with this. I also use a 'support group' in my head, of right-minded people with varying perspectives and roles, whose ethical acumen I admire. In this way I can step outside my own preoccupations and observe dilemmas from a range of standpoints.

Utu

Utu is a Maori word meaning restitution; the returning of what is due. The concept can provide a useful lens on the responsibilities of researchers to participants. Briefly, it links with honour, is fundamental to the reciprocity of social relations and historically could be significant in a group's survival. Often translated as 'revenge', it is in fact much broader. Providing something in response to what you have been given maintains status. Giving is done freely in the knowledge that an appropriate return will occur when the time is right. The value of the gift is related to the extent of the giver's sacrifice. *Utu* links people together not just for the present, but over generations; it is the glue of interpersonal relations.

In research there is a tendency for participants, usually portrayed as having less status than their researchers, to give but to receive little in return. Narrative research demands much of participants, far more than the completing of a questionnaire, for example. In return more must be given back. Part of this is in the gift to the future, the need for the research to have some purpose that relates to others like the participant, but there also must be a benefit for the actual participant. The experience of the event may be valuable (White, 2002), with its value enhanced by gifts that celebrate the contribution, for example a copy of the research, a bound transcript, photographs or a video. Participants' expressed needs must also be addressed.

Interviewing a mother and daughter together as part of my anorexia research, it became clear that the daughter was in need of therapeutic help. She had revealed more in the interview than her mother had expected and the latter wanted me to do some counselling, since I now seemed to have her daughter's trust. I could not do this, but I could talk through with them both what was needed, check the possibilities and make initial contact with the service they selected.

A beautifully bound small study of a New Zealand-based Pacific Island community was delivered to the university by the student who had undertaken the study, accompanied by representatives of the community. The study was handed over in a formal ceremony, with both sides making speeches accompanied by songs. A morning tea also honoured their contribution.

Informing and Consenting

I have intentionally left informed consent until last. It is of course thought about first, included in applications to ethics committees and developed as part of the initial proposal. While it certainly belongs there and needs planning with great care at that stage, in fact it operates as a thread through everything I have written about. Keeping participants informed about what is happening as it develops, and ensuring that they are in agreement, are processes that sit alongside the importance of connection and trustworthiness. Attention to this must be accompanied by a careful analysis of how power relations may be influencing participants' understanding and choices (Pugsley, 2002) and an awareness of how perceptions of the researcher may influence their decisions (Welland, 2002).

Conclusion

In summary, how do I bring all this to bear on my own research? Relationship, connection with self and others and trustworthiness should sit at the centre of my activities. Ethical functioning is lived, not just planned, and is based upon principles to apply rather than rules to adhere to. Being ethically mindful is necessary throughout. I need to affirm and promote the healing and confirming aspects of people's stories, while being open to their likely responses to other perspectives on what they have told me. I should not rely on my own judgement alone but make good use of the views of others too, through supervision and consultation, formal and informal. If I can recognise the familiarity of difficult situations as these arise, I can apply lessons from elsewhere. I want to be open and flexible to the needs of others, honouring the gifts they provide. I have a responsibility to share my narrative as researcher, in order to set participants' narratives in context.

The qualities needed for all this are humility, openness to seeking and receiving feedback, transparency, self-awareness, sense of perspective, sensitivity to others' needs, a sense of humour and patience. Finally, the traditional Rogerian core conditions for the counselling relationship, empathy, respect and genuineness, are as central to the narrative research endeavour as they are to counselling itself.

In the many 'villages' in which our narrative studies are situated, we all need to attend to ongoing connection and membership, the inevitable multiplicity and layering of relationships and the ways in which actions in one quarter have an inevitable impact on others. Reciprocity over time maintains relationships and responsibility for each other forms the currency of village life.

References

Berg, B. (2004) *Qualitative Research Methods for the Social Sciences*, 5th edn. Boston: Pearson.

Birch, M., Miller, T., Mauthner, M. & Jessop, J. (2002) Introduction, in M. Mauthner, M. Birch, J. Jessop & T. Miller (Eds) *Ethics in Qualitative Research*, pp. 1-13. London: Sage.

Bond, T. (2004) *Ethical Guidelines for Researching Counselling and Psychotherapy*. Rugby: British Association for Counselling and Psychotherapy.

British Association for Counselling and Psychotherapy (2002) *Ethical Framework for Good Practice in Counselling and Psychotherapy*. Rugby: British Association for Counselling and Psychotherapy.

Cohen, L., Manion, L. & Morrison, K. (2000) *Research Methods in Education*, 5th edn. London: RoutledgeFalmer.

Cram, F. (1997) Developing Partnerships in Research: Pakeha researchers and Maori research. *Sites: a journal for radical perspectives on culture*, 35, pp. 44-63.

Crano, W. & Brewer, M. (2002) *Principles and Methods of Social Research*, 2nd edn. Mahwah: Lawrence Erlbaum Associates.

David, M. & Sutton, C. (2004) *Social Research: the basics*. London: Sage.

Edwards, R., & Mauthner, M. (2002) Ethics and Feminist Research: theory and practice, in M. Mauthner, M. Birch, J. Jessop & T. Miller (Eds) *Ethics in Qualitative Research*, pp. 14-31. London: Sage.

Johnson, J., Joslyn, R. & Reynolds, H. (2001) *Political Science Research Methods*, 4th edn. Washington: CQ Press.

May, T. (1997) *Social Research: issues, methods and process*, 2nd edn. Buckingham: Open University Press.

New Zealand Association of Counsellors (2002) Code of Ethics, in *Handbook of the New Zealand Association of Counsellors.* Hamilton: New Zealand Association of Counsellors.

Pugsley, L. (2002) Putting Your Oar In: moulding, muddling or meddling? in T. Welland & L. Pugsley (Eds) *Ethical Dilemmas in Qualitative Research*, pp. 19-31. Aldershot: Ashgate.

Pugsley, L., & Welland, T. (2002) Introduction, in T. Welland & L. Pugsley (Eds) *Ethical Dilemmas in Qualitative Research*, pp. 1-3. Aldershot: Ashgate.

Punch, M. (1994) Politics and Ethics in Qualitative Research, in N. Denzin & Y. Lincoln (Eds) *Handbook of Qualitative Research.* Thousand Oaks: Sage.

Rogers, C.R. (1980) *A Way of Being.* Boston: Houghton Mifflin.

Selwyn, N. (2002) Telling Tales on Technology: the ethical dilemmas of critically researching educational computing, in T. Welland & L. Pugsley (Eds) *Ethical Dilemmas in Qualitative Research*, pp. 42-56. Aldershot: Ashgate.

Smith, C. & Wincup, E. (2002) Reflections on Fieldwork in Criminal Justice Institutions, in T. Welland & L. Pugsley (Eds) *Ethical Dilemmas in Qualitative Research*, pp. 108-120. Aldershot: Ashgate.

Weatherall, A., Gavey, N. & Potts, A. (2002) So Whose Words Are They Anyway? *Feminism and Psychology*, 12(4), pp. 531-539. http://dx.doi.org/10.1177/0959353502012004012

Welland, T. (2002) Research and the 'Fate of Idealism': ethical tales and ethnography in a theological college, in T. Welland & L. Pugsley (Eds) *Ethical Dilemmas in Qualitative Research*, pp. 135-148. Aldershot: Ashgate.

White, P. (2002) They Told Me I Couldn't Do That: ethical issues of intervention in careers education and guidance, in T. Welland & L. Pugsley (Eds) *Ethical Dilemmas in Qualitative Research*, pp. 32-41. Aldershot: Ashgate.

CHAPTER FOURTEEN

Narrative Conversation between Cultures: a novel approach to addressing an ethical concern

TIM BOND
University of Bristol, United Kingdom
DIONE MIFSUD
University of Malta, Malta

Introduction

Comparative studies between dissimilar cultures pose many ethical and technical challenges, and the study featured in this chapter was no exception. The task we set ourselves was to communicate and examine each other's lived experience of our respective national cultures in order to inform the decisions about the applicability of professional knowledge from one culture to another. The recent history of the relationships between our countries, the United Kingdom (UK) and Malta, meant that there were national sensitivities concerning identity and independence that needed to be taken into account. To be effective, we needed to find a way of relating that did not replicate the dynamics of coloniser and colonised, as these were still within living memory for both of us and many others. Malta had achieved independence from British rule in 1964 and closed the last British military base in 1979. This recent history of Malta explained why Britain was an obvious natural source of professional information, but also cautioned against assuming too readily that what worked in one context could be transferred uncritically to the other.

Much of the government infrastructure and public services in Malta are a continuation of those developed during 150 years of British rule. However, one of the characteristics of British rule was a complex set of relationships with the Maltese culture. The Maltese culture and language was encouraged, if it helped to resist those who wished to oust British influence by forming closer links with Italy. In the early twentieth century, the Maltese Nationalist Party favoured links with Italy over the UK, due to geographical proximity, continuing the Italian legacy left by the Knights and the shared religious commitment to Catholicism in opposition to British Protestantism. The attraction of 'Italianisation' for the Maltese was extinguished when Italy bombed Malta during the Second World War. On the other hand, the British approach to Maltese culture may have helped to create an underclass of poor and uneducated people, perhaps 'because it suited their purposes' (Mitchell, 2002, p. 9). The ending of the British occupation was the result of political struggle.

One of the outcomes of this complicated and paradoxical history was that both Maltese and English were adopted as the official languages of the State of Malta when independence was achieved in 1964. Since then interest in Maltese culture and language has grown. When we conducted this project, both our countries had become members of the European Union: Britain in 1973 and Malta in 2004. This provided us with a new and potentially equalising context in which to understand our respective national cultures. In common with much of the Mediterranean region, it is the Maltese way to be passionate and assertive and so we will set out our ethical orientation to this study in that spirit.

Ethical Orientation

Our approach to comparative studies and the transfer of insights and practices between dissimilar cultures is proudly pluralistic. We are *proud* because we assert the desirability of constructing comparative work on the basis of dialogue that is reciprocally respectful of cultural difference and engages with the complex task of *mutual* understanding of each other. The emphasis on 'mutual' is a determined rejection of any easy assumptions about the superiority of one culture over another. The task of seeking mutual understanding is envisaged as a two-way process between equals and any disruptions to this, whether conscious or unconscious, are worthy of critical examination.

We are committed to *pluralism* because of the human significance attached to differences in identity and culture. Pluralism is adopted as the preferred terminology because it conveys an acceptance of diverse practices in their own right without either being diminished because of the acknowledgement of difference. (In contrast, the widely used alternative term 'relativism' has negative overtones, by implying the inferiority of difference in comparison to anything that is universal or absolute.) In pluralism, differences are not only valued but viewed as opportunities for reciprocal and mutual learning.

The purpose of this chapter is to provide a case study that examines some of the ethical and technical aspects of how we conducted a conversation designed to communicate the lived experience of two men in different national cultures within our ethical aims of proud pluralism. The conversation that follows was undertaken by email following a series of face-to-face discussions in Bristol before Tim visited Malta to deliver a series of lectures and workshops on developing pastoral care and counselling for young people under the auspices of the Malta Association for the Counselling Professions. The style of narrative conversation, communicating primarily by short narratives of personal experience, grew naturally out of our shared interest in narrative approaches to research and a belief that recounting stories is truly universal even if the form and content varies. They emerged organically and spontaneously. In the final sections of this chapter we will reflect on what we have learnt from this process.

Note that Tim's parts of the dialogue are shown in Roman typeface, and Dione's in italics.

Narrative as Cross-Cultural Conversation

The food was served. The noise of over-excited eight-year-old boys at the birthday party subsided for a moment. Sam looked at James, his best friend for many years and smiled. Sam was enjoying his party and, as his dad, I could relax. I moved over to where James's dad had paused to eat a few well-earned nibbles from the party table. We were on the last lap. The swimming party had gone well. The kids had cooperated in building a giant float. There had been no quarrels or tears. Sam's mum and his sister were getting the cake ready with candles and chatting happily on the other side of the room. The party room bubbled with happy sounds.

Paul and I have got to know each other through our sons' friendship. One of the pleasures of children is the way they draw you into new networks of friends. I offer Paul a ham sandwich and for a moment or two we lean on the wall and eat contentedly. Paul pauses and looks up and starts to speak. I see his lips move but I cannot catch the sounds. Paul looks perplexed and says something as he moves away from one of the round deeply recessed portholes designed to give the room a futuristic feel. I catch the last few words: '... must move away from the echo in that window. That's better, I can hear myself clearly again.'

Something resonates. The tricks of echoes evoke powerful memories of a few days earlier in another country. They flood my consciousness and drown out the present. I am in an underground chamber, the last of a series of passages and caves. The air is musty and dank. The walls are limestone and the variations in grey are tinted with red patterns, painted by ancient hands. This chamber is particularly carefully carved. It is as though it had been built above ground from large stones. I experience the illusion of the lintels carrying the full weight of close-fitting slabs of rock to form the roof. The guide moves to a corner of the chamber. As he does so, his bass speaking voice gains resonance. He stands close to a square hole in the wall and suddenly the chamber is full of sound. He starts to intone a few notes. As they modulate, an empty chamber is transformed into the place of ancient ritual and beliefs. I look at my companion, Dione, and can see that he is deeply moved. Our eyes are moistened by surges of emotion. I am feeling privileged to be present in such an ancient site and to share something that is from the origins of a culture of another people and place. The enveloping sound seems to draw us closer together in a flow of timelessness. I don't know if that is how Dione is experiencing what feels like sacred moments.

I am standing inside the Hypogeum with Tim. I am aware I have brought him to this sacred place to show him one of our prehistoric monuments but I can feel the build-up of emotions that connect me to this place. As we make our way to the Oracle Chamber I am transported back to that day when, as an eight-year-old, I set foot in this place for the first time. I remember the guide speaking through the oracle hole and his voice becoming an amplified bass as it reverberated through the whole complex. That visit had made me aware that people in some form of distress used this chamber for solace 5000 years ago. They yearned for understanding, they cried, they hoped, they waited. I am aware I share this yearning for understanding with my ancestors, who do not seem to be so far removed from today. It is a very special moment. And I understand that, as a counsellor, I am in some way continuing the work of the ancient oracle. I am overwhelmed by the significance of it all. Suddenly I become aware of the present and look at Tim. He too seems overwhelmed by the poetic beauty of the place, the chambers, the red ochre stylised patterns, the dressed stones. I feel connected to Tim as well. I had heard so much about him before I actually met him. And now he is here sharing this vast experience with me. An oracle who has come from abroad to help a young association of counsellors, sharing this moment with me, where it all started.

Outside again as we walk back to my car we are silent, still trying to grasp the significance of it all. It is a celebration of humanity, an understanding of how frail and vulnerable we are, but also of how strong and creative we can be.

Back home as I recount the experience to my wife and children, with whom I have visited this place many times, I find it easy to explain the connectedness with the past to them. I can share with them the awareness that being inside the oracle chamber reminds me of my personal internal chamber where I feel free to yearn, to share, to cry and to hope.

The air is dank and there is the musty smell of damp stone. The guide talks about the chamber being a mirror image of temples above ground that are now ruins, piles of rocks that merely hint at their former splendour. Above ground in the warm sunshine these ancient buildings seem to celebrate life but underground suggest death and loss. A metaphorical shudder shakes my soul. I try to imagine people entering the chamber, perhaps to place the bones of relatives in the nearby ossuary or to honour the dead. I wonder if their grief is as gut-wrenching and heartbreaking as my own has been at the death of close relatives. I try to imagine what it must be like to have such a sense of place tied to a rocky island in the middle of fertile seas that simultaneously provide both food and isolation. The carefully shaped walls suggest a strong and confident tradition that can reproduce the interiors of its temples underground. The mingling of the bones of people who would have known each other in life suggests a sense of community that is outside my experience. I think of my relatives buried in well-ordered cemeteries scattered across northern England and the Isle of Man. The regimented symmetry puts physical and spiritual space between the dead and the distance between graveyards emphasises the fracturing of family networks. This seems so different from a people who are willing to place the bones of their dead together. I find myself wondering what ways of living together make the mixing of bones in death acceptable. Do the implied links between people in a jumbled intimacy of bones suggest such strength of community that the boundaries between the living and dead are minimised? Does the sense of community, continuity and place change the experience of dying and bereavement?

I feel powerfully the quality of death and loss of existence in my own culture. Death has a deep and hopeless finality, a deeply personal tragedy, when it is stripped of sense of place or traditions and community that links the coming and going of generations. I am feeling powerfully the lack of anywhere in which to experience the depth of continuity between the dead and the living suggested by this place. I look at Dione and wonder whether this place has these qualities for him.

It is Sunday evening and I am sitting on a chair in the house of my wife's parents. It is extremely noisy and I can hardly hear myself speak. Every Sunday it is like this. Ten brothers and sisters with their spouses and offspring all together in the same house, narrating what has gone on throughout the week, agreeing, disagreeing, cracking jokes, admonishing 'naughty' children ...

Ah, the children! Some are not children any more but sit quietly in a corner trying to speak about their experiences at school or at work or maybe about present or possible boyfriends or girlfriends. The younger ones are all playing in the yard amid a cacophony of noises: whistles, jeers, shouting and laughter. The brothers and brothers-in-law sit around a table reading the Sunday papers and discussing the latest in local politics, gossip, and football. The sisters and sisters-in-laws are all huddled inside the kitchen making tea or coffee and bread for everyone, and sharing the latest about their children's education and anything that is connected to their daily lives.

Amidst this entire hullabaloo, a lone figure of an 83-year-old man can be seen, hands crossed, watching television. He cannot listen to what is being said. He can only see the visuals. He hardly says a word. Life has been quite tough on him. He was a farmer who married a farm girl and fathered ten children. All his children became professionals, none wanted to continue farming. Ultimately when he retired he had to sell his fields and settle into a world that has been quite alien.

One person is significantly missing. His wife, the mother and grandmother to all this family, passed away two years ago. Ironically, she died of lung cancer after spending her life ploughing fields and rearing children in the pure air of those fields. She had been the person who had reared the family and stood by her children through thick and thin. Everyone loved her. Now she is no more.

I remember her funeral vividly. She had died at home. All the children wrote letters and poems that they sealed in plastic folders and placed in her coffin. Her funeral mass was another great family meeting. It was now not just the large immediate family that attended but the extended family, most of the village and friends of family members. The normal chaotic atmosphere of the house meetings became a sad gathering of heartbroken sons, daughters, in-laws, nephews and nieces.

She was buried in the family vault in the main cemetery in Malta. In Malta, most families own a vault and all family members are buried there. Normally a family member would choose into which side of the family s/he would like to be buried. If the deceased would not have voiced an opinion, the two families would agree upon which vault to use. Some years after a deceased person has died, the vault is opened and the bones are collected and put in small boxes to make space for new arrivals. Thus, even in death Maltese families stay together. Those who are not lucky enough to own their own vault are buried in a common one with their bones ending up in a common ossuary.

It seems to be a continuation of the practice of gathering bones together and putting them in a repository like the Hypogeum people. It is a celebration of togetherness of an island people who survived countless invasions and colonisations to preserve their own cultural, societal and familiar set-up.

I find the continuation of family identity and proximity after death very powerful. I am curious to know something of how one family chooses the boundary between being buried in one family grave or another. For example, is this choice made at the time of marriage? How is this experienced by the person who changes family? I ask this because one of the things that struck me was the way people would open conversations by explaining complex genealogical links between the living. One of the ways people would approach me would be to say, 'You were talking to my second cousin on my mother's side yesterday at …', or 'Do you know my aunt … ?'

Initially I heard this as an attempt to orient me socially in a society where blood ties are ever-extending, like filaments that bind island life together. The repetition of these genealogies in relation to different people left me with a strong impression of the impossibility of living on the island unattached and unobserved. Incomers may be unattached, at least for a while, but they stand out and may be closely observed. This feels qualitatively different from my experience as teenager in rural north-west England. The sense of being an 'incomer' until my family had lived there for three generations has some parallels. We only lived there for seven years. I never resolved how the generations were counted. Did it start on arrival, in which case we were two generations co-existing, or did it start at birth, in which case neither my parents nor their children counted: only my generation's offspring would count? Either way, I was an incomer and would be reminded of this status in the adolescent squabbles and fights on the school bus. There were times when I was hurt by being excluded, and felt more vulnerable because I didn't belong to a family clan who could rally round to protect me, and other times when I was relieved by the sense of freedom that can come from social disconnectedness. I sense in your account of family gatherings and from what I observed that there is warmth and celebration of family identity in Malta that changes how people view themselves. The repeated genealogies seemed to be communicating something more than a concern to orient me. As they became more familiar, I started to hear them as an assertion of identity that is rich in a sense of connectedness to others.

I started to realise this when we were eating together with your friends. I think it was the rabbit stew (*Stuffat tal-Fenek*) at the local football club. Someone mentioned a teacher who was remembered for her strictness and someone declared distant blood relationship to her. The accidental discovery of previously undisclosed blood relationships was embraced with interest and elaborated. There appeared to be genuine curiosity until the relationship to your shared knowledge of each others' family relationships was established. It is as though the Maltese sense of self reaches out wider than mine to include an ever-extending family. In contrast, my sense of identity is a defended space into which I choose to let others or not as I like. Where I have walls with battlements, you seem to have relationships bound by blood ties. I wonder if this fits your sense of English identity.

I arrived in Bristol for the first time in October 2002. I stayed in a guest house used by workers coming from other parts of the country. We met mechanically during breakfast. Communication was limited to a salutary good morning while their statements focused mostly on the weather and why on earth I had left Malta's stereotyped depiction as a sunny holiday country to come to England. Then I found out that if I had no friends my evenings were going to be extremely lonely. I found a pub in Southville which was close to the guesthouse and had a meal there every evening. I made friends with the owners, who were willing to communicate more than the usual salutary clichés. However, eating alone at a table for four was a daily occurrence. The pub's clientele was almost the same every evening and I felt as if I was intruding in a ritualised social activity.

Later I started to lodge with an elderly couple in Clifton. My experience here was completely different. Mark and Hazel have gone out of their way to make me feel at home. I have been invited to meals and other family occasions and at times made to feel like an adoptive son. I have been introduced to their married sons and daughters and had a feel of an English family. Mark and Hazel have trusted me with stories connected to their family, including the untimely death of a child. These two different experiences tell me a lot about how life and connectedness can be experienced completely differently in the same English city.

With Mark and Hazel I felt pampered because sharing stories is so important in the Maltese way of life. When we shared those moments at the local football club together with other Maltese counsellors, we were sharing our ties with you.

In Malta family ties are rarely broken, neither are other allegiances. There is normally a close connection to both families after marriage, though the loyalty to the family of origin is considered quasi-sacred. Other ties involve adherence to the parish, the town or village and the political party that is traditionally supported by one's family of origin. Some loyalties go as far as to produce colourful skirmishes between people supporting different village feasts, band clubs, political parties or football clubs. These range from chanting to bottle-throwing. But then, trust the same people to be united in defending the same issue on one day and completely at loggerheads on another issue on another. Being Maltese also means living outside, being exposed and acceptance of being vulnerable. This may explain the connectedness: people are known and stories are known because people construct stories and people become stories …

The Communicative Potential of Narrative

Stories are the heart and mind of human experience. Dione concluded his last email in this series, 'people are known and stories are known because people construct stories and people become stories …' The powerful simplicity of this statement conveys the communicative potential of stories. They enable us to articulate and influence the way in which people create their lives in connection and disconnection with others. To date, the social sciences have struggled to find a language that enables us to communicate adequately the lived experience of cultural difference. The process of changing the register from narrative to propositional discourse strengthens the analytical possibilities, but at the price of communicative power. This observation applies equally to communicating the quality of relationships that surround us and exist in a reciprocal relationship to the culture.

Ruthellen Josselson (1996, p. 2), a pioneer in recognising the academic potential of storied lives, wrote, 'We become inarticulate when it comes to addressing how people intermingle with others, how we need others and how we need them'. The universal use of stories as a form of communication provides an opportunity to communicate those aspects of human existence that become elusive in propositional discourse. They simultaneously convey 'local knowledge' (Geertz, 1983/1993) in a narrative form of 'thick description' (Geertz, 1973/1993, pp. 3-30). Stories have the potential to convey human experience as closely as possible to how it is experienced. This is not to suggest that narratives have simple and direct relationship to human experience. That relationship is every bit as problematic as any other form of communication, but they do have the potential to convey the relational aspects of life within a cultural context as closely as it is possible to get, while retaining the idiosyncratic character of lived lives. Exchanging narratives of shared experiences across cultural differences is a powerful form of communication that both bridges and illuminates those differences.

During the process of our work together we accumulated a number of demographic and cultural characteristics that distinguish and help to explain some of the cultural differences between our respective countries. These are summarised in Table I. These features are interesting in their own right and provide a context for understanding the influences on our respective cultures. Differences in density of population, history, relationship with tradition and modernisation all help to illuminate significant differences.

	Malta	United Kingdom
Land type and area	Islands – 316 square kilometres	Islands – 244,820 square kilometres
Population	396,000	59,600,000
Density of population	1253 per square kilometre	243 per square kilometre
Cultural position	Western European. Traditional, valuing sense of historical continuity, strong Roman Catholic and national identity linked together.	Western European. Modernising and progressive, but aware of national history. Public life is largely secularised.

	Europeanisation, modernisation and secularisation of young people occurring.	
Attitude to European Union membership	Ambivalent. Referendum to join yielded a 54% Yes vote. Joined in 2004. Retains national currency.	Ambivalent. Favours a European trading area over developing a federal Europe. Joined in 1973. Retains national currency.
Religion	Roman Catholic influence is strong in public and private life, although weakening in its influence on young people.	Predominantly Protestant (Anglican) but strong Catholic presence and many other faith traditions. Religious belief is largely a private matter.
Family structure	Closely knit family structure, usually involving extended family members across generations. Growing number of separations and cohabitations (Malta does not allow divorce).	Nuclear families with growing number of single-parent families, and reconfigured families creating complex step-relationships and fracturing sense of continuity between generations.
Current foci of concern over young people	Sexual behaviour, drugs and alcohol, compounded by a large tourist influx. Victims of abuse. Mental health.	Sexual behaviour, alcohol and drugs. Anti-social behaviour. Deterioration in mental and physical health leading to reduction in life expectancy. Breaking the cycle of disadvantage for impoverished young people.
General attitude to education	Education is viewed as the key to professional success. There is a competitive attitude, which is bolstered by the	Mixed or ambivalent. Girls generally participating and achieving better than boys. Higher education

	importance given to exam results. The island is split into two, with an affluent academically oriented north and a working-class south.	in transition away from advancing an elite in favour of meritocracy and growth of human capital.
General attitude to available resources	The only available resource is Malta's people, who try to make good use of what is available in terms of land and opportunities. The Maltese are generally resilient, hardworking and mutually supportive.	People valued alongside other natural and technological resources. Working relationships tend to be competitive, individualistic and determined by market forces, especially in the south.

Table I. Comparisons between Malta and the UK.

However, it is in the stories we told each other that we began to understand how differently we experience our social space, ways of relating and sense of place. For example, we deploy nostalgia differently: Dione to convey continuity back to the Temple builders of Malta approximately 5000 years ago, and Tim to communicate a sense of discontinuity in time and location. The qualitative differences of living in our respective family circumstances are readily apparent but also hint at topics not yet explored, for example cultural boundaries between what may be disclosed appropriately to whom. There may be as yet unexplored cultural permissions and prohibitions between communications within the family, friends and in public places (Mitchell, 2002, p. 83). The similarity between our backgrounds as middle-aged professional male counsellors employed in universities and having young families of similar size, gender and ages is both an asset and a potential detriment. Differences in experience are thrown into sharper relief by the similarity of background. Equally, there may be significant topics that lie outside our awareness: topics that would become more apparent and accessible with greater biographical divergences between us. We could extend the discussions to include other members of our families to develop a sense of gendered space and space associated with age, both youth and old age. We are both aware that we have started something and that we have barely begun to exploit its potential as a methodology.

We started our version of narrative dialogue out of an ethical concern about equalising the basis for exchanging relational and cultural experience, by adopting a universal form of communication. However, as in any other area of professional endeavour, good intent does not necessarily lead to good outcomes unless there is a persistent attention to the ethical dimensions of the work being undertaken. There is the danger that the persuasive pull of the unfolding narrative will lead a participant to transgress his own cultural norms. For example, who decides what may be disclosed about whom? What is restricted information and only disclosed outside the formal exchange, as it were 'off the record'? These are familiar problems in any qualitative research. However, the nature of the narrative process means that concerns of this type may be difficult to anticipate in advance and may only become issues as they arise. The optimal ethic is a robust relational ethic based on trust, 'a quality of relationship ... that is sufficient to withstand any challenges arising from inequality, difference, uncertainty and risk' (Bond, 2004). An alternative ethic would be a sufficient quality of mutual respect to withstand the human challenges of difference and inequality (Sennett, 2003). In either case, both parties need to engage reflexively in both the subject matter and the ethical challenges to create the human circumstances that enable the research to flourish and to ensure the intellectual integrity of the project.

Our dialogue is incomplete and will continue. Following this email dialogue, we met again about six weeks later in Bristol, where Dione visited Tim's home and family. During this visit we decided spontaneously to read our passages to each other just as they have been presented in this text. We followed these presentations to each other with a conversation recorded on audiotape. Even at this early stage in the process we can see that our perceptions of each others' cultural roots are changing. For example, Tim has found it hard to believe that the legacy of British rule is not hostility and resentment. He is beginning to understand better the complex mixture of feelings in that legacy, which Dione characterises as being more like 'cousins'. This simile opens up a new area for exploration linked to different constructions of family and identity.

Dione has experienced English culture as less formal and rigid than he expected. In the taped conversation, he observed that 'going to a Bristol City Football match [gave me] a strong sense of Bristol community ... there were many people there ... contrary to my country, there were also many females in the football crowd and the whole football ground was singing together'. This observation opens up the themes of community and gender. However, it is interesting to compare the relative paucity of description in the taped conversations, which seem relatively 'thin' in comparison to communication by exchanging narratives. There were no passages that were as evocative as the emailed exchange of narratives, even though the conversation grew out of those passages and dealt with the same subject matter. Narrative conversation is a methodology that not only invites us to continue with our explorations, but could be applied to many other dialogues across cultures. Our original ethical concern was to meet on equal terms and to learn from the differences between our respective cultural backgrounds. Narrative conversation provided a method for achieving these ethical commitments in ways that have proved far more informative than we anticipated.

References

Bond, T. (2004) *Ethical Guidelines for Researching Counselling and Psychotherapy*. Rugby: British Association for Counselling and Psychotherapy.

Geertz, C. (1973/1993) *The Interpretation of Cultures*. London: Fontana.

Geertz, C. (1983/1993) *Local Knowledge*. London: Fontana.

Josselson, R. (1996) *The Space between Us: exploring the dimensions of human relationship*. Thousand Oaks: Sage.

Mitchell, J.P. (2002) *Ambivalent Europeans: ritual, memory and the public sphere in Malta*. London: Routledge.

Sennett, R. (2003) *Respect: the formation of character in a world of inequality*. London: Allen Lane.

CHAPTER FIFTEEN

The Gulbarrian College Gargoyles and the Narrative Gaze: landscapes of the future, imaginative learning and researcher identity

JANE SPEEDY
University of Bristol, United Kingdom

Oxford, where the real and the unreal jostle in the streets ... where the river mists have a solvent and vivifying effect on the stone of the ancient buildings so that the gargoyles of Magdalen College climb down at night and fight with those from Wykeham, or fish under the bridges, or simply change their expressions overnight: Oxford, where windows open into other worlds ... (Baedecker, date unknown, quoted in Pullman, 2003)

There was a fair amount of pre-conference hustle and bustle, of the usual high-tech construction tripping up admin-and-catering variety, but the college and grounds were in an otherwise unusually peaceful state. The junior scholars had already gone down for the summer recess and a number of academicals had already left for their season of conferences. The tall golden buildings cast deep shadows across the lawns in the evening sunshine and the nearby river flowed quietly, as if in need of some gentle reverie after the excesses of the summer balls and punting parties.

Gradually the conference council were beginning to arrive for their pre-conference supper. Inside the great hall things were still chaotic. A gaggle of technocrats were busying themselves with all manner of palmsofts and webcams. They were trying to beam a giant facsimile of an early twenty-first-century text over from the Bodleian library and onto the far wall above the dais. The top table was being set for the evening

Jane Speedy

meal and a mobile bar, complete with tan leatherette stools and mirrored backdrop, had already been established alongside the entrance.

Flanked by sleek perpendicular columns supporting a tall, ornately carved vaulted ceiling, the space was lit softly by hanging titanium gauze chandeliers. As the sun gradually sank behind the spires and buttresses of St Mary-by-the-Water, the room's main attraction, the finest collection of gargoyles and grotesques in Europe, seemed to appear out of the shadows, glowering and leering down on the commotion below.

* * * * *

It had been quite a substantial repast, accompanied by fine wines and vintage ports. The group of mostly middle-aged academicals were scattered around the bar and in the armchairs close to the fireplace. Lambert Pinkerton, the outgoing president of the Association,[1] was finishing off the last of the claret at the bar. His accomplice was Amy Plant, a considerably younger, Jewish critical-feminist auto-ethnographer from Harvard who appeared to be wearing her pyjamas, no doubt the height of sartorial East Coast elegance. Grace Martin, draped over a chair by the fireside, was a comparativist of Scottish African descent who had just been appointed to the Chair at Leiden (after a rather bitter contest). Paula Ratten, an indigenous English new reflexivist from Oxford, sat opposite Grace. She had arrived late and flustered, flapping along in her formal professorial gown, claiming a prior commitment at some arcane local gathering, but this had clearly been regarded as a display of ostentation by most of the others. John Bristow, a postcolonial oral historian from South Australia, had a background in applied linguistics and a commendable track record in aboriginal political activism. He had pulled one of the bar stools across to the thick Turkish rug where Naoko Saruko, a narrative analyst from Illinois and Tan Yi Ling, a narrative therapist from Hong Kong, were sprawled with their coffees.

It all looked sublimely mellow, but a quietly intense discussion was taking place, which was really what they had all come for. They still tended to stick to their own tribes during the day, narrative inquirers presenting papers to narrative inquirers and comparativists to other comparativists, but that was not why they returned year after year. They came back each year for the conversations in the bar, particularly those at the pre-conference supper. They came for the chance to step outside their territories and, although this sometimes consisted of passionately defending each carefully constructed patch, each defence troubled the edges of the territory it supported, so that bit by bit there was a blurring of genres.

Lambert: But for all its flaws and imperfections, I do think that the time-space-context three-dimensional model of narrative inquiry [2] still has a lot to offer international researchers. It's a multidisciplinary model that can be used across and between worlds as well as within specific cultural settings. It evokes richer descriptions of the stories of people's lived experiences than a more traditional events-plotted-over-time understanding of narrative construction. It has less linearity, more fluidity, and is more easily transferred across cultural settings than the kinds of analysis based on 'Hayden White-dependent'[3] versions of narrative: You know, those essentialist frameworks that rely on a predetermined set of archetypal stories: the tired old 'quest', 'chaos', 'redemption' and 'illness' narratives repertoire, for instance.[4]

Naoko: Well, nobody's interested in researching 'dead experience', are they? [Naoko paused briefly here to glance upwards at what she had sensed as a disgruntled rustling emanating from somewhere within the vaulted ceiling.] I suppose I find the three-dimensional model interesting and more tentative than some; at least there is no moment-by-moment prescription for the number of interviews required [5], etcetera ... and it is a context-dependent version, which suits comparative analyses. But their construction of 'space' seems more limiting than it might be, there's little attention to a poetics of space or the meaning of moments of reverie [6] as a learning space within narratives for both tellers and audience, or indeed, readers and writers. Let's face it, there's no such thing as the uncritical cross-cultural transfer of either research or educational practice, is there?[7] Polkinghorne (1988) and Sarbin's (1986) [8] universalist claims of 'living in a storied world' may or may not turn out to be so relevant, but in the meantime how does that help us classify and fathom the world's diversity of stories and their purposes? If in one version of Australian culture (whitefella culture) man is classified and given meaning in relation to woman, and in another version woman, fire and dangerous things, together with some non-dangerous animals such as bandicoots and echidnas, come under the same category [9], these are surely very differently storied worlds to live in, wouldn't you say, John?

John: Mmm, absolutely, although I'm a bit surprised to be brought into the conversation alongside you. I thought you were an unreconstructed traditionalist when it came to analysing narratives? I think the problems start, or at least my discomfort starts just here. My dis-ease button starts to flash red alert when comparison is made across cultures and nations. Why compare *balan* and woman at all? Surely to consider several readings of *balan*, for and against the grain, and perhaps also of woman, would give a much richer sense of living in a storied world, without attempting to cross cultures, but rather to celebrate and describe diversity. Then perhaps some kind of translation can emerge in the space between the diverse stories and perhaps this is more of an art than a social science. To quote Geertz:

> Translation here is not a simple recasting of other's ways of putting things in terms of our ways of putting them (that is the kind where things get lost) but displaying the logic of their ways of putting them in the locution of ours; a conception which again brings it rather closer to what a critic does to illumine a poem than what an astronomer does to account for a star. (Geertz, 1983, p. 10)

In fact I'd say that the whole comparative project has its roots in the traditional anthropological position of domesticising the exotic and I just wish the whitefellas, or at least the whitefella tradition, would concentrate a little more on 'exoticising the domestic', to quote Bourdieu (1988).

Amy: [Swinging around on her stool to face John] What about other ethnographic and comparative traditions? What about ethnographers from and of the margins of Western societies: are they not differently positioned from ethnographers from and of low-income worlds? The post-structuralist feminists had quite a bit to say about this at the turn of the century, especially the women of colour who were trying to write against the academic grain. Were they anthropologists, comparativists, auto-ethnographers or novelists? Did it matter? Who did it matter to, I wonder? (See Chaudry, 1997; Visweswaran, 1998; Villenas, 2000.)

But my goodness, we're getting a bit poetic and whimsical here, aren't we? Have you had too much claret or have you dropped the hard-line postcolonial critical stance? I thought you never quoted those whose first language was the master's language.[10] Where did Bourdieu spring from; don't you mean Edward Said?[11]

John: [Smiling laconically, not rising to any of this] I can only dismantle the master's house with imperfect translations. I, like Said, speak and write in the master's tongue. He had his own of course, but Kaurna [12], although in the process of reconstruction, may never be fully recovered. I can only speak and write English. It was the study of lost languages that brought me into this narrative work; because of course losing languages loses stories (see Nettle & Romaine, 2000). The excavation of traces, fragments and nuances of forgotten stories is a postcolonial project. Stories open windows to different knowledges. They are a very important source of knowledge against the dominant grain. I'm not talking here about collecting old forgotten stories and 'folktales' (although I'm not ruling that out). I'm talking about stories with contemporaneous meanings: stories as rhizomes [13] that we may now have too few words to express. Translation is just one of many border crossings in this kind of work: 'translation as negotiation', as Eco (2003) would have it. Much of the literature of my field is not academic text so much as local fiction and poetry. Just as you 'critical auto-ethnographers' have borrowed heavily from the life stories of the African Diaspora to piece together a methodology of 'scattered belongings' [14], I have borrowed from Oodgeroo's poetry (1990) every bit as much as I have from field notes, interview transcriptions and academic texts. This is where the stories of the border crossings and the spaces between them lie, don't you agree?

> Let no one say the past is dead
> The past is all about us and within
> Haunted by tribal memories, I know
> This little now, this accidental present
> Is not the all of me, whose long making
> Is so much of the past.
> Tonight here in Suburbia as I sit
> In easy chair before electric heater
> Warmed by the red glow, I fall into dream
> I am away. (Oodgeroo, 1990, p. 86)

I suppose this relates to some of your histories too. With the mid-twentieth-century destruction of the *shtetls*, Yiddish has almost disappeared, hasn't it?[15]

Amy: Interesting you should say that. I gave a pre-conference workshop earlier today and was showing 'Number Our Days', the film of Myerhoff's [16] work, just to illustrate some ways of engaging with the stories people tell about their lives in community contexts and to engender some discussion about researching amongst your own people: auto-ethnographic ethics if you like, expanding on Lieblich's (1996) more general narrative ethics, towards an interweaving of your own story in the text, not as a reflexive researcher, but as a separate, legitimate site for narrative inquiry. In her voiceover, Myerhoff described the film's elderly North American Jews as having come from amongst the *shtetls* of Northern Europe, but none of the audience knew what a *shtetl* was. This had me reflecting on the purposes of the twentieth-century Holocaust and how far they had in fact, been achieved, if only by default. In the New York hypertextuality and community project (see Earth & Plant, 2057) one of the projects was to develop new writings and rereadings of dybbuk [17] stories, but maybe nobody knows what a dybbuk is any more, either. As you said, Naoko, nobody wants to research 'dead' experience.

Mmm, that was strange: did anyone feel a sort of gush of cold air just then? I'm really roasting in front of this fire, but I just felt a really cold tingle down the back of my neck.

Jane Speedy

Paula: [Sitting bolt upright suddenly] Hang on a minute, what's wrong with reflexive research? I'd argue that all research is reflexive, whether that is made explicit or not. We are all reflecting on this conversation from different positions. Why is weaving your own story through the text, or using your own story as the research site, somehow more legitimate than a transparently reflexive relationship with the participant's stories? If I am both constituted by and constitutive of the stories I tell about my life, then surely a separated out 'weaving in' of personal narrative is an unnecessary differentiation. Unless of course you are from the 'personal narrative as self-indulgence' [18] school of narrative inquiry?

Lambert: [Draining the last drop of claret as he speaks] Blimey, how did we get here again, what did I miss? I do think this kind of either/or thinking closes down the discussion space between us. I think Amy was talking about *one* legitimate research site, not *the* legitimate site. Does this have to do with different readings of reflexivity? Your texts focus strongly on a continuous relationship between the research and moments of 'indwelling' on the part of the researcher as a sign of validity. Others, Chaudry (1997) for example, and Ruth Behar (1993), see reflexive movement happening between their own lived context and the context they are researching. As you know, I would agree that all research is reflexive, which is why I am unsure about so much of the text being devoted sometimes to the researcher's narrative, especially when the researcher is often culturally or economically, particularly in comparative educational research, more privileged in terms of age and stage in society and with regard to the world they inhabit. We could be talking about the subject positioning of the researcher in a text focusing on the interplay between the culture and agency of others, say the development of musical identity amongst the children of Timbuktu and Glasgow, for instance, to take a project that Grace and I have been working on (see Pinkerton & Martin, 2063). This entire text is negotiated and shaped into existence by Grace and myself and the other principal authors. It is therefore, our story. Why add another additional overlay of reflexive writings to these readings when the entire text already performs our researcher lives (see Macbeth, 2001, for this and other readings of reflexivity.) We are situated in relation to context, but ... but ...

Grace: [sitting upright for a moment] Well, we basically take up less of the text as personal narrative than you would, Paula. The purpose of the text is to explore the development and performance of the identity claims of others. It was also commissioned as that. Constructing yourself as a musician from an early age is not an infrequent occurrence in either cultural context, but the meanings of both constructions are very

258

different: different in each context and also different from family to family. There are gender differences, marked ones, if anything more so in Glasgow than Timbuktu (Martin & Pinkerton, 2063). There seems to be a lot more new ethnography and reflexivity coming out of the first- to third-world centres than from places like Mali, falling from the fifth into the sixth world. Perhaps this still has to do with funding issues, not only in terms of the research funding, but the low income and geospace of the country. Perhaps ... perhaps it also has to do with meanings of reflexivity in less individually determined cultural contexts.[19] In a way the conversation is still between Lambert and myself and the other three adult researchers. That is where ideas are generated and practices are problematised, indeed, where discourses are analyzed and some narratives are generated. Not all of this research was conducted as a narrative inquiry; it became part of a multi-storied text through the dialogue that transpired between us. Some of this conversation, for instance, was statistical. This is not necessarily less reflexive; there was still a conversation to be had with those statistics. As Josselson (1997) would say:

> Perhaps we can know a field of scholarship best when we can
> engage those areas of tension where multiple facets of
> understanding intersect, interweave, collide, contradict, and
> show themselves in their shifting and often paradoxical
> relation to each other. (Josselson et al, 1997, p. 152)[20]

Some of the more open space, well, I think that's between the two groups of children as much as anything and owes much to the layered approach that we took to the presentation of the text.[21] I'm not sure how I would feel about a higher profile for my own personal narrative in relation to the comparisons we were making in this text. Glasgow could learn a lot from the Djeliya traditions with regard to the holding and keeping of community memories [22], particularly after so much regeneration earlier in the century. Similarly the fusion going on in Glaswegian schools between traditional and modern music: there's a lot in that that might be interesting for the teachers in Mali and the project was as much about their exchanges (the students and teachers), both on the web and through the visits. Somehow that's where the stories were woven and where intertextuality occurred. It would seem really strange in the context of research about shared memory and community to place too much emphasis on individual narrative.

Yi Ling: You know, this is so interesting to hear; as a first-world narrative researcher I come from a fusion of cultural and political values in relation to agency. Something of Rushdie's (1994) 'east meets west' metaphor, although this oversimplifies the conversations that Hong Kong has shaped and is shaped by.[23] My work as a narrative therapist, or narrative co-researcher, takes practices that emerged out of discontent with individualistic notions of the therapeutic project and uses these in a different time and cultural space to tell and retell Hong Kong stories across communities. This storytelling practice has its routes in the work of White (1997, 2000) and White & Epston (1990) on 'definitional ceremony'. It owes something to ways of witnessing and retelling as a method of collaborative narrative inquiry (see Speedy & Thompson, 2004; Speedy, in press), but it consists of collaborations across communities and contexts rather than the concerns or positions taken up by individuals. I suppose you might call this collective reflexivity, except that it consists in evocation, resonance and retelling. It is the retelling that makes the difference.

Paula: [Suddenly overexcited] Well, that's fascinating. I like the idea of collective reflexivity, and the words you are using strike a chord with the ways I'd position my own work. Evocation and resonance speak to a more literary version of narrative studies as far as I am concerned. Not towards the 'tired old archetypes' that Lambert mentioned earlier (not that there's anything necessarily wrong with archetypes, just as long as we are prepared for an infinite, constantly varying and diverse collection), but rather towards the liminal spaces (see Broadhurst, 1999) between words where meanings are co-constructed; Derrida's (1976, 1978) 'Chora', the fruitful space between common-sense meanings, where multiple possibilities lurk. This was the space taken up by Julia Kristeva (1974) as the place of poetic revolutions. This is where cultural intertextuality should perhaps be investigated in respect of comparative and international narrative inquiry ...

Grace: [Yawning] Mmm. You said that last year; I didn't understand what you were on about then either. No, no, don't even think about it, I need to get to bed. I'm the opening keynote tomorrow and I need to organise my slides. Let's tackle international intertextuality and the place of liminality tomorrow ... goodnight, everybody.

And somehow, suddenly, the conversation was over. One by one all seven protagonists got to their feet and, leaving the empty glasses, cups and bottles on the bar, wandered off into the night. Only Paula remained for a short while to jot something down in a small black moleskin notebook and then she too was gone.

*****

They swooped down instantly, the rustling turning into a full-blown winged swish even before the door had closed on Paula. The space they now occupied by themselves became other, as if the walls and ceilings that had momentarily delineated the edges of the hall had been erased. Geranbuel immediately turned on the palm drivers and began playing with the visuals.

Innurez: [Scratching the fur under her forewing with a long manicured talon] What century are we in?

Parsifnos: Never mind the century ... what kind of text are we in? I mean is this fictionalised research, creative non-fiction [24], or simply lying through teeth?

Djangot: By the spirits, I thought they'd never go. I must have been waiting about fifteen years to shake out the dust from the fantail fins behind my ears. Actually if we're talking text I think it's 'performative ethnography' (Turner, 1982, 1997) and all that lot. Late twentieth-century, second world and going down the dimensions of power. I'd prefer 'performative gargoylography' myself, but they don't seem to have us in their sights ... although it does have traces of those 'reconstructed conversations': you know, the ones where the conversation is all with Bakhtin's super-addressee [25], the third party in the conversation. Bakhtin used to argue the third party was co-constructed, but of course it was one of us. Actually it can't be that kind of text ... this isn't Russia.

'Excuse me', Pllanka interrupted, as she glided down and spread her long downy wings out to dry along the bar. 'I'm a replica of a small demon in Kiev ... they could all be addressing me.'

'Don't be ridiculous, Pllanka, nobody ever addresses you', said Geranbuel, still clicking on keypads with her foreclaws. 'Could you please move your haunches and tail feathers out of the beam path? You know, this could be the twenty-first century ... their lives still seem circumscribed by this archaic powerpoint display technology ... except that clearly there is no paper any more, which means the trees have gone. All the texts are hyperblogs or webdocs ... I'm not sure how to plot this in time, any ideas? They've been here before, haven't they? Haven't changed much.'

Parsifnos: I think it might be a narrative inquiry into their future; are they allowed to do that? Are humans permitted to story their futures? I thought their academicals were condemned to the present and to present histories of the past. Did you notice how dismissive they were about the discourses of the dead? I couldn't help rustling and frustling a bit at that .. but I do think they've changed a bit, I must say. I think they have more of a shared language than the last time they were here. They may stay in their territories by day, but they cross the borders by night. We could help that along a smidgen, expand the nomadic tendencies in their enquiry so that they could move across each others borders' respectfully.[26]

Innurez: Two smidgens. They could certainly do with some sustenance from us, even though they were so rude about dead experience. I think we should at least open a few more doors and windows and expand their dimensions a little. They may not come back here in centuries. If we open up their landscape of dreams tonight, their landscapes of action and meaning [27] will hum with points of entry to alternative stories [28] by morning, which of course they may not notice ...

Geranbuel: [Scrolling down the visuo-text] Well, it says here that the next gathering is in Beijing, in the Forbidden City. That's a substantially multi-storied and diverse-worlded city, full to the brim of the likes of us, if they want to extend their thinking beyond what they describe as 'lived experience'. Of course they have to know there are borders to cross. They seemed quite oblivious of us. Yet ... I'm sure it was one of theirs, twentieth-century French I think, who said: 'The person who doesn't tremble crossing a border doesn't know there is a border and doesn't cast doubt on their definition' (Cixous, 1993, p. 131).

Pllanka: Oh, I think they had some sense of the borders available to them here. I saw them trembling. Why do they move their mouths all the time; can't they communicate properly between minds?

Parsifnos: Apparently not. Poor creatures. I think this might be magical realism, is that permitted? I know they have critical realism as academical thinking. Is magical realism permitted or is that restricted to what they describe as 'make-believe'? I love that expression 'make-believe'. Still, I suppose this is Oxford, not Oaxaca, where the dead are closer, if only for a day.

Innurez: I have a cousin holding up Oaxaca Cathedral; should I call her over? Maybe we could salsa ... maybe not.

Pllanka: Shall we go then and open up their worlds a tiny morsel ... are you making any differences to what they might believe tomorrow at all, Geran?

Geranbuel: Indeed I am, my dears, Just leave that to me ... I'm rearranging their texts and ending the whole event with the words of an old student I was very fond of ... one of the rare ones who appreciated my tricks.

The more agile of the gargoyles took off without delay, their gawkiness on the ground compensated for by an eerie grace in flight. The largest, oldest and most grotesque remained. She was focused intensely on the console. Slides and graphics swirled across the walls as Geranbuel (see Geranbuel, 3039, for a retrospective exploration of these moments) clacked away at the keypads with renewed intensity.

Faint traces of daylight began to trickle through the long mullioned windows. One by one the creatures returned through the open oriels and ascended to their stations, although it might have appeared in the half-light, at first glance, as though some of them had changed places. Eventually Geranbuel joined them. She collapsed exhausted onto the only remaining plinth and folded down her wings, just before the doors re-opened for the morning session.

* * * * *

The second Oxford conference was generally regarded as something of a turning point. The opening keynote on 'comparative reflexivities of the future' took even the speaker by surprise, and set the tone for a series of highly innovative panels, including 'Postcolonial Poetics and the Longing for Water'; 'Positioning Ourselves amongst the Gargoyles: geopolitics and magical narratives'; 'Collective Reflexivity as a Comparative and International Methodology'; and 'International Perspectives on Liminal Space: threshold stories in cross-cultural contexts'. It seemed as though all the papers they had intended to give had been given. Nothing that anyone had intended to say was left unsaid or unsayable, and yet it had all been rather surprisingly reconceptualised. It was as if the original thinking had been thrown up in the air and had landed somewhat differently in relation not only to time, space and discipline, but also to versions of reality. It was as if someone or something had crept in, in the dark of the night, and rearranged the shape of the spaces that these conversations inhabited.

You might have thought, given the extraordinary success of this particular event, that the newly re-elected conference council would have returned to their respective countries, worlds and power dimensions feeling more than a little pleased with themselves. And yet, as they journeyed back, each one of them was overcome with an unprecedented sense of the modesty of their joint enterprise. It seemed as if the very last words of the conference, which had appeared in mid-air above their heads, apparently written in startlingly wet green ink with a quill or talon, had been inscribed forever on their memories:

> The stories I want to tell you will light up part of my life and
> leave the rest in darkness. You don't need to know everything.
> There is no everything. The stories themselves make the
> meaning. The continuous narrative of existence is a lie. There

is no continuous narrative, there are lit up moments and the
rest is dark. (Winterson, 2004, p. 134)

Author's Note

Some of the research projects referred to in this paper appear not to have
taken place at the present time, and perhaps appear to have been
undertaken by persons whose existence might easily be brought into
question. Czarniawska (1998) offers a compelling critique of the'
shopping list referencing' school of validity within the social sciences.
This style of referencing has the intention of situating the text for readers
but also tacitly nods at the convention of 'the more references the better'.
Many readers find themselves interrupted and distracted by these lists.
Czarniawska (1998, pp. 59-63) somewhat playfully suggests that some of
her references might be 'make-believe' and invites her readers to work
this out for themselves. This is a brave and somewhat disconcerting
assertion within an otherwise conventionally scholarly text, which forms
part of the International Qualitative Research Methods series published
by Sage. The author of this chapter is equally mindful of hooks' (1994)
contention that people at the educational margins (in North American
urban cultures at the turn of the century) do not perceive the reading of
footnotes as a culturally relevant activity.

Nonetheless, in order to allow the dialogue within this text to flow,
the majority of references have been placed in the Notes. The author can
only hope that the playfulness in the conversations will intrigue and
draw readers towards the Notes as well as the substantive text.
References to work conducted in the future have been dated
approximately and may be subject to forthcoming alterations.

Notes

[1] The Association of International and Comparative Narrative Research was
founded in the early twenty-first century. Several highly esteemed
journals were associated with its work and a bi-annual international
conference had been held since 2009. The geographical location for the
conference rotated between worlds and hemispheres. Third-world
countries were chosen about every four years, as the fifth and sixth
worlds were usually considered too politically and economically
unpredictable. This was the second Oxford conference, but the first in
Gulbarrian College.

[2] Clandinin & Connelly (2000) suggest this three-dimensional framework as
a tool for the narrative analysis of ethnographic field notes, interview
data, personal journals and other materials. Primarily educational
researchers, they and their team developed this way of working over a

number of years within urban, multicultural school environments, initially exclusively within first-world settings.

[3] Riessman (1993) had been a standard text on narrative analysis for some decades. Her early work under the supervision of Elliot Mischler (1986), on a line-by-line content and process analysis of interview texts, had been based on studies by Western literary theorists and narratologists such as Hayden White (1973).

[4] Narratology, conjoined with psychodynamic theory, had produced a number of models of narrative research that relied on an underlying infrastructure of archetypal human story lines or plotlines. These had been particularly popular among late twentieth-century studies of white Western first-world cultures and concerns (see McAdams, 1993; Frank, 1995; McAdams & Bowman, 2001). Gradually, as initially Europe and then the Northern Americas had slipped from first- to second- and thence third-world status, the certainties of these standpoints had faded from popularity.

[5] See Lieblich et al (1998) for a more manualised version of narrative research.

[6] See Bachelard (1992, 1994) on the poetics of reverie and space.

[7] See Crossley (1999) and Crossley & Jarvis (2000) for a critique of 'cargo-cult assumptions' about the uncritical continuation of traditional Western policies and practices within the postcolonial academy.

[8] Polkinghorne and Sarbin's studies were amongst the earliest contributions to a body of work emanating from Europe and the North Americas (including Bruner (1991, 2002) in social psychology and Geertz (1973, 1983) in cultural anthropology) in the late twentieth and early twenty-first century. This had heralded what became known as the 'narrative turn' (Denzin & Lincoln, 1994) within the human sciences.

[9] In his 1986 work *Women, Fire and Dangerous Things*, George Lakoff famously quoted the signifier *balan* as an illustration of the contingent and local nature of language, classification and meaning-making.

[10] Audre Lorde (1984), an African-American poet and feminist, wrestled with the constraints of only having the master's tools (the English language) with which to 'dismantle the master's house'.

[11] Edward Said, a Palestinian-American and author of *Orientalism* (1978), was the founding figure of postcolonial theory and practice. He died early in the twenty-first century.

[12] Kaurna: the language of the indigenous people of Tandanya, the land of the red kangaroo (the coastal plains of South Australia). The people survived but their language and the red kangaroos both came to the verge of extinction (see Wingard & Lester, 2001; Ralfs, 2002).

[13] Deleuze & Guattari's (1987) notion of rhizomatic language, stories and discourses was taken up by turn-of-the-century feminists and students of 'queer studies', and thence others whose narratives might have been languishing beneath cultural surfaces (see St. Pierre, 1997).

[14] 'Scattered belongings' refers to a late twentieth-century text by Ifegwunigwe (1999), a woman who described herself as 'metisse' (of multiple cultures) and stood outside constructs of alienation, hybridity and transition, advocating, or at least embodying, a constant, fluid, situated process of belonging and scattering.

[15] *Shtetl*: Yiddish for 'ghetto'.

[16] Myerhoff's (1980) extraordinary anthropological work, describing the multiple 'life as performance of identity' stories of a group of elderly Jews living in poverty in Venice Beach, California at the end of the twentieth century, was made into an Academy Award-winning film. The trace of a story within a story begins in the space occupied by Myerhoff's line in the film: 'I'll never be a Chicana, but I will be a little old Jewish Lady'. She died shortly after the film was made, but not before making another acutely auto-ethnographic film about her own death, from cancer, in her forties.

[17] *Dybbuk:* another Yiddish word, describing a kind of demon or spirit, found in the Kabbalah and other ancient texts.

[18] The turn of the century had witnessed fierce debate, which sometimes still raged, about whether constructs such as reflexivity and personal narrative (Mykhalovskiy, 1997; Sparkes, 2002) were forms of researcher self-indulgence or contributions to the development of situated research genres.

[19] This perhaps relates to a continuation of early twenty-first-century constructs of research funding in what was then known as 'the developing world' (see Crossley & Tikly, 2004). It may also have a connection with reflexivity in relation to individual, family and community sites and meanings of agency (see, for instance, Chaudry, 1997; Tuhiwai-Smith, 1999).

[20] Conversation as method (Josselson et al, 1997) is one approach, originating in Israel, which has continued to illustrate the ways in which several non-commensurate research stories can exist alongside each other.

[21] Originally a first-world poststructuralist feminist tradition that had been seen to work well in the production and representation of texts where power relations between researcher and researched had been particularly marked in terms of social privileges and access to narrating 'reality'; see Lather & Smithies, 1997; Lather, 2000.

[22] Women's voices are particularly valued within the Djeliya or *griot* tradition of Mali, which holds 'the people's memory: without which, everything would fade away in the mists of oblivion' (Kouyaté, 1997).

[23] See *International Journal of Narrative Therapy and Community Work* (2004) for an early twenty-first-century take on the shape of postcolonial pre-first world conversations from Hong Kong.

[24] Narrative inquiry, in particular, has a long-standing commitment to textual aesthetics and to 'troubling the edges' between 'fact' and fiction. Clough's (2002) work fictionalises research that might otherwise have remained unavailable within the public domain. Richardson (1997, 2000)

has an arts-based approach to narrative research. She pioneered the poeticising of interview texts, but was initially accused of 'making up' the data she had presented in stanza form.

[25] Bakhtin's work on dialogue (1981, 1986), identifying the super-addressee, was used by Gergen (2001) as part of her performative narratives.

[26] St. Pierre (1997) described respectful ways of investigating one cultural/theoretical group (elderly conservative/humanist) from the perspective of another (poststructuralist/feminist) as 'nomadic inquiry'.

[27] Bruner (1991, 2002) used the metaphor of different landscapes (meaning, action, etc.) navigated across time to illustrate narrative knowing (as opposed to paradigmatic knowing).

[28] White (2000) described absent but implicit interruptions to shared meanings in people's conversations as the 'points of entry' to alternative stories of their lives.

References

Bachelard, G. (1992) *The Poetics of Reverie*. Boston: Beacon.

Bachelard, G. (1994) *The Poetics of Space*. Boston: Beacon.

Baedecker, O. (date unknown) *The Coasts of Bohemia*, a book that fell through from Lyra's world. Quoted in P. Pullman (2003) *Lyra's Oxford*. Oxford: David Fickling.

Bakhtin, M. (1981) *The Dialogic Imagination: four essays*, trans. C. Emerson & M. Holquist. Austin: University of Texas Press.

Bakhtin, M. (1986) *Speech Genres and Other Late Essays*. Austin: University of Texas Press.

Behar, R. (1993) *Translated Woman: crossing the border with Esperanza's story*. Boston: Beacon.

Blackwood, J. (1996) *Oxford's Gargoyles and Grotesques*. Charleston: Charon Press.

Bourdieu, P. (1988) *Homo Academicus*. Stanford: Stanford University Press.

Broadhurst, S. (1999) *Liminal Performance*. London: Cassell.

Bruner, J. (1991) The Narrative Construction of Reality, *Critical Inquiry*, 18, pp. 1-21.

Bruner, J. (2002) *Making Stories: law, literature, life*. New York: Farrar, Straus & Giroux.

Chaudry, L. (1997) Researching 'My' People, Researching Myself: fragments of a reflexive tale, *International Journal of Qualitative Studies in Education*, 8, pp. 229-238.

Cixous, H. (1993) *Three Steps on the Ladder of Writing*. New York: Columbia University Press.

Clandinin, J. & Connolly, F.M. (2000) *Narrative Inquiry: experience and story in qualitative research*. San Francisco: Jossey-Bass.

Clough, P. (2002) *Narratives and Fictions in Educational Research.* Buckingham: Open University Press.

Crossley, M. (1999) Reconceptualising Comparative and International Education, *Compare*, 19, pp. 249-267.

Crossley, M. & Jarvis, P. (2000) Introduction: continuity, challenge and change in comparative and international education, *Comparative Education*, 36, pp. 261-265.

Crossley, M. & Tikly, L. (2004) Postcolonial Perspectives on Comparative and International Research in Education: a critical introduction, *Comparative Education*, 40, pp. 147-156. http://dx.doi.org/10.1080/0305006042000231329

Czarniawska, B. (1998) *A Narrative Approach to Organization Studies.* Thousand Oaks: Sage.

Deleuze, G. & Guattari, F. (1987) *A Thousand Plateaus: capitalism and schizophrenia.* Minneapolis: University of Minneapolis Press.

Denzin, N.K & Lincoln, Y.S. (Eds) (1994) *Handbook of Qualitative Research.* Thousand Oaks: Sage.

Derrida, J. (1976) *Of Grammatology.* Baltimore: Johns Hopkins University Press.

Derrida, J. (1978) *Writing And Difference.* Chicago: University of Chicago Press.

Earth, R. & Plant, A. (2057) Technobiography, Hypertextuality and the Jewish Communities of New York. Available at: http://www/technobiographies.com/NYstories

Eco, U. (2003) *Mouse or Rat? Translation as Negotiation.* London: Weidenfeld & Nicholson.

Frank, A. (1995) *The Wounded Storyteller: body, illness and ethics.* Chicago: University of Chicago Press.

Geertz, C. (1973) Thick Description: towards an interpretative theory of culture, in C. Geertz, *The Interpretation of Cultures.* New York: Basic Books.

Geertz, C. (1983) *Local Knowledge.* London: Fontana.

Geranbuel, G. (3039) My Lives as a Gargoyle: an auto-ethnographic study. Available at: http://www.adobereader/wingblogs/2_14

Gergen, M. (2001) *Feminist Reconstructions in Psychology: narrative, gender and performance.* Thousand Oaks: Sage.

hooks, b. (1994) *Teaching to Transgress: education as the practice of freedom.* London: Routledge.

Ifegwunigwe, J. (1999) *Scattered Belongings: cultural paradoxes of 'race', nation and gender.* London: Routledge.

International Journal of Narrative Therapy and Community Work (2004) Part One: stories from Hong Kong, 1, pp. 3-40.

Josselson, R., Lieblich, A., Sharabany, R. & Wiseman, H. (1997) *Conversation as Method: analysing the relational world of people who were raised communally.* Thousand Oaks: Sage.

Kouyaté, M. (1987) Quoted in B. Wrenger (Ed.) *The Divas of Mali* (CD album text). Cologne: WDR-Funkhaus.

Kristeva, J. (1974) Revolution in Poetic Language, in K. Oliver (Ed.) *The Portable Kristeva*. New York: Columbia University Press.

Lakoff, G. (1986) *Women, Fire and Dangerous Things: what categories reveal about the mind*. Chicago: University of Chicago Press.

Lather, P. (2000) Drawing the Line at Angels: working the ruins of feminist ethnography, in E. St. Pierre & W. Pillow (Eds) *Working the Ruins: feminist poststructuralist theory and methods in education*. London: Routledge

Lather, P. & Smithies, C. (1997) *Troubling the Angels: women living with HIV/Aids*. Boulder: Westview.

Lieblich, A. (1996) Some Unforeseen Outcomes of Conducting Narrative Research with People of One's Own Culture, in R. Josselson (Ed.) *Ethics and Process in the Narrative Study of Lives*. Thousand Oaks: Sage.

Lieblich, A. Tuval-Mashiach, R. & Zilber, T. (1998) *Narrative Research: reading analysis and interpretation*. Thousand Oaks: Sage.

Lorde, A. (1984) *Sister Outsider*. New York: Crossing Press.

Macbeth, D. (2001) On 'Reflexivity' in Qualitative Research: two readings, and a third, *Qualitative Inquiry*, 7, pp. 35-69.

Martin, G. & Pinkerton, L. (2063) Narrative Comparisons in the Development of Musical Identities in Childhood: engendered experiences in Scotland and Mali. Available at: http://www/InternationalE-Journal/Narrative studiesinEducation_42/35/7_71

McAdams, D. (1993) *The Stories We Live By*. New York: Guildford Press.

McAdams, D. & Bowman, P. (2001) Narrating Life's Turning Points: redemption and contamination, in D. McAdams, R. Josselson & A. Lieblich (Eds) *Turns in the Road: narrative studies of lives in transition*. Washington, DC: American Psychological Association.

Mischler, E.G. (1986) *Research Interviewing: context and narrative*. Cambridge, MA: Harvard University Press.

Myerhoff, B. (1980) *Number Our Days*. New York: Simon & Schuster.

Myerhoff, B. (1986) Life Not Death in Venice, in V. Turner & E. Bruner (Eds) *The Anthropology of Experience*. Champaign: University of Illinois Press.

Mykhalovskiy, E. (1997) Reconsidering Table-Talk: critical thoughts on the relationship between sociology, autobiography and self-indulgence, in R. Hertz (Ed.) *Reflexivity and Voice*. Thousand Oaks: Sage.

Nettle, D. & Romaine, S. (2000) *Vanishing Voices: the extinction of the world's languages*. Oxford: Oxford University Press.

Oodgeroo (1990) *My People*. Milton, QLD: Jacaranda Wiley.

Pinkerton, L. & Martin, G. (2063) The Construction of Musical Identities in Glasgow and Timbuktu: towards a comparative narrative study. Available at: http://www/MusicalInquiry/29/4/27_35

Polkinghorne, D. (1988) *Narrative Knowing and the Human Sciences*. New York: State University of New York Press.

Pullman, P. (2003) *Lyra's Oxford*. Oxford: David Fickling.

Ralfs, C. (2002) Who Am I? Who are My People? And Where Do I Belong? in D. Denborough (Ed.) *Queer Counselling and Narrative Practice.* Adelaide: Dulwich Centre Publications.

Richardson, L. (1997) Skirting the Pleated Text: de-disciplining an academic life, *Qualitative Inquiry,* 3, pp. 295-303.

Richardson, L. (2000) Writing: a method of inquiry, in N.K. Denzin & Y.S. Lincoln (Eds) *Handbook of Qualitative Research,* 2nd edn. Thousand Oaks: Sage.

Riessman, C.K. (1993) *Narrative Analysis.* Newbury Park: Sage.

Rushdie, S. (1994) *East, West.* New York: Vintage Books.

Said, E. (1978) *Orientalism.* New York: Vintage Books.

Sarbin, T.R. (1986) The Narrative as a Root Metaphor for Psychology, in T.R. Sarbin (Ed.) *Narrative Psychology: the storied nature of human conduct.* New York: Praeger.

Sparkes, A. (2002) Auto-ethnography: self indulgence or something more? in A. Bochner & C. Ellis (Eds) *Ethnographically Speaking: autoethnography, literature and aesthetics.* Walnut Creek: Alta Mira Press.

Speedy, J. (in press) *Narrative Inquiry in Counselling and Psychotherapy.* Basingstoke: Palgrave.

Speedy, J. & Thompson, G. (2004) Living a More Peopled Life: definitional ceremony as inquiry into psychotherapy 'outcomes', *International Journal of Narrative Therapy and Community Work,* 3, pp. 43-53.

St. Pierre, E. (1997) Nomadic Inquiry in the Smooth Spaces of the Field, *International Journal of Qualitative Studies in Education,* 10(3), pp. 365-383.

Tuhiwai-Smith, L. (1999) *Decolonising Methodologies: research and indigenous peoples.* Dunedin: Otago Press.

Turner, V. (1982) Dramatic Ritual/Ritual Drama: performative and reflexive anthropology, in J. Ruby (Ed.) *A Crack in the Mirror: reflexive perspectives in anthropology.* Philadelphia: University of Pennsylvania Press.

Turner, V. (1997) *The Anthropology of Performance.* New York: Performing Arts Journals Publications.

Villenas, S. (2000) This Ethnography Called My Back: writings of the exotic gaze, 'othering' Latina and recuperating Xicanisma, in E. St. Pierre & W. Pillow (Eds) *Working the Ruins: feminist poststructuralist theory and methods in education.* London: Routledge.

Visweswaran, K. (1998) Race and the Culture of Anthropology, *American Anthropologist,* 11, pp. 70-83. http://dx.doi.org/10.1525/aa.1998.100.1.70

White, H. (1973) *Metahistory.* Baltimore: Johns Hopkins University Press.

White, M. (1997) *Narratives of Therapists' Lives.* Adelaide: Dulwich Centre Publications.

White, M. (2000) *Reflections on Narrative Practice: essays and interviews.* Adelaide: Dulwich Centre Publications.

White, M. & Epston, D. (1990) *Narrative Means to Therapeutic Ends.* New York: Norton.

Wingard, B. & Lester, J. (2001) *Telling Our Stories in Ways That Make Us Stronger.* Adelaide: Dulwich Centre Publications.

Winterson, J. (2004) *Lighthousekeeping.* London: Fourth Estate.

Postscript

In the final chapter of this book the conversations in the bar brought the delegates back year after year to the conference of the Association of International and Comparative Narrative Research. It was in those conversations that narrative inquirers and comparativists risked bridging and dissolving their borders, gradually blurring their genres. The contributors to this book have bridged their diverse cultural contexts, backgrounds and disciplines and engaged in innovative conversations like those carried out in the hypothetical bar to show how developments in narrative research have much to offer comparative and international research in education.

In their chapter, Cortazzi & Jin discuss narrative variability – the different ways of sharing stories in different cultures. The place of the audience is particularly important in the sharing of stories, but the positioning of that audience differs from culture to culture. Cortazzi & Jin refer to the Athabascan people of North America, who wait for their audience to anticipate the conclusion of a story and to give it both an ending and a meaning. I am mindful of some of the last words of the post-2009 conference inscribed in the memories of the participants: 'You don't need to know everything. There is no everything. The stories themselves make the meaning'.

I imagine that, as you read each chapter in this book, you will have been reminded of stories from your own life, and will have attributed a range of meanings to the stories you have read. You may also have been reflecting on how you can use the original ideas presented here in your own work. I hope that the book has stimulated you to engage with the process of strengthening the use of narrative approaches in the field of comparative and international research in education. Perhaps it has also caused you to reflect on yourself as a researcher, a practitioner, a person. It is up to you now to provide endings and meanings to the stories we have told – or to let 'the stories themselves make the meaning'.

Sheila Trahar
University of Bristol, United Kingdom

Notes on Contributors

George Bailey is a member of two research centres in the Graduate School of Education, University of Bristol, UK – the Centre for International and Comparative Studies and the Centre for Globalisation, Education and Societies. Dr Bailey's research interests focus on communities and individuals' accessing and experiencing of education. He is also a member of the Ethics Committee for the Faculty of Health and Social Care, University of the West of England and is interested in the processes, thinking and outcomes of the drive by governments to link education and health policies.

Angeline Barrett worked for a number of years as a mathematics and physics teacher in further education colleges in England and in secondary schools in Uganda and Tanzania, before studying for a Master's in Education at Leeds University. This led her into a PhD at Bristol University, comparing Tanzanian with English primary school teacher identity. She is now a research fellow within a research programme funded by the British Department for International Development – Education Quality in Low Income Countries – collaborating with colleagues within a consortium of higher education institutions in Sub-Saharan Africa and the UK.

Tim Bond is Reader in Counselling and Professional Ethics in the Graduate School of Education, University of Bristol, UK. Dr Bond is the author of *Standards and Ethics for Counselling in Action* (Sage, 2000) and *Ethical Guidelines for Researching Counselling and Psychotherapy* (British Association for Counselling and Psychotherapy, 2004), as well as many articles on professional ethics. Recurrent themes in his work are developing contextually and culturally appropriate ethics and the ethical challenges of communicating across cultural difference. He is also a member of the Executive Council of the International Association for Counselling.

Nell Bridges is currently undertaking doctoral research at the University of Bristol, UK, exploring counsellors' experiences of being pressured to practise unethically. She is particularly interested in challenging boundaries between art, science, therapy and spirituality, for example by using narrative methods and autoethnographic, creative and therapeutic writing. Nell has many years of experience as a counsellor, supervisor and counselling educator in a wide variety of settings.

Martin Cortazzi is Visiting Professor at the University of Warwick, UK. He has taught applied linguistics courses and trained teachers in the UK, China, Turkey, Lebanon, Malaysia, Singapore and elsewhere. He has published many books and articles on narrative analysis and language and education, literacy, vocabulary learning, discourse analysis and cultures of learning.

Beth Cross is a Research Fellow at the Centre for Educational Sociology, University of Edinburgh, UK, with an interest in children's literacy issues, popular culture and the interface between formal and informal learning. Dr Cross's work also includes consulting widely across Scotland with local authorities developing projects to re-integrate storytelling into the culture of the classroom.

Kim Etherington is Reader at the University of Bristol, UK, and a British Association for Counselling and Psychotherapy accredited senior counsellor and supervisor in private practice. Prior to retraining in the counselling field, she worked for more than twenty-five years as an occupational therapist for the UK National Health Service, social services and charitable organisations. Her work at the university includes teaching and supervising research students on Master's and doctoral programmes, as well as undertaking and writing about her own research. She is particularly interested in using, teaching and supervising reflexive narrative research methodologies, and in exploring the researcher's personal and professional development through using these methods. As a practitioner researcher her aim is to bridge the gap between practice and research through writing, editing and publishing accessible texts, and to encourage and assist others in doing the same. Her book *Becoming a Reflexive Researcher: using our selves in research* (Jessica Kingsley) was published in 2004.

Christine Fox is a senior academic in comparative and international education, based at Wollongong University, Australia. Dr Fox has extensive experience teaching and supervising students in narrative research methodology. She has worked and lived as an educational consultant for over twenty years in various countries in the Asia-Pacific region, as well as in the UK, the USA and Latin America. Her expertise lies in working in partnership with in-country educational personnel to appraise and formulate policies and programmes that are appropriate to the sociocultural context. She has published widely on critical intercultural communication theory and practice and on the subaltern voice. Dr Fox is immediate past-President of the Australian and New

Zealand Comparative and International Education Society and is a former Vice-President of the World Council of Comparative Education Societies.

Ruth Hayhoe is a professor at the Ontario Institute for Studies in Education of the University of Toronto and president *emerita* of the Hong Kong Institute of Education. She has written extensively on higher education in China and on educational relations between China and the West.

Lixian Jin is Principal Lecturer in Linguistics at De Montfort University, UK. She has taught applied linguistics courses and trained teachers and speech and language therapists at universities in China, Cyprus, Turkey, Hong Kong and the UK. Her research publications are in narrative analysis, intercultural communication, cultures of learning, second-language development and bilingual clinical assessment.

Richard Kiely has a PhD in programme evaluation from the University of Warwick, UK, and has published on ethnographic approaches in language programme evaluation and applied linguistics. A book, *Programme Evaluation in Language Education* (with Pauline Rea-Dickins), was published in 2005 by Palgrave Macmillan. He is currently involved in research projects into learning to do research and the impact of language proficiency on international students. Dr Kiely currently coordinates the Master of Education TESOL Pathway at the University of Bristol, UK, and has worked as a teacher and teacher educator in Zambia, Malaysia, Hong Kong, France and Ireland, as well as in the higher education sector in the UK.

Elizabeth McNess is a Senior Lecturer in Education in the Graduate School of Education, University of Bristol, UK. Dr McNess is Joint Co-ordinator of the Centre for International and Comparative Studies and Head of the Document Summary Service. Her main research focus has been on a sociocultural explanation of the unintended consequences of policy. She has an interest in developing qualitative methodologies such that their capacity to illuminate the 'private' can be set against the 'public' concerns manifest at a macrostructural level.

Dione Mifsud works as a counsellor at the University of Malta, where he also lectures in counselling skills and career counselling. He was involved in the establishment of the Malta Association for the Counselling Professions in 2002. His research interests involve contextualised counselling supervision, cross-cultural counselling and ethical issues around counselling. He is currently pursuing doctoral studies at the University of Bristol, UK.

Jane Speedy is a Senior Lecturer in Education at the University of Bristol, UK. She coordinates CeNTRAL, a multidisciplinary research centre in narratives and transformative learning, as well as a doctoral programme in narrative and life-story research and a Master's programme in narrative therapy. Her research interests include 'troubling the edges' between therapy and research methodologies such as autoethnographies, collective biographies and fictional accounts.

Sheila Trahar is a Lecturer in Education at the University of Bristol, UK. She is co-Director of the Master of Education programme and teaches on this programme in Bristol and in Hong Kong. She also teaches on the Doctor of Education programme and is a trained counsellor and counsellor educator. A committed practitioner researcher, Sheila is currently pursuing doctoral research, exploring her own and students' experiences of teaching and learning in an international higher education community. She is particularly interested in developing ways of teaching research methodology that are creative and accessible and that encourage students to critique the Eurocentric epistemological and ontological perspectives underlying many paradigms.

Sue Watson has had a varied career, from a secondary school teacher of English to her present post as Lecturer in the Department of Health and Human Development at Massey University in New Zealand. She teaches undergraduate and postgraduate courses in adult development, narrative as a research methodology and attachment theory and research. Her main research interest is the nature of the cognitive/emotional environment provided by parents to their infants, especially as revealed in their autobiographical stories.

Sue Webb was born and brought up in Leicestershire, UK, and worked as a secondary school teacher in Bristol, but has lived in New Zealand for the last thirty years. She is now Senior Lecturer in counselling at Massey University. She has interests in counselling process research, women's issues, school counselling and counselling ethics as well as narrative approaches to research. She is a former President of the New Zealand Association of Counsellors and serves on the Association's Ethics Committee.